T0222505

Enterprise Cyber Risk Management as a Value Creator

Leverage Cybersecurity for Competitive Advantage

Bob Chaput

Foreword by Phil Gardner, CEO, IANS Research

Apress®

Enterprise Cyber Risk Management as a Value Creator: Leverage Cybersecurity for Competitive Advantage

Bob Chaput
Belleair Beach, FL, USA

ISBN-13 (pbk): 979-8-8688-0093-1   ISBN-13 (electronic): 979-8-8688-0094-8
https://doi.org/10.1007/979-8-8688-0094-8

Copyright © 2024 by Bob Chaput

This work is subject to copyright. All rights are reserved by the Publisher, whether the whole or part of the material is concerned, specifically the rights of translation, reprinting, reuse of illustrations, recitation, broadcasting, reproduction on microfilms or in any other physical way, and transmission or information storage and retrieval, electronic adaptation, computer software, or by similar or dissimilar methodology now known or hereafter developed.

Trademarked names, logos, and images may appear in this book. Rather than use a trademark symbol with every occurrence of a trademarked name, logo, or image we use the names, logos, and images only in an editorial fashion and to the benefit of the trademark owner, with no intention of infringement of the trademark.

The use in this publication of trade names, trademarks, service marks, and similar terms, even if they are not identified as such, is not to be taken as an expression of opinion as to whether or not they are subject to proprietary rights.

While the advice and information in this book are believed to be true and accurate at the date of publication, neither the authors nor the editors nor the publisher can accept any legal responsibility for any errors or omissions that may be made. The publisher makes no warranty, express or implied, with respect to the material contained herein.

Managing Director, Apress Media LLC: Welmoed Spahr
Acquisitions Editor: Susan McDermott
Development Editor: Laura Berendson
Coordinating Editor: Jessica Vakili

Distributed to the book trade worldwide by Springer Science+Business Media New York, 233 Spring Street, 6th Floor, New York, NY 10013. Phone 1-800-SPRINGER, fax (201) 348-4505, e-mail orders-ny@springer-sbm.com, or visit www.springeronline.com. Apress Media, LLC is a California LLC and the sole member (owner) is Springer Science + Business Media Finance Inc (SSBM Finance Inc). SSBM Finance Inc is a **Delaware** corporation.

For information on translations, please e-mail booktranslations@springernature.com; for reprint, paperback, or audio rights, please e-mail bookpermissions@springernature.com.

Apress titles may be purchased in bulk for academic, corporate, or promotional use. eBook versions and licenses are also available for most titles. For more information, reference our Print and eBook Bulk Sales web page at http://www.apress.com/bulk-sales.

Any source code or other supplementary material referenced by the author in this book is available to readers on the Github repository: https://github.com/Apress/Enterprise-Cyber-Risk Management-as-a-Value-Creator. For more detailed information, please visit https://www.apress.com/gp/services/source-code.

Paper in this product is recyclable

I dedicate this book to my wife, Mary.

It's like deja-vu all over again.

—Yogi Berra (1925–2015), American professional baseball catcher, manager, and coach.

Table of Contents

Endorsements for *Enterprise Cyber Risk Management as a Value Creator*

Throughout my 28 years in CISO roles at two of the highest-risk organizations in the world, I have sweated through countless budget and resource challenges and struggled to connect my cybersecurity program to business objectives in the minds of business leaders and our board. A major hurdle was that cybersecurity was viewed as risk avoidance—a cost center that did not add value, that is, a painful but necessary overhead. This book lays out the holy grail for cybersecurity, how to flip that script to make cybersecurity a business enabler and part of the core growth strategy, and how to integrate that approach into business strategy.

No one is more knowledgeable and qualified to make this case than Bob Chaput, who is a living legend in cybersecurity and an unmatched thought leader in enterprise cyber risk management (ECRM). He lays out a compelling case, with details on how to apply this thinking to your organization, and then provides a detailed road map for making it happen.

This should be mandatory reading for CISOs, CFOs, CEOs, and board members. It will close communication gaps and change the mindset because it shines a light on the opportunities to expand and accelerate business transformation and earn customer and stakeholder trust— through cybersecurity.

—Paul Connelly, First CISO at the White House and
HCA Healthcare

Bob Chaput picks up where most books leave off by providing powerful insight into ECRM engagement by providing a factual background coupled with strategic examples that can and will have positive impacts on any company's cyber risk strategy and approach. This resource should become the standard guidebook for every risk manager, general counsel, CISO, CTO, C-suite, and board member who has an interest in or a concern around cyber and privacy liability and entire ECRM protocols.

—Kevin Hewgley, Senior Vice President,
Financial Services at Lockton Companies

In *Enterprise Cyber Risk Management as a Value Creator*, Bob Chaput's latest contribution to simplifying the often impenetrable field of cybersecurity, Bob turns from calling attention to the problem to helping us think differently about it. Are investments in cybersecurity a cost of doing business, with cost containment as the overarching goal? Is cybersecurity a "check the box" exercise, allowing us to throw up our hands if an adverse event occurs after we've checked all our boxes? Or is cyber a strategic priority meriting an offensive rather than defensive mindset? As always, Bob doesn't just pose the questions. He provides practical and timely answers alongside a wealth of real-world examples. A must-read for everyone from the cybersecurity novice to the seasoned pro looking for proper organizational focus on a business pandemic that has no miracle cure in sight.

—Ralph W. Davis, Independent Director/Board Advisor,
Operating Partner, The Vistria Group

Bob Chaput's latest book is a powerful read that explains cybersecurity in a new context, one that will be helping business leaders, including corporate directors, reframe cybersecurity as a critical part of the need for every organization to drive and create value. With so much economic growth and output already dependent upon complex digital systems, this mindset will help leaders understand the importance of cybersecurity to the organization's future.

—Bob Zukis, CEO, Digital Directors Network

Enterprise Cyber Risk Management as a Value Creator delves deep into the critical realm of enterprise cyber risk management, providing a comprehensive guide to not just safeguarding against digital threats but also harnessing the power of cybersecurity as a catalyst for growth and innovation. Today, businesses and organizations are more reliant on technology and data than ever before, and the need for robust cybersecurity practices cannot be overstated. This book serves as an indispensable resource, offering both practical wisdom and strategic insights to navigate the ever-evolving landscape of cyber risks.

Authored by Bob Chaput, a seasoned expert in the field, this material is backed by a wealth of knowledge derived from real-world experiences. It's not merely a theoretical exercise but a hands-on manual for organizations seeking to proactively protect their digital assets and leverage them for strategic advantage. The lessons to be learned from this book are not confined to a single sector or industry. Its principles are universally applicable, ensuring that both large and small organizations can find applicable and valuable takeaways. It's not just about fortifying defenses; it's about adopting a proactive stance toward cybersecurity.

As data breaches and cyberattacks continue to make headlines, this book is a timely and crucial resource for organizations looking to safeguard their integrity and reputation. Moreover, it provides the tools and strategies needed to turn cyber risk management into a value creator, helping organizations thrive amid an era of digital transformation.

Enterprise Cyber Risk Management as a Value Creator is a guiding light in the intricate maze of cybersecurity. It's a valuable asset for organizations of all sizes, empowering them to not only withstand digital threats but emerge stronger, more resilient, and ready to seize the boundless opportunities of the modern digital age.

—Michael E. Whitman, PhD, CISM, CISSP
Executive Director, Institute for Cybersecurity Workforce Development
Professor of Information Security and Textbook Author

Having performed dozens of risk analyses for companies during my career at a public accounting firm, this book is a masterclass in strategic management of digital risks in an enterprise and provides great insight to turn digital risk management into a competitive advantage. This is a good resource for business leaders, security professionals, and anyone seeking to navigate the complex landscape of digital security. With profound insights and practical wisdom, it successfully highlights the critical role of cyber/digital risk management in driving business value. Bob Chaput's expertise shines through as he presents a comprehensive and forward-thinking approach to managing cyber/digital risks. The inclusion of actionable insights and practical frameworks adds immense value to the content, ensuring that readers can immediately apply what they've learned.

—Raj Chaudhary, Independent Director, Board Advisor,
Retired Cybersecurity Partner, Crowe LLP

Someone told me recently that "cybersecurity is boring." Cybersecurity *is* boring if it is other people listening to CIOs, CISOs, and other IT people talking about it. They understand the issues, the risks, the solutions. Cybersecurity *should not be boring* to people who don't live it but must make decisions about it—big decisions like staffing, funding, prioritization against other business issues. How do you talk about cybersecurity in meaningful ways with the full C-suite, with your board of directors or trustees?

Bob Chaput has answered that question and solved the problem with his latest book: *Enterprise Cyber Risk Management as a Value Creator*. For too long, cybersecurity has been viewed as a defensive play, a cost center. What if the tables were turned and executives and boards thought about cybersecurity in a positive light and as an opportunity to create competitive advantage and add value to the organization and drive business growth?

This book, using data, statistics, and real business examples, is a primer for redirecting and refocusing those discussions for the leaders who must be engaged in cybersecurity but for too long have stayed out of the fray. The book provides lots of guidance and many questions—in each chapter—to get the business to start answering the right questions and asking their own. Multiple studies (many cited in this book) clearly indicate that business leaders and consumers agree that establishing trust in products and experiences (AI, digital technology, data) that meet expectations will deepen trust and promote growth.

This is the book to start those conversations, up and down the organization. Cybersecurity isn't boring if you have the right people talking about it—here is how to engage those "right" people in your organization. You'll need to arm your IT, security, risk management, operational, and innovation leaders, but you'll use the learning to deeply engage the C-suite, the boards, and committees of the board in positive discussion around cybersecurity and how to leverage a more secure organization to move faster and drive new opportunities.

—David Finn, Health IT Advocate,
Recovering Healthcare CIO, Security and Privacy Officer
Baldrige Foundation Award for Cybersecurity Leadership Excellence

Enterprise risk management, and cybersecurity risk management in particular, is more important now than ever. Bob's book takes the reader through easy-to-follow steps and provides "food for thought" when implementing an ERM program. A compliment to any bookshelf.

—Rachel V. Rose, JD, MBA, Principal at
Rachel V. Rose—Attorney at Law, PLLC

Chaput's new book on enterprise cyber risk management is a tour de force on this subject. Building a value-creating ECRM culture is not a sprint or a marathon, but a relay. Making this book an all-team read for your leadership and the first part an all-board read is an excellent way to start building that culture.

—Nancy Falls, Independent Board Director and CEO,
The Concinnity Company

I heard a friend recently bemoaning the state of ECRM within their organization, "We do risk management as an art, not a science." Bob breaks ECRM down to science. Bob's prescription for ECRM is on point and execution-ready. I looked at the Table of Contents and jumped right to Chapter 8. Each organization I've been part of has had a different ECRM strategy. Bob's book helps distill what success looks like. Bob coaches the reader through aligning business strategy and ECRM strategy—I especially appreciated his wisdom on what "HOW your organization will conduct ECRM?" means. Now, the challenge is ours to learn and implement.

—Dan Bowden, Global CISO, Marsh

Where others have focused primarily on the defensive aspects of cyber risk management, Bob Chaput sees opportunities in ECRM. Mr. Chaput states: "Companies with a strong security posture are more likely to retain existing customers and attract new ones, as they value their data protection. This customer trust and brand loyalty can increase revenue and market share for the organization." C-suite and board members will ignore this timely advice at their peril. This book provides a road map for the actions necessary to turn defensive thinking and processing into positive and value-creating actions and programs. Mr. Chaput makes the case for competitive and reputational advantage with logic, intelligence, and wit and draws from a depth of personal knowledge and experience in ECRM. Each chapter includes a set of "Questions Management and the Board Should Ask and Discuss," and these provide a great agenda of items worthy of consideration. You need this on your reading list.

—Stephen R. Rusmisel, JD, NACD.DC, 12-Year Independent Director and Former Lead Director of Life Storage, Inc.

Enterprise Cyber Risk Management as a Value Creator is a wide-ranging, thought-provoking book on an often-overlooked topic. Bob not only lays out why executives should care about ECRM but gives meaningful advice on how to get it done, and done well. He shares lessons, learned from years in the trenches, on how companies can get a handle on this vital yet often-misunderstood topic. This book addresses the key success factors as well as the common pitfalls in world-class risk management. It focuses on what leaders need to know and do, rather than get lost in the minutia of "this configuration of this system." This focus makes this book applicable across any industry that has to manage its cyber risk, which is, of course, all of them. The questions for the board of directors alone make this a worthwhile read—merely asking these questions will, at the very least, start you on the right path.

—William Niner, CISO

Bob Chaput in his latest book, *Enterprise Cyber Risk Management as a Value Creator,* works magic by revealing why cybersecurity risk is an essential ingredient of enterprise risk management. He introduces a new paradigm with enterprise cyber risk management (ECRM) being not just a defensive play, but as a proactive business enabler that can improve customer trust and stickiness through security services and increasing revenue sources by way of security capabilities. Bob lays out a well-understood foundation by elegantly taking us through a comprehensive survey of the changing cybersecurity governance landscape. He skillfully reveals timely concepts such as the new federal regulations, the evolving financial industry governing body trends, and the quiet but growing court system precedents. Bob makes a sound case for why ECRM is a must-have concept that is to be understood and adopted by organizations today.

With tight financial margins facing many organizations, it is critical that business value is achieved with every dollar spent. Bob shows us how ECRM goes well beyond just being an IT problem. He clearly explains how ECRM can serve to propel an organization forward with a host of benefits, some of which are by facilitating digital transformation and innovation, attracting higher-quality investments, bringing in more talent, supporting mergers and acquisitions (M&A) activities, reducing regulatory exposure, assuring operational continuity and resiliency, and creating increased competitive advantage.

Bob makes it easy for us to not only comprehend this evolving topic but practically take steps forward to implement the ECRM strategy by outlining a simple five-step approach. He sheds light on how small and large organizations can justify and practically build out an appropriate budget needed to establish a successful ECRM program, with specific guidance on how to educate and win over the C-suite and board, including key questions to ask and discuss. Bob deftly reveals the role of ECRM Program and Cybersecurity Strategy within the context of ERM, tying cybersecurity strategy into the board's responsibilities. His insights on the business ownership of risk through authorization to operate and use are particularly compelling.

This text is a must-have for boards of directors, senior management, IT and security leaders, and anyone who wants to know just how vital ECRM can be in ensuring the future success of your organization.

—James Brady, PhD, Healthcare CIO/CTO/CISO

Legal Disclaimer

Although the information provided in this book may be helpful in informing you and others who have an interest in data privacy, security issues, and cyber risk management issues, it does not constitute legal advice. This information may be based in part on current international, federal, state, and local laws and is subject to change based on changes in these laws or subsequent interpretative guidance. Where this information is based on federal law, it must be modified to reflect state law where that state law is more stringent than the federal law or where other state law exceptions apply. Information and informed recommendations provided in this book are intended to be a general information resource and should not be relied upon as a substitute for competent legal advice specific to your circumstances. Furthermore, the existence of a link or organization reference in any of the following materials should not be assumed as an endorsement by the author. YOU SHOULD EVALUATE ALL INFORMATION, OPINIONS, AND RECOMMENDATIONS PROVIDED IN THIS BOOK IN CONSULTATION WITH YOUR LEGAL OR OTHER ADVISORS, AS APPROPRIATE.

Acknowledgments

First, I must start by thanking my wonderful wife, Mary, to whom I dedicate this book. From coffee, food, patience, and encouragement to keeping the cats off my lap so I could write, she was as important to this book getting done as I was. Thank you so much, Mary.

I would also like to thank all the colleagues, executives, and board members with whom I've had an opportunity to work over the course of my career at GE, Johnson & Johnson, Healthways, and Clearwater. Those career opportunities helped me develop as an information technology and cyber risk management executive, entrepreneur, and educator and, ultimately, prepared me to write this book. Everyone with whom I worked contributed to this book in some way. Thank you.

When I first considered writing this book, I prepared a book proposal and turned to several cybersecurity, regulatory, and risk management veterans to provide feedback on the concept of a book on positive cyber risks or cyber opportunities. I sincerely appreciate Jim Brady, Raj Chaudhary, David Finn, Rachel Rose, and Paul Connelly for their careful reviews and constructive and encouraging feedback.

I want to thank the entire publishing team at Apress and, specifically, Susan McDermott and Laura Berendson for their support and guidance throughout the process.

Finally, I would like to thank my friend, former colleague, and technical reviewer of this book, Jon Stone, for skull sessions on the subject matter in this book that go back to our early work on Clearwater Security together.

About the Author

 **Bob Chaput, NACD.DC**, is the author of *Stop the Cyber Bleeding: What Healthcare Executives and Board Members Must Know About Enterprise Cyber Risk Management (ECRM).* He is also Founder and Executive Chairman of Clearwater, a leading provider of cybersecurity, cyber risk management and compliance software, consulting, and managed services. As a leading authority in cybersecurity regulatory compliance and enterprise cyber risk management, Bob has assisted dozens of organizations and their business partners, including Fortune 100 organizations, wanting to improve their risk posture. Bob's degrees include an MA in mathematics from Clark University and a BA in mathematics from the Massachusetts College of Liberal Arts. In addition to the NACD Directorship Certification (NACD.DC), Bob holds numerous privacy, security, and cyber risk management certifications. He is a faculty member at IANS Research.

About the Technical Reviewer

 **Jon Stone** is Senior Vice President and Chief Product Officer for Clearwater. In this role, he leads product innovation and product development.

Formerly, Jon served in numerous roles at Healthways, Inc., including Senior Portfolio and Project Management Director. He provided leadership of complex projects, product development, product strategy, and health information management consulting services to healthcare, managed care, and health information technology companies.

Before joining Healthways, Jon served as Director of Project Management and Healthcare Quality Metrics at Cigna Healthcare.

Jon has a master's in public administration and healthcare regulatory policy from the University of Tennessee at Chattanooga. He is certified as a Project Management Professional and has a Project Management for Information Systems certification from the University of Colorado.

Foreword

The issue of value creation has long been a contentious topic in cybersecurity. In this book, Bob Chaput makes a compelling argument that cybersecurity executives can function as value creators by taking on a leadership role in enterprise cyber risk management (ECRM). Bob then articulates a road map for how infosec executives, business leaders, and board members can work together to develop an ECRM-driven approach to security.

This book couldn't have come at a more critical time. The release of new cyber breach disclosure rules from the US Securities and Exchange Commission in July 2023 accelerated a growing movement among boards to govern cyber in a more strategic manner. Public companies are expected to identify the materiality of breaches and report on any material incidents within four days of determining materiality. To meet this need, the board, business executives, and CISOs must work together to develop a cohesive ECRM strategy. While the mandate only extends to public companies, the impact is expected to extend well beyond that jurisdiction.

Moving the cybersecurity conversation away from a focus on controls to an emphasis on ECRM is essential, and Bob is perfectly positioned to provide guidance here. From his executive technical leadership positions at GE, Johnson & Johnson, and Healthways to his work as CEO and, since 2018, Executive Chairman at Clearwater Compliance, not to mention his essential contribution as a member of the IANS Faculty, Bob has been exposed to countless executive cyber risk conversations. Bob is also a member of the National Association of Corporate Directors and has served as a board advisor. This blend of experience allows Bob to not only speak with authority about ECRM issues but also provide practical guidance on how to deliver value to the business.

On a personal note, I've found Bob to be one of the best active listeners that I've ever met. Bob's other great skill is in his ability to distill his conversations with CISOs, business leaders, board members, and regulators into compelling, actionable insights. He cares deeply about this topic and it shows.

The wisdom he passes on in this book is not just for CISOs. Anybody with a responsibility to manage or govern enterprise cyber risk can benefit from Bob's guidance.

This work is essential in the industry today, especially because it is not an academic work. Instead, Bob provides real, practical guidance on how to build out an ECRM program and use that to influence the business effectively. It takes what is often a theoretical idea and presents tangible ways to make that value a reality. That actionability makes it stand out and turns it into a necessary read for executives seeking a perspective on enterprise cyber risk.

—Phil Gardner, CEO, IANS Research

Preface

It feels like we're going through a similar positive cycle to what I experienced early in my career in the mid-1980s when businesses recognized that information and information technology were an asset that companies could leverage for competitive advantage. In 1985, Michael E. Porter and Victor E. Millar published their seminal article, "How Information Gives You Competitive Advantage." In it, they highlighted how the information revolution critically affected competition, including changing industry structure, altering competition rules, creating competitive advantage by giving companies new ways to outperform their rivals, and spawning whole new businesses.

In this book, I highlight parallels between what happened over the course of the last 40 years and what is underway today with cybersecurity. In short, with the explosion in data, systems, and devices in connection with massive digitization programs that businesses have undertaken, it has become clear that organizations must safeguard these new information assets. Organizations, their C-suites, and boards must now realize that they can leverage a robust Enterprise Cyber Risk Management (ECRM) Program and Cybersecurity Strategy to create a competitive advantage for their organization. As Yogi said, it's like déjà vu all over again.

I was gratified to see how well executives, board members, and many stakeholders in the healthcare ecosystem received my book *Stop the Cyber Bleeding* in 2020. I appreciated the opportunity to give something back to the healthcare industry in the form of practical, tangible recommendations to establish, implement, and mature an ECRM program. For many organizations, building such a program represented paying off "ECRM debt" after having gone on a spending binge as they digitized what were, in many cases, ancient clinical and administrative information systems. Most of that book focused on basics to build defenses to assure the confidentiality, integrity, and availability of data, systems, and devices against adversarial and other threat sources.

To a lesser extent, I addressed the possibility of a strong ECRM program becoming a business enabler. I discussed that not only is ECRM not an "IT problem," it can become a business enabler if appropriately handled. I briefly discussed how a robust ECRM Program and Cybersecurity Strategy might be leveraged as a competitive advantage. I presented several possible cyber opportunities, such as facilitating M&A, reducing the cost of capital, lowering executive risk insurance premiums, and helping their organizations compete with "technology invaders."

In *Enterprise Cyber Risk Management as a Value Creator*, I go further. I wrote this book to encourage organizations in all industries to start to move away from ECRM and cybersecurity strategy as a purely defensive play. I think most organizations are overdue to proactively seek ways to use their ECRM Program and Cybersecurity Strategy to not only manage risks or "manage the downside" but also identify ways to use their ECRM Program and Cybersecurity Strategy to identify and exploit opportunities or "manage the upside" and create competitive advantage.

This book provides an overview of why a robust ECRM Program and Cybersecurity Strategy is a strategic imperative for your organization and how executives and board members should think more positively about ECRM and cybersecurity and, finally, outlines how to develop your ECRM Program and Cybersecurity Strategy, including a discussion of the contents of documentation that will help establish, implement, and mature your program and meet increasingly more stringent requirements legislators, regulators, and the courts are setting.

My goal is that C-suite executives, board members, and their Chief Information Security Officers (CISOs) use this book to bridge communication gaps and meet at the intersection of where boards focus:

talent management, strategy, and risk management. As an existential risk to most organizations, they need to manage these risks and leverage their programs' strengths to create value and drive business growth.

For ECRM to be effective, the entire organization must be engaged in the program. Although this book is written primarily for C-suite executives, board members, and CISOs, I am confident that the information I present will also be helpful to other leaders, managers, and professionals in all functional areas in all organizations in all industries.

Bob decided to write this book to help facilitate the role of Chief Information Security Officers (CISOs) to better integrate into their businesses and interact with C-suite executives and board members. As happened when Chief Information Officers (CIOs) began to "earn a seat at the table" decades ago, there is a significant communication gap between this newly discovered role, the C-suite, and the board. Bob's goal is to make CISOs and their boards successful in better understanding one another and better managing cyber risks and cyber opportunities. The aim of this book is to help close the communication gap by linking CISOs with the three main topics that boards deal with: talent management, strategy, and risk management.

—Bob Chaput, Founder and Executive Chairman, Clearwater

Abbreviations

- AI: Artificial Intelligence

- ANSI: American National Standards Institute

- BIA: Business Impact Analysis

- BT: Business Technology

- CAE: Chief Audit Executive

- CapEx: Capital Expenditures

- CCA: Certified CMMC Assessor

- CCP: Certified CMMC Professional

- CCPA: California Consumer Privacy Act

- CDI: Covered Defense Information

- CFR: Code of Federal Regulation

- CFTC: Commodity Futures Trading Commission

- CGEIT: Certified in Governance of Enterprise IT

- CIA: Confidentiality, Integrity, and Availability

- CIO: Chief Information Officer

- CIRCIA: Cyber Incident Reporting for Critical Infrastructure Act of 2022

- CISA: Certified Information Systems Auditor

- CISA: Cybersecurity and Infrastructure Security Agency, US Department of Homeland Security

ABBREVIATIONS

- CISM: Certified Information Security Manager

- CISO: Chief Information Security Officer

- CISSP: Certified Information Systems Security Professional

- CMMC: Cybersecurity Maturity Model Certification

- CMS: Centers for Medicare and Medicaid Services

- COBIT: Control Objectives for Information and Related Technologies

- COOP: Continuity of Operations Plan

- COSO: Committee of Sponsoring Organizations of the Treadway Commission

- CPA: Certified Public Accountant

- CRISC: Certified in Risk and Information Systems Control

- CSO: Chief Security Officer

- CSRC: Computer Security Resource Center (at NIST)

- CUI: Controlled Unclassified Information

- CVE: Common Vulnerability Enumeration

- DBIR: Data Breach Investigations Report (Verizon)

- DFARS: Defense Federal Acquisition Regulation Supplement

- DHHS: Department of Health and Human Services

- DOJ: Department of Justice

- DIB: Defense Industrial Base

- ECRM: Enterprise Cyber Risk Management

- ECRMS: Enterprise Cyber Risk Management System

- ED&I: Equity, Diversity, and Inclusion

- EDP: Electronic Data Processing

- EDR: Endpoint Detection and Response

- EHR: Electronic Health Record

- ePHI: Electronic Protected Health Information

- ERP: Enterprise Resource Planning

- ERM: Enterprise Risk Management

- ESG: Environmental, Social, and Governance

- EU: European Union

- FAR: Federal Acquisition Regulation

- FBI: Federal Bureau of Investigation

- FCC: Federal Communications Commission

- FCI: Federal Contract Information

- FDA: Food and Drug Administration

- FDIC: Federal Deposit Insurance Corporation

- FERPA: Family Educational Rights and Privacy Act

- FFIEC: Federal Financial Institutions Examination Council

- FISMA: Federal Information Security Management Act

- FSB: Financial Stability Board

- FSOC: Financial Stability Oversight Counsel

- FTC: Federal Trade Commission
- GDPR: General Data Protection Regulation
- GISS: Global Information Security Survey
- GLBA: Gramm-Leach-Bliley Act
- GRC: Governance, Risk Management, and Compliance
- HIMSS: Healthcare Information and Management Systems Society
- HIPAA: Health Insurance Portability and Accountability Act
- HITECH Act: Health Information Technology for Economic and Clinical Health Act
- HVAC: Heating, Ventilation, and Air Conditioning
- IAM: Identity and Access Management
- IDN: Integrated Delivery Network
- IM: Information Management
- IRM|Pro: Information Risk Management | Professional, Clearwater's ECRMS solution
- ISA: Internet Security Alliance
- ISACA: Information Systems Audit and Control Association
- ISAC: Information Sharing and Analysis Center
- ISC2: International Information System Security Certification Consortium
- ISCM: Information Security Continuous Monitoring

- ISO/IEC: International Organization for Standardization and International Electrotechnical Commission
- ISS: Institutional Shareholder Services
- ISSA: Information Systems Security Association
- IT: Information Technology
- M&A: Mergers and Acquisitions
- MD&A: Management's Discussion and Analysis of Financial Condition and Results of Operations
- MFA: Multifactor Authentication
- MNPI: Material Non-public Information
- MIS: Management Information Services
- MIT CISR: Massachusetts Institute of Technology Center for Information Systems Research
- MPL: Medical Professional Liability
- NACD: National Association of Corporate Directors
- NASDAQ: National Association of Securities Dealers Automated Quotations Stock Market
- NATO: North Atlantic Treaty Organization
- NCUA: National Credit Union Administration
- NIS2: Network and Information Security Directive 2 2022/2555
- NIST: National Institute of Standards and Technology
- NIST SP: NIST Special Publication
- NIST CSF: NIST Cybersecurity Framework

- NPRM: Notice of Proposed Rulemaking

- NYDFS: New York Department of Financial Services

- NYSE: New York Stock Exchange

- OCC: Office of the Comptroller of the Currency (OCC), US Federal Reserve

- OCR: HHS Office for Civil Rights

- OpEx: Operating Expenses

- PAM: Privileged Access Management

- PB: Petabytes

- PCI: Payment Card Information

- PCI DSS: Payment Card Industry Data Security Standard

- PDLC: Product Development Life Cycle

- PE: Private Equity

- PHI: Protected Health Information

- PI Program: CMS' Promoting Interoperability Program

- PII: Personally Identifiable Information

- PIN: Personal Identification Number

- PMO: Project Management Office

- RIMS: Risk Management Society

- ROI: Return on Investment

- ROSI: Return on Security Investment

- SaaS: Software-as-a-Service

- SDLC: Systems Development Life Cycle or Security Development Life Cycle

- SEC: US Securities and Exchange Commission

- SIEM: Security Information and Event Management

- SOC: Security Operations Center

- SOC2: System and Organization Controls (SOC)

- TB: Terabytes

- TCO: Total Cost of Ownership

- TPRM: Third-Party Risk Management

- VC: Venture Capital

- XDR: Extended Detection and Response

PART I

A Case for Action

CHAPTER 1

Enterprise Cyber Risk Management as a Value Creator

Once you replace negative thoughts with positive ones, you'll start having positive results.

—Willie Nelson[1]

Over the last 40 years, I've enjoyed helping organizations comply with various privacy, security, and breach notification regulations and standards and improve their enterprise cyber risk management and cybersecurity posture. These efforts have been primarily defensive. The focus of my defensive work with healthcare organizations, for example, is captured in the subtitle of my book *Stop the Cyber Bleeding,*[2] as *How to Save Your Patients, Preserve Your Reputation, and Protect Your Balance Sheet.* The verbs "save," "preserve," and "protect" are about safeguarding, assuring, and "managing the downside." Although critically important, "managing the downside" does not align with the language of most companies' strategic objectives, which include creating value, driving revenue growth, and enabling their business. In other words, those

© Bob Chaput 2024
B. Chaput, *Enterprise Cyber Risk Management as a Value Creator,*
https://doi.org/10.1007/979-8-8688-0094-8_1

defensive verbs are not about using cybersecurity to "create and manage the upside." You need to think about cyber opportunities that can help achieve your business goals.

Risk management and especially cyber risk management (both of which I will further define) are too often only focused on preventing the bad things that may happen in your organization. That's a good thing. At the same time, I recommend you expand your thinking, policies, procedures, and practices to incorporate opportunity and specifically cyber opportunities in your risk management work. Although I may not always link "risk and opportunity" together in phrases like risk and opportunity management, risk and opportunity assessment, or risk and opportunity treatment, know that the intent of this book is to provoke your thinking always to consider opportunities or upside outcomes from your ECRM work. Also, keep in mind that while cybersecurity regulations such as HIPAA, SEC, and NYDFS focus on risk (i.e., the downside) when they use the term risk management, there are compelling reasons to include your cyber opportunities (i.e., the upside) in your work to meet these regulatory requirements.

This chapter addresses an essential consideration for all companies regarding their ECRM Program and Cybersecurity Strategy—pivoting from regarding cybersecurity as solely a cost-centered defensive program to a profit-centered transformational core growth strategy. With global estimated cybercrime costs forecasted to exceed \$23B globally by 2027,[3] there are already enough good reasons to be defensive and establish, implement, and mature a strong ECRM program. Progressive-thinking organizations are going beyond being defensive. Missed cyber opportunities can be as costly to your organization as exploited vulnerabilities.

In its "2023 Global Future of Cyber Survey," Deloitte observes:

Today, we are seeing the emergence of powerful new attitudes when it comes to cyber. Leaders are looking at cyber through a sharp, new lens—one that reveals the inherent business value that can come by embedding cyber. Not only across the enterprise, but as a crucial part of a powerful growth strategy.[4]

A strong ECRM Program and Cybersecurity Strategy can facilitate business strategy, value creation, and growth. To do so, you must change your thinking to regard cybersecurity as a potential profit center rather than a cost center.

The Next Cybersecurity Pivot

I wish I could readily recall how often I wrote or said that ECRM is not an "IT problem," but, indeed, an enterprise risk management issue. I've written that it can be a business enabler.[5] I am now "tripling down" by adding that it can be a value creator and growth driver. Your ECRM Program and Cybersecurity Strategy can support your strategic business objectives and growth. Suppose you've reached the board by connecting to their risk oversight responsibilities. In that case, you can now pivot to focus on one of their other top three responsibilities, strategy, which is about growing market share, revenues, and profits.

Of course, timing is everything, and the maturity level of your ECRM Program and Cybersecurity Strategy is a critical consideration as you make this pivot. I would be reluctant to dive into an all-out cyber media campaign to increase customer trust in your company (a value creator) if you've not yet completed a comprehensive, enterprise-wide risk and opportunity assessment. You need to assess your current ECRM maturity before pivoting.

I've written about the transformational importance of an ECRM program, the resultant cybersecurity strategy, and the core capabilities organizations must develop around governance, people, process, technology, and engagement.[6] Pivoting from an "IT problem" to an "enterprise risk management matter" to a "core part of business strategy" not only requires these capabilities but can help further mature these capabilities.

In 2020, Hepner and Powell published an article in the MIT Sloan Management Review that examined, among other topics, why the C-suite and board treat ECRM and cybersecurity as operational rather than strategic issues. They cited four top reasons: cybersecurity is delegated to IT, companies misunderstand the strategic nature of cybersecurity, companies keep attacks under wraps of cybersecurity risk, and executives assign strategic priorities based on their own areas of expertise. Like my call for a pivot in thinking, they recommend flipping the narrative on cybersecurity.[7]

Digital Transformation Is Not Slowing Down

The Chip War[8] continues, Moore's Law[9] has not yet stretched the laws of physics, technology rapidly evolves, and organizations continue their digital transformation programs. Whether your digital priorities involve quantum computing, artificial intelligence/machine learning, 5G, data analytics, cloud, blockchain, Internet of Things (IoT), or replacing more traditional IT applications, ongoing digitization is driving the need for better ECRM programs and the maturing of your cybersecurity strategy. Cybersecurity protects investments and business value and enables digital initiatives to drive growth.

Research by the MIT Center for Information Systems Research has shown that information technology units are more important than ever to building a company's success, citing how leveraging four key capabilities can result in higher profitability of as much as 24% greater than competitors.[10] None of the four capabilities (the CIO working strategically with the company's executive committee on the role of digital, building digital discipline across the enterprise, improving external customer engagement, and relentlessly delivering operational efficiencies) would be possible without a strong ECRM Program and Cybersecurity Strategy.

Creating Business Value

The following sections provide examples of positive business outcomes that may result from a strong ECRM Program and Cybersecurity Strategy.

Increasing Customer Trust and Brand Loyalty

In the digital age, customers are increasingly concerned about the security of their data. Businesses investing in cybersecurity demonstrate their commitment to protecting customer information and fostering trust and loyalty. Companies with a strong security posture are more likely to retain existing customers and attract new ones, as they value their data protection. This customer trust and brand loyalty can increase revenue and market share for the organization. A Harvard Business Review article highlighted the positive outcomes for a trusted organization:

> *The most trustworthy companies have outperformed the S&P 500, and high-trust companies are more than 2.5 times more likely to be high-performing revenue organizations. Our own research shows that trusted companies outperform their peers by up to 400% in terms of total market value, that customers who trust a brand are 88% more likely to buy again, and that 79% of employees who trust their employer are more motivated to work and less likely to leave.[11]*

Companies that invest in robust cybersecurity measures enjoy an enhanced reputation in the market, which can translate to a competitive advantage, discussed later in this chapter. When a company demonstrates its commitment to protecting sensitive customer information and business data, it fosters trust and confidence in its brand. This commitment is essential in industries where data privacy and security are paramount, such as finance, healthcare, and ecommerce.

According to a McKinsey survey, consumer faith in cybersecurity, data privacy, and responsible AI hinges on what companies do today—and establishing this digital trust just might lead to business growth.[12] The survey results of more than 1,300 business leaders and 3,000 consumers globally suggest that establishing trust in products and experiences that leverage AI, digital technologies, and data meet consumer expectations and could promote growth.

Increasing customer trust and brand loyalty creates value and drives growth.

Improving Social Responsibility

Elevating your ECRM Program and Cybersecurity Strategy can strengthen your environmental, social, and governance (ESG) program. The SEC has proposed significant changes to ESG disclosures. It is already monitoring required filings and voluntary statements such as those made in corporate sustainability reports, on websites, or in marketing materials.[13] Figure 1-1 illustrates the relationship of regulatory compliance, cybersecurity, and privacy with ESG.

Figure 1-1. *Relationship of Compliance, Cybersecurity, and Privacy with ESG*

Privacy, cybersecurity, and cyber risk management exposures and oversight are material ESG issues (MEIs) and should be considered critical to an organization's overall ESG risk rating. An MEI is an ESG issue with the most significant potential to affect a company's bottom line.[14] As companies work to build investors' and other stakeholders' trust and confidence, expect ESG to influence privacy and security programs and vice versa.

A recent World Economic Forum article admonishes:

Companies need to start looking at cybersecurity as part of ESG. Cyber risk is the most immediate and financially material sustainability risk that organizations face today.[15]

In "Cyber security: Don't report on ESG without it," KPMG presents the case that cybersecurity is part of all three elements of ESG—environmental, social, and governance.[16] A recent Harvard Law School Forum on Corporate Governance article also aligns cybersecurity closely with E, S, and G. The paper proposes how NASDAQ might incorporate cybersecurity into its voluntary ESG Reporting Guide under the Corporate Governance subsection.[17]

A strong ECRM Program and Cybersecurity Strategy can create value and a competitive advantage by improving your organization's social responsibility posture and ESG reporting.

Driving Revenue Growth

As previously discussed, a progressive and robust ECRM Program and Cybersecurity Strategy can increase customer trust and brand loyalty, retaining existing customers and attracting new ones, which means revenue growth. In the MIT Sloan Management Review article "Improving Your Bottom Line with Cybersecurity," the author Matthew Doan cites three specific ways in which cybersecurity may increase revenue:

- *Providing a differentiating and marketable trait to gain customers, increase transaction size, and charge premium prices.*

- *Accruing new revenue sources by adding security capabilities (for example, monitoring, response) into an existing product/service portfolio.*

   Using security services for long-term "stickiness" with customers, keeping sales channels open for a range of offerings.[18]

Your organization may be able to create premium pricing or offer individual dedicated security or privacy products. "Cybersecurity-by-design" has long been a catchphrase to underscore the importance of developing secure information systems and applications as part of the systems development life cycle (SDLC). Organizations must consider cybersecurity a design element in their manufacturing processes and product development life cycle (PDLC) to drive revenue growth. In some cases, it may be a matter of having created the ability to charge premium pricing; in others, it may be a matter of creating a strategic differentiator in your offering.

A strong ECRM Program and Cybersecurity Strategy should enable your organization to earn a cybersecurity certification, such as those associated with SOC2, ISO 27001, HITRUST, PCI DSS, NIST, and CMMC. With the increase in cybersecurity spending, which I discuss further in Chapter 5, organizations seeking your services will likely consider relevant certifications for your industry. For example, when the final regulatory rulemaking is complete, without a Cybersecurity Maturity Model Certification (CMMC), your organization cannot contract with the Department of Defense.[19] As another example, consider the movement to the cloud that most organizations undertake. Authors of a *CPA Journal* article observed that organizations are shifting from concerns over migrating to the cloud due to cloud security to business resiliency benefits due to the increased maturity of cloud offerings and the attendant attention to cybersecurity certifications.[20] Producing the proper certifications in your sales or business development process will help drive revenue.

Companies prioritizing cybersecurity grow revenue by expanding into new markets, as they can confidently address the diverse security requirements and regulations in different regions. A strong security posture can also attract new customers and partners who value the protection of their data, further facilitating market expansion and growth.

A robust cybersecurity program can help an organization build trust with prospective customers in new markets by demonstrating a commitment to protecting their data and privacy, as discussed in the preceding separate section. In the context of expanding into new markets, think about the power you place in the hands of your marketing, sales, and investor relations team by publishing the highlights of your ECRM Program and Cybersecurity Strategy in alignment with your company values. Equifax has been doing exactly that for several years now with its Security Annual Report.[21]

Expanding into new markets often requires adherence to international regulations and data protection laws, such as Europe's General Data Protection Regulation (GDPR). A robust cybersecurity program can help an organization ensure a secure and dependable supply chain, which is crucial when entering new markets and working with new suppliers and partners. The digital transformation underway in all industries and increasing supply chain complexity driven in no small part by the COVID-19 pandemic have highlighted cybersecurity supply chain risks. Comparitech, a pro-consumer website founded in 2015, analyzed the most significant software supply chain attacks (i.e., SolarWinds, Log4j, Codecov, and Kaseya), finding thousands of downstream customers attacked with a variety of techniques, including counterfeiting, drive-by compromise, malware infections, phishing, etc.[22]

Securing your supply chain through a solid third-party risk management program that is part of your strong ECRM Program and Cybersecurity Strategy ensures the continuity of operations, ongoing customer service, and continued revenue growth.

Facilitating Digital Transformation and Innovation

A strong ECRM Program and Cybersecurity Strategy can give your organization the confidence to pursue its digital transformation and innovate. The absence of proactive ECRM slows new technology adoption and innovation. Over 300 senior technology decision-makers cited cybersecurity solutions as the most critical factor affecting business transformation.[23] A major loss of shareholder value can result from ECRM failure. The August 2023 Clorox attack reportedly occurred in the middle of a $500M digitization project. Among other costly consequences was a stock price drop from ~$160 per share to $125 per share resulting in a $4.3 billion loss of shareholder value.[24]

As businesses undergo digital transformation to improve efficiency and gain a competitive edge, the importance of cybersecurity becomes even more apparent. Integrating cybersecurity into the core of the digital transformation process can streamline the adoption of new technologies, protect against emerging threats, and create a resilient digital infrastructure that can adapt to evolving business needs. By incorporating cybersecurity as a critical pillar of digital transformation, companies can derive more value from their investments in new technologies and platforms.

Secure digital infrastructure empowers companies to leverage emerging technologies, such as quantum computing, artificial intelligence/machine learning, 5G, data analytics, blockchain, cloud computing, data analytics, and the Internet of Things (IoT), to drive innovation and improve their products and services. By investing in a robust ECRM Program and Cybersecurity Strategy, organizations can adopt new technologies, ensuring that they remain at the forefront of their industry, thereby creating a competitive advantage.

Lowering the Cost of Capital

Access to capital is vital for all types of organizations, including public, private, and not-for-profit. Without capital, organizations would be unable to acquire new technologies, start new lines of business for alternative sources of revenue, renovate facilities, and offer new products and services. Organizations must maintain access to capital at low rates to stay competitive.

Lowering the cost of capital or maintaining access to capital at a competitive interest rate is another potential benefit of implementing a strong ECRM program, creating value by positively impacting your organization's bottom line.

ECRM is playing an increasingly important role in this arena. Credit-rating agencies—including Standard and Poor's (S&P), Moody's, and Fitch Group—have all implemented consideration of the financial impact of a cyberattack on an organization's credit rating.

In 2018, Moody's named Derek Vadala (Moody's CISO) to a newly established role as Head of Cyber Risk for Moody's Investors Service (MIS).[25] In a press release announcing the appointment, Rob Fauber, president of MIS, said:

> *As with environmental, social, and governance risks, we see cyber risk as an area of increasing relevance to issuers, investors, counterparties, and government authorities as it impacts operational and credit risk. Moody's unique perspective can help enhance market understanding of how credit and cyber risk intersect.*[26]

In February 2019, Moody's Investors Service Research Announcement indicated one of the critical factors in Moody's credit analysis could include "…the extent of an entity's investment in cyber defenses before an event …"[27] The announcement went on to say:

> *When assigning a credit rating, we consider cyber risks in the context of all other risks an issuer faces. A significant cyber event could lead to lower scoring for factors such as cost structure, market position, profitability, coverage, and leverage. When we believe an emerging risk is highly likely to weaken a company's credit quality, we incorporate these expectations into our ratings. Consistent with this long-standing approach, we expect to incorporate the credit effects of cyber risk as our understanding of issuer-level exposures and mitigation strategies evolves and well before the effect of a significant cyber event is fully evident in financial and operating results.*[28]

Moody's downgraded the credit rating for Equifax from "stable" to "negative" based on the massive data breach the company experienced in 2017.[29] SolarWinds had its rating lowered by S&P from a B+ to a B in April of last year after a cyberattack in 2020.[30]

A robust ECRM program may positively impact your credit rating and help your organization obtain more competitive rates for capital.

Attracting Higher-Quality Investments

Beyond borrowing, businesses with robust cybersecurity measures can attract more venture or private equity investors, as these businesses are better equipped to manage risks and safeguard assets. Increased and sustained investment in public or private markets can help drive growth and innovation.

A robust ECRM Program and Cybersecurity Strategy helps mitigate cybersecurity risks, which are a primary concern for investors. As I have discussed, cyberattacks and data breaches can lead to significant financial losses, damage to reputation, and legal liabilities. By proactively addressing these risks, companies can demonstrate a commitment to protecting their assets and investors' interests. Investors place a premium on trust and reputation. Companies with a strong cybersecurity posture are less likely to experience damaging cyberattacks and data breaches that erode trust. This trust is crucial for attracting long-term investments and retaining existing shareholders.

Investors conduct thorough due diligence before making investment decisions. Companies with transparent cybersecurity practices and a willingness to share information about their security measures are more likely to attract investments.

A robust cybersecurity program is no longer a tool for "managing the downside" or a technical necessity; it has become crucial in attracting higher-quality investments. Investors are increasingly aware of inadequate cybersecurity's financial and reputational risks, making it a critical consideration in their investment decisions. Companies prioritizing cybersecurity can position themselves as attractive investment opportunities by mitigating risks, building trust, ensuring compliance, and enhancing their overall competitive posture.

A robust ECRM Program and Cybersecurity Strategy may help your organization attract higher-quality investments from other sources.

Assuring Operational Continuity and Resilience

Business interruption insurance generally replaces business income lost in a disaster such as a fire, hurricane, or another natural disaster. In addition to covering lost net profits, it may also cover items like rent and other fixed costs, alternate or temporary location costs, employee wages, taxes, training costs, etc.[31] There are many items it does not cover. For many reasons, it's best not to test your policy. It's better to invest in your business continuity and resilience initiative, which should be part of your ECRM program.

The National Institute of Standards and Technology (NIST) defines a continuity of operations plan (COOP) as "a predetermined set of instructions or procedures that describe how an organization's mission-essential functions will be sustained within 12 hours and for up to 30 days as a result of a disaster event before returning to normal operations."[32] NIST defines resilience as "the ability to prepare for and adapt to changing conditions and withstand and recover rapidly from disruption. Resilience includes the ability to withstand and recover from deliberate attacks, accidents, or naturally occurring threats or incidents."[33]

Operational continuity and resilience are crucial for organizations, as disruptions can result in significant financial losses and damage their reputation. A strong ECRM program and cybersecurity posture help maintain operational continuity by protecting critical infrastructure, preventing data breaches, and ensuring the availability of essential services. Progressive organizations can use ECRM to identify strategically important operations and ensure operational continuity. A foundational element of your ECRM program is a framework, such as the NIST Cybersecurity Framework,[34] which originally included five core functions—Identify, Protect, Detect, Respond, and Recover.[35] In August 2023, NIST released the Public Draft: The NIST Cybersecurity Framework 2.0, which includes many changes, including the addition of a core function called Govern.[36]

As you may infer, with core functions such as Detect, Respond, and Recover, resilience is a core focus of the NIST Cybersecurity Framework. Regarding the idea of pivoting to consider cyber opportunities and to support the case for consideration of the positives of your ECRM Program and Cybersecurity Strategy, note the addition of the subcategory under the Risk Management category in the NIST Cybersecurity Framework 2.0 under the new Govern function:

> *GV.RM-07: Strategic opportunities (i.e., positive risks) are identified and included in organizational cybersecurity risk discussions.*[37]

This new subcategory is all about the pivot in thinking that I am calling for.

Operational continuity and resilience derive from a robust ECRM Program and Cybersecurity Strategy, creating business value, preserving revenue, and enabling your organization to continue serving customers. Additionally, this allows you to focus on your core business activities and maintain your competitive position.

Creating Competitive Advantage

As I write this section, I recall the analogous journey many of us made progressing through our information technology (IT) careers. Developing and deploying IT solutions was primarily about automation, efficiency, and cost savings. In the early days, the function was called electronic data processing (EDP) and usually originated in the finance department with projects to implement batch processing solutions to automate payroll, accounts payable, fixed assets accounting, etc.

The IT function became increasingly more critical as it evolved through name changes like EDP to information systems (IS) to IT to information management (IM), management information services (MIS), and, one I adopted, business technology (BT) after hearing George Colony of Forrester Research advocate its use.[38] And then, I recall attending a two-week class at the GE Executive Development Center at Crotonville, New York, taught by Harvard professor Jim Cash in the mid-1980s. Wow! Wait! What? Use the information to create a competitive advantage? Around that time, Professor Michael Porter (Mr. Competitive Advantage himself) co-authored a seminal Harvard Business Review article with then Arthur Andersen & Co managing partner Victor Millar titled "How Information Gives You Competitive Advantage."[39] Call it what you will— EDP, IT, IS, MIS, BT—the information technology function was off to the races. Business leaders invited CIOs to have a seat at the table to discuss how to leverage information for competitive advantage.

One of my favorite definitions of strategy is "the means to create economic value by gaining competitive advantage through a unique value proposition"[23] because it connects value creation with a competitive advantage. Organizations with a strong cybersecurity posture can differentiate themselves from competitors by showcasing their commitment to data protection and security. This differentiation can increase market share and value creation in the long term.

Advocating a risk-based approach to cybersecurity, a recent article by the World Economic Forum advises:

> *Adopting a risk-based cybersecurity model also confers benefits beyond simply preventing cyber-attacks. It builds resilience and agility, and this method of continuously assessing and adapting makes for more streamlined and competitive organizations more generally.*[40]

A comprehensive ECRM Program and Cybersecurity Strategy that considers both cyber risks and cyber opportunities—the focus of this book—conveys a commitment to your industry, the marketplace, and current and prospective customers that distinguishes your organization from your competitors.

Attracting and Retaining Talent

Companies prioritizing cybersecurity can attract and retain top talent, as employees value working for organizations committed to protecting their and their customers' data and digital assets. This protection commitment can increase employee satisfaction and productivity, further creating value.

COVID-19, the "Great Resignation," significant technology company layoffs, and "quiet quitting" have created a new set of dynamics for organizations striving to attract and retain talent for their organizations. Organizations with tainted reputations due to material cybersecurity incidents will likely have a more difficult time with talent management, a vital C-suite and board issue. Existing workforce members and candidates may conclude that management and the board either don't know or don't care about managing cyber risks. Who wants to work there? In general, members across the workforce will think twice. Specific to your organization's cybersecurity talent, how competitive will your organization be in attracting cybersecurity professionals in the face of the current shortage of 3.4 million cybersecurity workers worldwide?[41]

A strong ECRM Program and Cybersecurity Strategy can help your organization attract and retain talent in several ways. Organizations with robust cybersecurity measures are perceived as more reliable and trustworthy, making them more attractive to prospective employees. A good reputation can help attract top talent. ADP, one of the world's largest comprehensive providers of cloud-based human capital management (HCM) solutions, has advanced the notion of a TRUST model of communication (*trust, regulation, usage, security, and technology*) to underscore the importance of protecting employee information for all employees at scale.[42]

A strong ECRM Program and Cybersecurity Strategy demonstrates an organization's commitment to safeguarding employees' personal and sensitive information, increasing their trust and satisfaction. As mentioned earlier in this chapter, 79% of employees who trust their employer are more motivated to work and less likely to leave.[43]

Implementing a cybersecurity program requires ongoing employee training and development, which can be an attractive incentive for potential employees seeking career growth. The Swiss Cyber Institute, for example, suggests cybersecurity training for employee training and development, which increases employee engagement and, ultimately, promotes greater profitability.[44]

An organization that adheres to cybersecurity regulations and standards, such as PCI DSS, GLBA, CCPA, GDPR, SEC, DFARS/CMMC, or HIPAA, can reassure potential employees that they will protect their personal information, making them more likely to join and stay with the company. Employees (and consumers and business leaders) cited protecting data and cybersecurity as the principal element of trust, according to PwC's 2021 Trust in Business Survey.[45] A subsequent PwC article connected the talent management challenges all executive teams face, citing the turbulent labor market over the past two years and how employees have commanded the C-suite's attention, suggesting that this could point to a shift in workers becoming more like customers and clients than like employees.[46]

A secure working environment allows employees to collaborate more effectively and share information without fear of unauthorized access, enhancing productivity and team cohesion. Teamwork is critical to business success, especially as we migrate to hybrid and fully remote work environments. More and more information is shared virtually by members of your workforce, and, at the same time, as Verizon's 2022 Data Breach

Investigations Report (DBIR) shows, 82% of breaches involved the human element, including incidents like the use of stolen credentials, phishing, misuse, or simply errors.[47]

Unfortunately, organizations with weak ECRM programs can drive talent away. Nurses at two CommonSpirit hospitals are suing CommonSpirit for $1.5 million due to a ransomware attack last fall that allegedly resulted in unpaid wages.[48] As a result of a cyberattack on UKG Inc.'s Kronos timekeeping system in late 2021, a dispute with employees at Ascension Health Alliance in St. Louis, Missouri, a customer of UKG, resulted in one of its hospitals agreeing to pay $19.7 million to settle disputes over employee wages. In another ongoing UKG-driven case at Honda Motor Co.'s US subsidiary, four employees sued the automaker last year for allegedly failing to properly track their hours and pay them appropriately.[49] These events will drive employees away rather than help retain them and attract new ones.

Establishing, implementing, and maturing your ECRM Program and Cybersecurity Strategy can become a powerful talent management tool for your organization.

Facilitating M&A Activity

Mergers and acquisitions (M&A) activity has long been a priority for public and private companies. Executives and boards have a critical role in M&A activities, as both a tool used in disruption and an often-used strategic alternative to organic growth. Of course, M&A activity involves divestitures as well as mergers and acquisitions. Therefore, board members may find themselves overseeing either buying or selling activity. In either case, strong ECRM capabilities can be vital.

In Deloitte's 2022 Future of M&A Trends Survey, 92% of respondents expected deal volume to increase or stay the same over the next 12 months.[50] Cyber risk is an increasingly significant part of M&A due diligence activity. About three-quarters of respondents (77%) in an ISC2 study have recommended to proceed with an M&A deal based on the strength of the target company's cybersecurity program.[51]

Lots of things can go and do go wrong in M&A work. A Harvard Business Review article stated that, according to most studies, between 70% and 90% of acquisitions fail.[52] A strong, proactive ECRM program can facilitate M&A activity by helping avoid making bad M&A decisions. Acquirers can experience a loss of shareholder value due to concerns of earnings dilution, poor fit, or excessive diversification.[53]

After Verizon agreed to acquire Yahoo, Yahoo disclosed two massive data breaches had occurred in 2013 and 2014.[54] Due to the disclosure, the two companies negotiated a reduction of $350 million in the purchase price.[55] Spirit AeroSystems announced that the acquisition of Asco had been pending since 2018, with a delayed closing mainly due to a ransomware attack on Asco. In June 2019, Asco experienced a ransomware attack that forced temporary factory closures, ultimately causing a 25% purchase price reduction of $150 million from the original $604 million.[56] In September 2020, the parties terminated the acquisition due to the deal's unsatisfied conditions.[57]

A mature ECRM program can facilitate M&A transactions by enabling creating scale and competitive advantage. A mature ECRM program can ensure that cybersecurity issues will not stand in the way of whether your organization wants to acquire or to be acquired.

Whether your organization is acquiring another organization or is the target of an acquisition effort, it is essential to have your cyber risk management house in order. A strong ECRM program can ensure that M&A negotiations are successful. Potential buyers will likely subject your organization to a rigorous cybersecurity due diligence review as a seller.

To maintain your sales price and, potentially, shareholder value, you want to show a strong ECRM position, with cyber risks well understood and managed.

As a buyer, you may be acquiring substantial cyber risk. If you have a strong ECRM position, your organization will be able to conduct more rigorous due diligence on your target, allowing you to factor weaknesses into your purchase price. Most private equity firms I have worked with requested an ECRM assessment as part of their due diligence when considering new portfolio company investments.

Strengthening your ECRM program will improve the quality of your M&A activities.

Leveraging Regulatory Compliance Requirements

Regulatory compliance is an important factor in the development of your ECRM Program and Cybersecurity Strategy. Uber Health is an example of an organization that took a proactive approach to ECRM that leveraged a compliance requirement. In 2017, Uber began partnering with healthcare organizations to address the need for reliable patient transportation. Studies have shown that lack of reliable transportation can be a barrier to healthcare access.[58] Uber addressed regulatory compliance and cybersecurity head on when it developed the Uber Health platform. Uber Health makes clear in its marketing that it has developed its platform with attention to HIPAA compliance, including HIPAA's cyber risk management requirements.[59]

In fact, prior to launching the business, Uber Health executives proactively met with the Department of Health and Human Services (DHHS) Office for Civil Rights (OCR) to lay out their program and present their accomplishments. I had the opportunity to speak with Roger Severino who was the OCR director at the time about the unusual circumstance of a business setting such a meeting, and he applauded their effort as smart business-building tactic. By taking this approach to ECRM, Uber has been able to earn the trust of provider partners as well as of patients. As of early 2022, Uber Health boasted more than 3,000 provider partners.[60]

The takeaway is that organizations and their business partners can leverage a strong, proactive ECRM Program and Cybersecurity Strategy to comply with regulations, create business value, gain market share, and compete more effectively.

Conclusion

In this chapter, I emphasized the importance of prioritizing ECRM and cybersecurity within your organization. Having a strong ECRM Program and Cybersecurity Strategy is now table stakes for ensuring the growth of your business. Just as, over the last five decades, information technology has become a strategic asset, cybersecurity has become one now. You cannot continue your digitization efforts without transforming your approach to ECRM. Almost all business-critical processes are at risk of cyberattacks.

I call for a pivot or shift in thinking so that you go beyond explaining the value of ECRM and cybersecurity in terms of defensive risk reduction, loss prevention, and regulatory compliance. You need to frame the discussion around "creating and managing the upside" and focus on the positive business benefits of ECRM, including creating value, enabling the business, and driving growth.

Businesses can thrive in an ever-evolving digital landscape by enhancing their reputation, facilitating digital transformation, and promoting customer trust. A strong ECRM Program and Cybersecurity Strategy is critical in doing so. Forbes recently published its first ever America's Most Cybersecure Companies list in which the research compared companies within their specific sectors. The top two hundred companies out of 12 million analyzed comprised the list.[61] Where would your organization rank on a list like this one? The visibility of lists like this may create a competitive advantage.

Investing in a comprehensive ECRM Program and Cybersecurity Strategy is essential for long-term success, as it protects against potential threats and can drive business growth and innovation. To better understand the opportunity to leverage cyber regulatory requirements, in Chapter 2, I cover the growing number of cybersecurity regulations, with a focus on the new SEC cybersecurity disclosure requirements.

Questions Management and the Board Should Ask and Discuss

1. What is the nature of your ECRM and cybersecurity discussion today along a continuum ranging from cost-centered and "managing the downside" to profit-oriented and "managing the upside"?

2. Which of the following topics represent your organization's three (3) most significant opportunities to view your ECRM Program and Cybersecurity Strategy in a value-creating, business-enabling, and growth-driven light?

    a. Increasing customer trust and brand loyalty

    b. Improving social responsibility

    c. Driving revenue growth

    d. Facilitating digital transformation and innovation

    e. Attracting higher-quality investments

      f. Assuring operational continuity and optimization

      g. Creating competitive advantage

      h. Attracting and retaining talent

      i. Enabling market expansion

      j. Facilitating M&A activity

3. What will your executive team's role be in advancing the discussion of the three (3) opportunities you identified?

4. What will your board's role be in advancing the discussion of the three (3) opportunities you identified?

5. Do you have the internal resources with the appropriate skills, knowledge, and experience to undertake this work?

6. Would your organization benefit from a session reviewing these and related ECRM programs and cybersecurity strategy opportunities with competent outside counsel and cyber risk and opportunity management experts?

7. Where would your company be positioned on Forbes' America's Most Cybersecure Companies list?

Endnotes

1. Nelson, Wille. BrainyQuote. "Once you replace negative thoughts with positive ones, you'll start having positive results." (n.d.) Accessed July 10, 2023. Available at https://www.brainyquote.com/quotes/willie_nelson_184361

2. Chaput, Bob. *Stop the Cyber Bleeding: What Healthcare Executives and Board Members Must Know About Enterprise Cyber Risk Management (ECRM).* 2021. Clearwater. Available at https://amzn.to/33qr17n

3. Petrosyan, Ani. Statistica. "Estimated cost of cybercrime globally 2016-2027." December 2, 2022. Available at https://www.statista.com/statistics/1280009/cost-cybercrime-worldwide/

4. Deloitte. "2023 Global Future of Cyber Survey." January 27, 2023. Accessed September 9, 2023. Available at https://www.deloitte.com/content/dam/assets-shared/legacy/docs/analysis/2022/deloitte_future_of_cyber_2023.pdf

5. Chaput, Bob. The Governance Institute's E-Briefings. "Cyber Risk Management: A Business Enabler (Not an IT Issue)." September 2019. https://www.governanceinstitute.com/page/EBriefings_V16N5Sep2019#hide2

6. Chaput, Bob. *Stop the Cyber Bleeding: What Healthcare Executives and Board Members Must Know About Enterprise Cyber Risk Management (ECRM)*. 2021. Clearwater. Available at https://amzn.to/33qr17n

7. Hepfer, Manuel and Powell, Thomas C. "Make cybersecurity a strategic asset." MIT Sloan Management Review 62, no. 1 (2020): 40–45. Accessed July 15, 2023. Available at https://blog.sodipress.com/wp-content/uploads/2020/10/MITSMR-Cloudera-Reboot-Your-Strategy-0920.pdf#page=15

8. Miller, Chris. *Chip War*. Simon & Schuster. October 4, 2022. Available at https://www.simonandschuster.com/books/Chip-War/Chris-Miller/9781982172008

9. Moore's law. *Wikipedia*. March 31, 2023. Available at https://en.wikipedia.org/wiki/Moore%27s_law

10. Woerner, Stephanie L. and Weill, Peter. MIT Center for Information Systems Research (CISR). "Companies with a digitally savvy IT unit perform better." March 12, 2019. Accessed April 20, 2023. Available at https://cisr.mit.edu/publication/2019_0301_ITUnitDigitalSavvy_WoernerWeill

11. Reichheld, Ashley and Dunlop, Amelia. "4 Questions to Measure—and Boost—Customer Trust." November 1, 2022. Available at https://hbr.org/2022/11/4-questions-to-measure-and-boost-customer-trust

12. Boehm, Jim, Brennan, Liz, Singla, Alex, and Same, Kate. McKinsey & Company. "Why Digital Trust Truly Matters." September 12, 2022. Available at https://www.mckinsey.com/capabilities/quantumblack/our-insights/why-digital-trust-truly-matters

13. Gibson, Kelly, Hacker, Michael, and Goldberg, Liz. "ESG enforcement is on the rise: Are you ready?" November 16, 2022. Available at https://www.reuters.com/legal/legalindustry/esg-enforcement-is-rise-are-you-ready-2022-11-16/

14. ESG, The Report. "What Is an MEI in Business Sustainability?" Accessed December 2, 2022. Available at https://www.esgthereport.com/what-is-an-mei-in-business-sustainability/

15. Sarnek, A. and Dolan, C. World Economic Forum. "Cybersecurity is an environmental, social and governance issue. Here's why." March 1, 2022. Available at https://www.weforum.org/agenda/2022/03/three-reasons-why-cybersecurity-is-a-critical-component-of-esg/

16. Govindankutty, Prasanna. KPMG. "Cyber security: Don't report on ESG without it." October 13, 2021. Available at https://advisory.kpmg.us/articles/2021/cyber-security-report-on-esg.html

17. Everhart, Jonathan R. Harvard Law School Forum
     on Corporate Governance. "Cybersecurity + ESG
     for the Global Capital Markets." September 15,
     2022. Available at https://corpgov.law.harvard.
     edu/2022/09/15/cybersecurity-esg-for-the-
     global-capital-markets/

18. Doan, Matthew. MIT Sloan Management Review.
     "Improving Your Bottom Line With Cybersecurity."
     October 23, 2018. Available at https://
     sloanreview.mit.edu/article/improving-your-
     bottom-line-with-cybersecurity/

19. 48 CFR 252.204-7021 Contractor Compliance with
     the Cybersecurity Maturity Model Certification
     Level Requirement. Accessed April 7, 2023.
     Available at https://www.ecfr.gov/current/
     title-48/chapter-2/subchapter-H/part-252/
     subpart-252.2/section-252.204-7021

20. Lanz, Joel and Susan, Bruce. The CPA Journal.
     "ICYMI | Information Security Program
     Management in a COVID-19 World." August
     2020. Available at https://www.cpajournal.
     com/2020/08/18/icymi-information-security-
     program-management-in-a-covid-19-world/

21. Equifax, Investor Relations. "Equifax Releases
     2022 Security Annual Report." March 21, 2023.
     Available at https://investor.equifax.com/news-
     events/press-releases/detail/1283/equifax-
     releases-2022-security-annual-report

22. Comparitech. "Worldwide software supply chain attacks tracker (updated daily)." April 7, 2023. Available at https://www.comparitech.com/software-supply-chain-attacks/

23. Greenberg, Elizabeth. DIGIT News. "How Critical Is Cybersecurity to Digital Transformation?" January 26, 2023. Available at https://www.digit.fyi/cybersecurity-key-to-digital-transformation/

24. Stupp, Catherine and Nash, Kim S. "Clorox Warns of Accruing Costs From Cyberattack." October 5, 2023. Accessed October 9, 2023. Available at https://www.wsj.com/articles/clorox-warns-of-accruing-costs-from-cyberattack-a0bc5b6a

25. "Moody's names Derek Vadala as Global Head of Cyber Risk for MIS." Moody's Investor Relations. October 17, 2018. Accessed February 2, 2020. https://ir.moodys.com/news-and-financials/press-releases/press-release-details/2018/Moodys-Names-Derek-Vadala-as-Global-Head-of-Cyber-Risk-for-MIS/default.aspx

26. "Moody's names Derek Vadala as Global Head of Cyber Risk for MIS." Moody's Investor Relations. October 17, 2018. Accessed February 2, 2020. https://ir.moodys.com/news-and-financials/press-releases/press-release-details/2018/Moodys-Names-Derek-Vadala-as-Global-Head-of-Cyber-Risk-for-MIS/default.aspx

27. Cross-Sector—Global: Credit Implications Of
     Cyber Risk Will Hinge On Business Disruptions,
     Reputational Effects. Moody's Investors Services.
     February 28, 2019. Accessed February 14, 2020.
     https://www.moodys.com/research/Moodys-
     Credit-implications-of-cyberattacks-will-
     hinge-on-long-term--PBC_1161216

28. Cross-Sector—Global: Credit Implications Of
     Cyber Risk Will Hinge On Business Disruptions,
     Reputational Effects. Moody's Investors Services.
     February 28, 2019. Accessed February 14, 2020.
     https://www.moodys.com/research/Moodys-
     Credit-implications-of-cyberattacks-will-
     hinge-on-long-term--PBC_1161216

29. Lindsey, Nicole. CPO Magazine. "Equifax
     downgrade shows the lasting financial impact of
     a massive data breach." June 3, 2019. Accessed
     February 3, 2020. https://www.cpomagazine.com/
     cyber-security/equifax-downgrade-shows-
     the-lasting-financial-impact-of-a-massive-
     data-breach/

30. Stupp, Catherine. WSJ. "Credit-Raters Look
     More Carefully at How Companies Respond to
     Cyberattacks." October 27, 2022. Available at
     https://www.wsj.com/articles/credit-raters-
     look-more-carefully-at-how-companies-
     respond-to-cyberattacks-11666863002

31. Kagan, Julia. Investopedia. "Business Interruption Insurance: What It Covers, What It Does Not." May 31, 2021. Available at https://www.investopedia.com/terms/b/business-interruption-insurance.asp

32. "Continuity of Operations Plan (COOP)." Glossary. Computer Security Resource Center (CSRC). National Institute of Standards and Technology (NIST). Accessed April 6, 2023. Available at https://csrc.nist.gov/glossary/term/continuity_of_operations_plan

33. "Resiliency." Glossary. Computer Security Resource Center (CSRC). National Institute of Standards and Technology (NIST). Accessed April 6, 2023. Available at https://csrc.nist.gov/glossary/term/resilience

34. Framework for Improving Critical Infrastructure Cybersecurity, Version 1.1. National Institute of Standards and Technology (NIST). April 16, 2018. Accessed July 10, 2023. Available at https://nvlpubs.nist.gov/nistpubs/CSWP/NIST.CSWP.04162018.pdf

35. Framework for Improving Critical Infrastructure Cybersecurity, Version 1.1. National Institute of Standards and Technology (NIST). April 16, 2018. Accessed July 10, 2023. Available at https://nvlpubs.nist.gov/nistpubs/CSWP/NIST.CSWP.04162018.pdf

36. Public Draft: The NIST Cybersecurity Framework
     2.0. National Institute of Standards and Technology.
     August 8, 2023. Accessed August 28, 2023. Available
     at https://nvlpubs.nist.gov/nistpubs/CSWP/
     NIST.CSWP.29.ipd.pdf

37. Public Draft: The NIST Cybersecurity Framework
     2.0. National Institute of Standards and Technology.
     August 8, 2023. Accessed August 28, 2023. Available
     at https://nvlpubs.nist.gov/nistpubs/CSWP/
     NIST.CSWP.29.ipd.pdf

38. Colony, George. Forrester Research Blog. "My View:
     The CIO And The CEO." February 27, 2007. Available
     at https://www.forrester.com/blogs/08-01-30-
     my_view_the_cio_and_the_ceo/

39. Porter, Michael E. and Millar, Victor E. Harvard
     Business Review Magazine. "How Information
     Gives You Competitive Advantage." July 1985.
     Accessed April 6, 2023. Available at https://hbr.
     org/1985/07/how-information-gives-you-
     competitive-advantage

40. Etoom, Adham. World Economic Forum. Centre for
     Cybersecurity. "Strategising cybersecurity: Why a
     risk-based approach is key." April 2, 2023. Available
     at https://www.weforum.org/agenda/2023/04/
     strategizing-cybersecurity-why-a-risk-based-
     approach-is-key/

41. ISC2. "(ISC)2 Cybersecurity Workforce Study 2022."
     October 17, 2022. Available at https://www.isc2.
     org//-/media/ISC2/Research/2022-WorkForce-
     Study/ISC2-Cybersecurity-Workforce-
     Study.ashx

42. Bonderud, Doug. ADP. "The TRUST Model:
     Delivering on the Promise of Employee Data
     Privacy." January 2020. Available at https://www.
     adp.com/spark/articles/2020/01/the-trust-
     model-delivering-on-the-promise-of-employee-
     data-privacy.aspx

43. Reichheld, Ashley and Dunlop, Amelia. "4
     Questions to Measure—and Boost—Customer
     Trust." November 1, 2022. Available at https://
     hbr.org/2022/11/4-questions-to-measure-and-
     boost-customer-trust

44. Swiss Cyber Institute. Blog. "5 Benefits of Cyber
     Security Training for Employees in 2022."
     December 17, 2021. Available at https://
     swisscyberinstitute.com/blog/5-benefits-of-
     cyber-security-training-for-employees/

45. PwC. "PwC's Trust in US Business Survey".
     September 16, 2021. Available at https://www.
     pwc.com/us/en/library/trust-in-business-
     survey.html

46. PwC. "Trust: the new currency for business." June
     16, 2022. Available at https://www.pwc.com/us/
     en/services/consulting/library/consumer-
     intelligence-series/trust-new-business-
     currency.html

47. Verizon. "Data Breach Investigations Report (DBIR). "June 3, 2022. Available at https://www.verizon.com/business/resources/Tdb/reports/dbir/2022-data-breach-investigations-report-dbir.pdf

48. Strupp, Catherine. WSJ Pro. "Nurses Sue CommonSpirit Hospital Chain Over Unpaid Wages After 2022 Cyberattack." April 12, 2023. Available at https://www.wsj.com/articles/nurses-sue-commonspirit-hospital-chain-over-unpaid-wages-after-2022-cyberattack-ba800349

49. Strupp, Catherine. WSJ Pro. "Nurses Sue CommonSpirit Hospital Chain Over Unpaid Wages After 2022 Cyberattack." April 12, 2023. Available at https://www.wsj.com/articles/nurses-sue-commonspirit-hospital-chain-over-unpaid-wages-after-2022-cyberattack-ba800349

50. Deloitte. "2022 M&A Trends Survey: The Future of M&A." January 2022. Available at https://www2.deloitte.com/us/en/pages/mergers-and-acquisitions/articles/m-a-trends-report.html

51. ISC2. "Cybersecurity Assessments in Mergers and Acquisitions." September 20, 2019. Available at https://www.isc2.org/-/media/E6C334079C1F48E4974368CCA4C18D18.ashx

52. Kenny, Graham. Harvard Business Review. "Don't Make This Common M&A Mistake." March 16, 2020. Available at https://hbr.org/2020/03/dont-make-this-common-ma-mistake

53. Kengelbach, Jens et al. Boston Consulting Group. "The 2019 M&A Report: Downturns Are a Better Time for Deal Hunting." September 25, 2019. Available at https://web-assets.bcg.com/img-src/BCG-Downturns-Are-a-Better-Time-for-Deal-Hunting-September-2019_tcm9-230008.pdf

54. Snider, Mike. USA Today. "Verizon shaves $350 million from Yahoo price." February 21, 2017. Available at https://www.usatoday.com/story/tech/news/2017/02/21/verizon-shaves-350-million-yahoo-price/98188452/

55. Snider, Mike. USA Today. "Verizon shaves $350 million from Yahoo price." February 21, 2017. Available at https://www.usatoday.com/story/tech/news/2017/02/21/verizon-shaves-350-million-yahoo-price/98188452/

56. Gruzeev, Rob. TechCrunch. "It's time to better identify the cost of cybersecurity risks in M&A deals." September 10, 2020. Available at https://techcrunch.com/2020/09/10/its-time-to-better-identify-the-cost-of-cybersecurity-risks-in-ma-deals/

57. Shaikh, Niloofer. Seeking Alpha. "Spirit AeroSystems' acquisition of Asco." September 25, 2020. Available at https://seekingalpha.com/news/3617313-spirit-aerosystems-cancels-acquisition-of-asco-industries

58. Syed, Samina T., Gerber, Ben S., and Sharp, Lisa K. "Traveling towards disease: transportation barriers to health care access." Journal of Community Health. Vol. 38, 5 (2013): 976–993. doi:10.1007/s10900-013-9681-1. Accessed August 18, 2019. https://www.ncbi.nlm.nih.gov/pmc/articles/PMC4265215/

59. Uber Health. "Built with compliance." March 4, 2018. Accessed October 29, 2023. https://clearwatercompliance.com/wp-content/uploads/2018/03/Uber_OnePager_safety_SM.pdf

60. Wetsman, Nicole. The Verge. "Uber and Lyft are taking on healthcare, and drivers are just along for the ride." February 17, 2022. Accessed August 29, 2023. Available at https://www.theverge.com/2022/2/17/22937849/uber-lyft-health-transport-safety

61. Schwarz, Alan. Forbes. "America's Most Cybersecure Companies." June 8, 2023. Accessed July 17, 2023. Available at https://www.forbes.com/lists/most-cybersecure-companies/

CHAPTER 2

SEC and Other Important Cyber Regulations

If you have ten thousand regulations, you destroy all respect for the law.

—Winston Churchill[1]

I haven't counted to see if we're close to 10,000 privacy, security, compliance, and risk management regulations, but it feels like it to many global organizations. This chapter focuses on the Securities and Exchange Commission's cybersecurity disclosure requirements. However, before I focus on those changes, here's a quick recap of emerging regulations as of this writing:

- New and updated US state privacy laws are going into effect in several states across the United States, including California, Colorado, Connecticut, Utah, and Virginia. The state legislatures designed these laws to increase consumer protection and require data protection (think: risk) assessments.[2]

© Bob Chaput 2024
B. Chaput, *Enterprise Cyber Risk Management as a Value Creator*,
https://doi.org/10.1007/979-8-8688-0094-8_2

- In the financial services sector, several agencies, including the Federal Deposit Insurance Corporation (FDIC), Federal Reserve, Office of the Comptroller of the Currency (OCC), Federal Trade Commission (FTC), Commodity Futures Trading Commission (CFTC), National Credit Union Administration (NCUA), and New York Department of Financial Services (NYDFS), are tightening requirements around cyber incident reporting.[3]

- For organizations in the Defense Industrial Base (think: Department of Defense [DoD] contractors and subcontractors), the proposed rules on the Cybersecurity Maturity Model Certification (CMMC) and Defense Federal Acquisition Regulation Supplement (DFARS) were submitted to the Office of Information and Regulatory Affairs (OIRA) in July and are slated for release for public comment in October 2023.[4] Implementation and enforcement are expected to start in 2024.[5]

- For businesses contracting with federal agencies outside the DoD, fasten your seatbelts as an active discussion is underway to modify the existing Federal Acquisition Regulation (FAR) to look more like the CMMC/DFARS requirements. This future change means that if you do business with any of the dozens of departments in the executive branch (think: Commerce, Education, Health and Human Services, Agriculture, Energy, Interior, etc.), you will likely be required to implement and be assessed on implementation of 110 basic controls in National Institute of Standards and Technology (NIST) Special Publication (SP) 800-171.[6]

- Globally, in the UK, the Product Security and Telecommunications Infrastructure Act goes into effect in March 2024. Across the European Union (EU), the Digital Operational Resilience Act, the Network and Information Security Directive 2 (NIS2) 2022/2555, and the EU-US Privacy Framework will be implemented or updated.[7]

As the old, classified ads used to read, many other regulations "too numerous to list here" are coming to an enforcement agency near you soon. And at the same time, in a recent survey of a panel of high-level digital security experts from across government, the private sector, and the security research community, almost a majority, 49%, indicated that cyber regulators aren't going far enough.[8] Watch this space.

In the rest of this chapter, I will focus on the Securities and Exchange Commission's cybersecurity disclosure requirements because they elevate the matter to where it belongs, to your organization's C-suite and board of directors.

Overview of the SEC "Cybersecurity Risk Management, Strategy, Governance, and Incident Disclosure" Final Rule

I recently co-authored an article in which I cited two critical trends related to enterprise cyber risk management (ECRM):

1. The emergence of a de facto "standard of care" related to cyber risk management

2. The increasing possibility that legislatures, regulators, and the courts will hold executives and directors responsible for enterprise cyber risk management (ECRM) failures

This section addresses increased regulations and specific changes made by the Securities and Exchange Commission (SEC) to significantly increase reporting and disclosure requirements around cybersecurity and ECRM for publicly traded companies. Remember that while the SEC regulations apply to publicly traded companies, all organizations should consider adoption as I discuss later in this chapter.

Why Are These Changes Being Made?

Cybersecurity risks and incidents can impact a company's financial performance or position. Consistent, comparable, and decision-useful disclosures regarding an organization's cybersecurity risk management, strategy, and governance practices, as well as a company's response to material cybersecurity incidents, will allow investors to understand such risks and incidents, evaluate a company's risk management and governance practices regarding those risks, and better inform their investment and voting decisions.

In February 2022, before the notice of proposed rulemaking (NPRM) was issued, SEC Chairman Gary Gensler stated:

[T]he proposed amendments are intended to better inform investors about a registrant's risk management, strategy, and governance and to provide timely notification of material cybersecurity incidents.[9]

The cybersecurity disclosure rule changes are all about what the SEC believes are full, fair, and truthful disclosures:

The Commission observed that cybersecurity threats and incidents pose an ongoing and escalating risk to public companies, investors, and market participants. It noted that cybersecurity risks have increased alongside the digitalization of registrants' operations, the growth of remote work, the ability of criminals to monetize cybersecurity incidents, the use of digital payments, and the increasing reliance on third party service providers for information technology services, including cloud computing technology. The Commission also observed that the cost to companies and their investors of cybersecurity incidents is rising and doing so at an increasing rate. All of these trends underscored the need for improved disclosure.[10]

When Will the SEC "Cybersecurity Risk Management, Strategy, Governance, and Incident Disclosure" Changes Be Implemented?

The SEC published the notice of proposed rulemaking on March 9, 2022, and requested comments back to the SEC by May 9, 2022. The comment period was extended, with over 150 comments submitted.[11] The SEC's timetable for these changes initially showed final rulemaking by April 2023.[12] The US GSA Office of Information and Regulatory Affairs then released the updated SEC calendar and scheduled final action on the cybersecurity governance rules in October 2023.[13] However, in late July 2023, the SEC issued the final rule.[14]

The final rules become effective 30 days following publication of the adoption release in the Federal Register. Certain requirements related to your risk management processes discussed in the following require disclosure beginning with annual reports for fiscal years ending on or after December 15, 2023. Material cyber security incidents, again discussed in the following, require disclosure 90 days after the publication date of the final rule in the Federal Register or December 18, 2023, whichever is later.

Who Is Covered?

Publicly traded companies or SEC registrants and so-called foreign private issuers ("FPIs") are required to comply with the changes. US-based publicly traded companies are required to comply with the Securities Act of 1933 ("Securities Act"), the Securities Exchange Act of 1934 ("Exchange Act"), and regulations promulgated under these and other federal securities laws. These organizations typically file Forms 8-K, 10-Q, 10-K, and others as part of their regular filings with the SEC.

What Changes Are Being Made?

Four specific changes were proposed, but not all made it into the final rule:

1. Reporting of Cybersecurity Incidents on Form 8-K

2. Disclosure About Cybersecurity Incidents in Periodic Reports

3. Disclosure of a Registrant's Risk Management, Strategy, and Governance Regarding Cybersecurity Risks

4. Disclosure Regarding the Board of Directors' Cybersecurity Expertise

In the final rule, the SEC streamlined the proposed disclosure requirements related to risk management, strategy, and governance. The requirement to disclose board cybersecurity expertise was dropped. Instead, there are requirements to describe the board's oversight of risks from cybersecurity threats and management's role and expertise in assessing and managing material risks from cybersecurity threats.[15]

I discuss each of these disclosure requirements in the sections that follow. Meanwhile, know that the proposals call for specific changes to disclosures made to existing regulations (e.g., PART 229—STANDARD INSTRUCTIONS FOR FILING FORMS UNDER SECURITIES ACT OF 1933, SECURITIES EXCHANGE ACT OF 1934 AND ENERGY POLICY AND CONSERVATION ACT OF 1975—REGULATION S-K) by adding or amending existing language.

The SEC summarized where changes were being made in the regulations in Table 2-1.

Table 2-1. *Summary of Amendments to SEC Regulations*

Commission Reference		CFR Citation Where Changes Are Made (17 CFR)
Regulation S-K		§§229.10 through 229.1305
	Items 106 and 601	§§229.106 and 229.601
Regulation S-T		§§232.10 through 232.903
	Rule 405	§232.405
Securities Act of 1933 ("Securities Act")[1]	Form S-3	§239.13
Securities Exchange Act of 1934 ("Exchange Act")[2]	Rule 13a-11	§240.13a-11
	Rule 15d-11	§240.15d-11
	Form 20-F	§249.220f
	Form 6-K	§249.306
	Form 8-K	§249.308
	Form 10-K	§249.310

Source: Bob Chaput, Executive Chairman, Clearwater. Adapted from SEC "Final Rule: Cybersecurity Risk Management, Strategy, Governance, and Incident Disclosure." July 26, 2023. Accessed July 30, 2023. Available at *https://www.sec.gov/files/rules/final/2023/33-11216.pdf*

As a simple, specific example, the SEC added definitions for terms like *cybersecurity incident, cybersecurity threat,* and *information systems* at 17 CFR §229.106(a):

Cybersecurity incident means an unauthorized occurrence, or a series of related unauthorized occurrences, on or conducted through a registrant's information systems that jeopardizes the confidentiality, integrity, or availability of a registrant's information systems or any information residing therein.

Cybersecurity threat means any potential unauthorized occurrence on or conducted through a registrant's information systems that may result in adverse effects on the confidentiality, integrity, or availability of a registrant's information systems or any information residing therein.

Information systems means electronic information resources, owned or used by the registrant, including physical or virtual infrastructure controlled by such information resources, or components thereof, organized for the collection, processing, maintenance, use, sharing, dissemination, or disposition of the registrant's information to maintain or support the registrant's operations.[16]

Who Enforces These and Other SEC Regulations?

The Division of Enforcement within the SEC administers the Securities and Exchange Commission's Enforcement Program. The Division of Enforcement is responsible for detecting and investigating potential federal securities law and regulation violations.[17] In November 2022, the SEC announced that it filed 760 total enforcement actions in the fiscal year

2022, representing a 9% increase over the prior year. Out of the 760, 462 were new or "stand-alone," which represented a 6.5% increase over the prior year.[18] The combination comprising civil penalties, disgorgement, and prejudgment interest totaled $6.439 billion, the most on record in SEC history and up from $3.852 billion in fiscal year 2021.[19]

Will CISOs, under duress, aid in SEC enforcement of cyber disclosures? The SEC Office of the Whistleblower was established to manage the program whereby individuals with knowledge of securities law violations can be rewarded when they assist in prosecuting violators.[20] In fiscal year 2022, adding about $229 million, total cumulative SEC whistleblower awards grew to more than $1.3 billion since the program began.

In August 2022, Peiter Zatko, Twitter's former head of security, filed whistleblower complaints with the SEC, the Federal Trade Commission, and the Justice Department alleging "'extreme, egregious deficiencies by Twitter in every area of his mandate,' including privacy, digital and physical security, platform integrity and content moderation."[21] If investigations show that his allegations were true, they represent serious privacy and security concerns for millions of Twitter, now X, users. We might see this whistleblower trend continue.

What Happens If Your Company Doesn't Comply?

An organization making false, incomplete, or misleading statements about security incidents, risk management, strategy, and governance in its public statements or its required SEC disclosures could result in an SEC violation and, additionally, potential violations of other federal (e.g., HIPAA), state (e.g., NYDFS), or even international privacy and security regulations (e.g., GDPR). These potential violations would be harmful to investors and bad for the company. SEC penalties can be severe. In 462 enforcement actions in 2022, the SEC total financial remedies ordered in enforcement actions totaled $6.439 billion, the highest ever and a nearly 70% increase over 2021.[22]

Disclosure of Cybersecurity Incidents on Current Reports

Ernst & Young recently published the results of their analysis of filings by 74 Fortune 100 companies and, comparing 40 material cybersecurity Form 8-K filings (of 74,098) in 2020 to the 2020 Verizon Data Breach Report's 3,950 confirmed data breaches in 2020, and observed a gap in disclosures.[23] The changes under "Reporting of Cybersecurity Incidents on Current Reports" aim to address this gap in reporting.

The SEC remains steadfast in its view that investors need timely, standardized disclosure regarding cybersecurity incidents materially affecting registrants' businesses and that the existing regulatory landscape is not yielding consistent and informative disclosure of cybersecurity incidents from registrants.[24] It requires registrants to "disclose material cybersecurity incidents in a current report on Form 8-K within four business days after the registrant determines that it has experienced a material cybersecurity incident."[25]

For those unfamiliar with Form 8-K, it is known as a "current report" and is generally used to announce significant events at a company that investors should know. Organizations must file a Form 8-K within four days of the incident that triggers the filing.[26] Examples of events that trigger a Form 8-K filing include but are not limited to a quarterly earnings announcement, a change in leadership, entry into a material definitive agreement, a material audit finding, bankruptcy, etc. These disclosures inform investors of material events that may influence their investment decisions.

The SEC amends Form 8-K filings by adding new Item 1.05 in "Section 1—Registrant's Business and Operations," entitled "Material Cybersecurity Incidents," which would require a registrant to disclose the following information on a Form 8-K filing within four business days:

- Material aspects of the nature, scope, and timing of the incident

- Material impact or reasonably likely material impact on the registrant, including its financial condition and results of operations[27]

Healthcare organizations will note some similarities to breach notification requirements under the HIPAA Breach Notification Rule with a notable difference in the reporting timeline (up to 60 days vs. four days).[28] Others may compare these seemingly overlapping requirements to what Congress has passed as the Cyber Incident Reporting for Critical Infrastructure Act of 2022 (CIRCIA).[29] The Cybersecurity and Infrastructure Security Agency (CISA) has issued a Request for Information (RFI) for public comment on new cyber disclosure rules expected to take effect in 2024. This Act would require operators to report major cyber incidents within 72 hours and ransom payments within 24 hours.[30]

Key terms to consider when submitting a Form 8-K filing and around which much discussion, if not debate, ensues are "material" and "cybersecurity incidents." According to the SEC, what constitutes "materiality" for purposes of the cybersecurity incident disclosure would be consistent with that set out in the numerous cases addressing materiality in the securities laws. Information is material if "there is a substantial likelihood that a reasonable shareholder would consider it important" in making an investment decision or if it would have "significantly altered the 'total mix of information made available.'" [31]

In the case of cybersecurity incidents, a company must conduct a materiality assessment "without unreasonable delay after discovery of the incident."[32] Companies do not need to report every cybersecurity incident; only those determined to be material must be disclosed. Undoubtedly, this will be a learning process, but consistent with Supreme Court rulings[33] and SEC enforcement, when in doubt about materiality, companies will be expected to err on the side of informing and protecting investors.

Based on the definition of a cybersecurity incident, the SEC appears to have a comprehensive understanding of potential threats. The definition encompasses all types of incidents, not just those caused by malicious hackers. It's important to consider incidents emanating from accidental, structural, and environmental threat sources, along with adversarial sources.

Although not-for-profit, private, startup, and emerging companies may not immediately face these incident disclosure requirements, I recommend that all organizations implement robust incident response and reporting policies, procedures, and practices starting today.

It is essential to note that both Institutional Shareholder Services (ISS)[34] and Glass Lewis[35], the two most prominent proxy advisory services in North America, have taken measures to include disclosures and other similar requirements to the SEC final cybersecurity disclosure requirements in their governance assessments of public companies. These firms provide research and analysis to institutional investors, among others, to assist with investment decisions. The point is that the SEC changes around Form 8-K filings and updates in periodic reports are in some ways finally catching up with investor demands.

Disclosure About Cybersecurity Incidents in Periodic Reports

Originally, in the notice of proposed rulemaking, under "Updates to Previously Filed Form 8-K Disclosure," the SEC had proposed changes that would have required registrants to "disclose any material changes, additions, or updates to information required to be disclosed according to Item 1.05 of Form 8-K" in quarterly Form 10-Qs or annual Form 10-Ks for the period (the company's fourth fiscal quarter in the case of a yearly report) in which the material change, addition, or update occurred.[36]

Instead of requiring updates in quarterly Form 10-Qs or annual Form 10-Ks, updates must be provided on Form 8-Ks, under the following instructions:

> *To the extent that the information called for in Item 1.05(a) is not determined or is unavailable at the time of the required filing, the registrant shall include a statement to this effect in the filing and then must file an amendment to its Form 8-K filing under this Item 1.05 containing such information within four business days after the registrant, without unreasonable delay, determines such information or within four business days after such information becomes available.*[37]

Periodic reporting means that cybersecurity incident disclosures are not a once-and-done matter. It would be best if you were both backward-facing and forward-looking when evaluating the impact of cybersecurity incidents on your business. It is essential to formalize your cybersecurity incident management and reporting processes. Be sure your organization has a mutually agreed-upon definition of key cyber risk terms (most organizations do not!) and can differentiate cybersecurity events from material cybersecurity incidents.

Disclosure of a Registrant's Risk Management, Strategy, and Governance Regarding Cybersecurity Risks

Previously, I cited SEC Chairman Gary Gensler, who stated that the SEC performs its work "...through a disclosure-based regime, not a merit-based one."[38] The current system, which requires the disclosure of certain types of business and financial data regularly to the SEC and the company's stockholders, is known as the integrated disclosure system.[39] Regulation S-K is an SEC regulation that spells out how registrants should disclose material qualitative or textual descriptions of their business on registration statements, periodic reports, and any other filings such as the 8-K, 10-Q, and 10-K.[40]

The SEC added to Regulation S-K at Item 106(b) a requirement for registrants to provide more consistent and informative disclosure regarding their cybersecurity risk management and strategy. I cannot overstate the importance of ongoing, comprehensive, enterprise-wide risk and opportunity assessments as a foundational step in establishing, implementing, and maturing an ECRM Program and Cybersecurity Strategy.

Under risk management and strategy, the final rule includes the following non-exclusive list of specific disclosure items related to your processes for "assessing, identifying, and managing material risks from cybersecurity threats in sufficient detail for a reasonable investor to understand those processes":

> *(i) Whether and how any such processes have been integrated into the registrant's overall risk management system or processes;*
>
> *(ii) Whether the registrant engages assessors, consultants, auditors, or other third parties in connection with any such processes; and*
>
> *(iii) Whether the registrant has processes to oversee and identify such risks from cybersecurity threats associated with its use of any third-party service provider.*[41]

It is also a requirement to describe whether any risks from cybersecurity threats have materially affected or are reasonably likely to materially affect the registrant, including its business strategy, results of operations, or financial condition and, if so, how.

Under governance, the final rule requires that the board's and management's roles in cyber risk management are specified. For the board, the disclosure requirements include a description of the board's oversight and identification of any specific committee or subcommittee charged with this responsibility.

For management, similarly, describing management's role along with the identification of management positions or committees responsible for assessing and managing cyber risks is required. At the management level, not the board level, you must disclose relevant cybersecurity expertise and the nature of the expertise of named individuals. You must disclose the processes by which you prevent, detect, mitigate, and remediate cybersecurity incidents. Finally, you must disclose whether you report cybersecurity risks to the board.

These are extensive and comprehensive disclosure changes. The activities represent sound cyber risk management and align with numerous industry guidelines and resources. For boards of directors, I will present NACD's most recent Principles for Board Governance of Cyber Risk[42] as a great resource in Chapter 9.

The following are six initial actions organizations can take to establish or improve their enterprise cyber risk management (ECRM) program. These actions will help meet cyber disclosure requirements regarding risk management, strategy, and governance:

1. Conduct ongoing enterprise-wide NIST-quality risk assessments.

2. Establish board and executive team governance.

3. Adopt the NIST Cybersecurity Framework.

4. Implement the NIST "Managing Information Security Risk" Process.

5. Engage your executive risk insurance brokers.

6. Measure the maturity of your ECRM program.[43]

Of course, these six items only represent a partial list of all cybersecurity practices. They are simply examples of the items that, if completed, should be disclosed. They would all meet the SEC's goal of providing greater transparency regarding the registrant's strategies and actions to manage cybersecurity risks. See Chapter 13 for additional implementation information.

Risk oversight is one of the top three responsibilities of a board of directors, along with strategy and leadership. Disclosing information about risk and risk management oversight is not new to public company boards. Public company boards have had to disclose their role in overall risk oversight since February 28, 2010, according to an SEC final rule, Proxy Disclosure Requirements.[44] As another specific example of risk-related disclosure, audit committees of New York Stock Exchange–listed companies must disclose policies concerning risk assessment and risk management.[45]

As part of Regulation S-K, at 17 CFR §229.401(e), companies must discuss the business experience of board directors.[46] Further, at 17 CFR §229.407(h), companies must "disclose the extent of the board's role in the risk oversight of the registrant, such as how the board administers its oversight function, and the effect that this has on the board's leadership structure."[47]

In an analysis of Form 10-K filings by 74 Fortune 100 companies in 2022, Ernst & Young found that disclosures about directors' cybersecurity expertise had increased significantly over the last five years before these SEC final rule changes. In 2018, only 20% of the companies disclosed cybersecurity expertise as a sought-after skill, compared with 46% in 2002. In 2018, only 28% cited existing cybersecurity expertise in at least one board member, compared with more than 50% in 2022. Progressive, forward-thinking organizations see the need for cybersecurity expertise and the value of disclosures.[48]

It is fair to think about the SEC's final rule related to Risk Management, Strategy, and Governance Regarding Cybersecurity Risks as simply an extension of existing requirements, in this case, to address one of the most severe risks facing our economy and public equity markets.

Disclosure Regarding the Board of Directors' Cybersecurity Expertise

Originally there was a proposed requirement of "Disclosure Regarding the Board of Directors' Cybersecurity Expertise." For this disclosure requirement, the SEC had proposed to amend Item 107 of Regulation S-K to require

> *disclosure about the cybersecurity expertise of members of the board of directors of the registrant, if any. If any member of the board has cybersecurity expertise, the registrant would have to disclose the name(s) of any such director(s) and provide such detail as necessary to fully describe the nature of the expertise.*[49]

Companies were to make this disclosure in proxy statements and the 10-K.

In the final rule, the SEC did not adopt the board cybersecurity expertise proposed changes. There is and will continue to be much discussion about cybersecurity expertise on the board. Comments received by the SEC and the SEC's rationale for not adopting the original proposed changes are included in the final rule. I believe that most boards would benefit from having individuals with cybersecurity, risk management, and other equally strong board qualifications serve their shareholders.

What Is Cybersecurity Expertise?

All US public companies must disclose whether their audit committees have at least one financial expert and, if they don't, tell why. These requirements came about in rulemaking following the passage of the Sarbanes-Oxley Act Of 2002 and may be found at 17 CFR §229.407(d)(5).[50] Now, 20+ (yes, 20+!) years later, the SEC had proposed similar disclosure requirements for cybersecurity expertise that were dropped. The cybersecurity disclosure requirement was similar but not the same.

The term "audit committee financial expert" is defined in terms of specific attributes at 17 CFR §229.407(d)(5)(ii).[51] The language at 17 CFR §229.407(d)(5)(iii) discusses how someone might have acquired these attributes.[52]

Pundits continue to debate the wisdom or the lack thereof of the final rule not having disclosure of board-level expertise. What had been an explicit proposed disclosure requirement about whether "...any member of the registrant's board of directors has expertise in cybersecurity"[53] shifted to the expertise disclosure requirement of "whether and which management positions or committees are responsible for assessing and managing such risks ..."[54] I believe it is only a matter of time before the board expertise disclosure requirement is back on the table. Wise organizations will see the need and value without the force of law.

Whatever constitutes "cybersecurity expertise," there is not enough of it on boards today. In late 2022, WSJ Pro Research analyzed the professional backgrounds of 4,621 board directors representing S&P 500 companies; only 86 directors (1.9%) had relevant professional experience of cybersecurity in the last ten years.[55] According to a more recent study published by Diligent Institute in September 2023

> *Our research confirms that, despite the rising risk and cost of cyberattacks, 88% of S&P 500 companies do not currently have an executive with specialized cybersecurity experience on their board to guide them on risk mitigation efforts, and 57% lack*

similar specialized experience in other technology categories. Boards have a direct responsibility to shareholders to mitigate risk to the organization, yet, as the data shows, many do not possess the background, education, or training to fluently "speak the language of cybersecurity" and adequately combat cyber risk.[56]

As a profession, cybersecurity is immature compared with the more mature taxonomy of knowledge, skills, abilities, and certifications in finance and accounting. Cybersecurity expertise is more difficult to define than financial expertise. Therefore, I am writing to clarify "cybersecurity expertise" in a manner that may help you recruit candidates for your board.

Ideally, you would find an individual with both CRISC, Certified in Risk and Information Systems Control,[57] and CISSP, Certified Information Systems Security Professional[58] certifications—the two preeminent cyber risk management and cybersecurity certifications. Of course, these cybersecurity certifications are simply table stakes. Certifications like these are in addition all other important board skills. My "skills matrix," then, for someone with "cybersecurity expertise" would include many broader business attributes to avoid onboarding a single-purpose director and instead someone who can contribute to fulfilling other board oversight responsibilities, including strategy and talent management:

- Board experience, preferably, NACD Directorship Certification (NACD.DC)

- CEO experience, preferably in a leading ECRM or cybersecurity company

- Strategy-, risk management-, leadership-savvy

- Financially literate

- Entrepreneur, executive, and educator experience

- Hands-on experience as or management experience of CIO, CISO, CTO, COO

- Certifications, in order of priority, CRISC, CISSP, NACD CERT Certificate in Cyber-Risk Oversight

- Degrees such as MBA or equivalent, MS—Cybersecurity

- Recognized expert through writing, teaching, or serving as an expert witness

Should Your Not-for-Profit and Private Company Care About SEC Cyber Disclosure Requirements?

The bottom-line-up-front (BLUF) is YES!

Over the last couple of years, I received feedback and questions from executives and board members at not-for-profit and private companies that essentially conveyed, "Not a problem. We don't deal with the SEC" or "Why bother with these requirements when we have a myriad of other regulations with which to comply."

As of September 2022, the NYSE had a combined total of 2,578 listed domestic and international companies, while the NASDAQ had 3,788 for a total of 6,366 publicly listed companies.[59] So the population of companies subject to SEC disclosure requirements is small, especially considering the approximately 32.6 million businesses in the United States.[60] The point is that private companies dominate the US economy and are not directly subject to SEC registration, reporting, and disclosure requirements. However, they are increasingly targeted by adversarial threat sources AND subject to the same accidental, structural, and environmental threat sources that public companies face. Getting one's cyber risk management ducks in a row is not just for SEC-regulated companies.

Within these millions of non-public organizations are an estimated 1.5 million nonprofit organizations,[61] which include many of our most prominent health systems and 16,000 PE-backed portfolio companies.[62] An argument can be made for all the millions of non-public US businesses to care about the SEC cyber disclosure requirements.

Here are my top six reasons not-for-profit and private companies should care about SEC cybersecurity disclosure requirements:

1. The SEC has the authority to investigate all companies that seek to raise capital from US investors. Among other avenues, investors in private companies often exit by way of an initial public offering and going public. SEC's oversight includes all public and private companies making any false or misleading statements as part of an offering process.[63] Any private company would be required to respond to the SEC cybersecurity disclosures in their registration statement. Therefore, private companies should eagerly work on their cybersecurity and cyber risk and opportunity management program to tell prospective investors a proactive and progressive story responsive to the SEC's cyber disclosures. As the authors point out in "The SEC Takes Aim at the Public-Private Disclosure Gap," "...the line between 'investors' and the 'public' has blurred in recent decades, as a majority of the American public is now exposed to both public and private market risk through pension funds, education savings plans, and company retirement programs."[64]

2. A strategic acquirer of a private company may
    already be public and currently subject to SEC
    disclosure requirements. In this case, any potential
    acquirer would already be filing required cyber-
    related reports and disclosures and would
    place value on any private company efforts not
    only to easily make the disclosures but, more
    importantly, to have a mature enterprise cyber
    risk and opportunity management program in
    place. According to a recent Forescout report, 48%
    of business leaders encountered a critical cyber
    issue or incident during an M&A transaction that
    jeopardized the deal.[65] Private companies should
    be attentive to the SEC's cyber disclosures and
    what's driving them—better enterprise cyber risk
    management.

3. Forget about acquisitions and IPOs; take care
    of your current stakeholders. As I've written
    throughout this chapter, the SEC disclosure
    requirements are important to investors. At the
    same time, they are a means to an end—driving
    improvements in cyber risk management. Not-for-
    profit and private organizations have customers,
    perhaps patients, investors, bankers, insurers,
    employees, and regulators (think: NYDFS, HIPAA,
    GLBA, FERPA, GDPR, etc.), all of whom expect your
    organization to have and benefit from a robust cyber
    risk and opportunity management program.

4. The cost of capital is lower for all organizations that establish, implement, and mature an enterprise cyber risk management program. As I discussed in Chapter 1, all credit-rating agencies consider the financial impact of a cyberattack on an organization's credit rating. The SEC cyber disclosure requirements provide a north star for improved cybersecurity and, therefore, access to capital at a lower cost, whether you are private or public. You have an opportunity to improve your credit rating with a strong, proactive ECRM Program and Cybersecurity Strategy.

5. Most private companies are part of public company supply chains. Heads up, even though you may serve on the board of a private company, your customers and vendors may be public companies. Now that the SEC has finalized the cybersecurity disclosure requirements, expect to have your public company stakeholders raise the ante in terms of your incident response and reporting to them. The Omnibus Final Rule codifying the HITECH Act tightened similar provisions for the healthcare supply chain when it was published in the Federal Register in 2013.[66] Public companies, private companies, and nonprofit organizations must strengthen and be more transparent about their cyber risk management programs. Public companies are likely to become more discriminating about the partners with whom they choose to work, looking for them to disclose detailed information like that required by the SEC about their cyber risk management programs.

6. Manage the expectations of your board members
    from public companies. Many private and nonprofit
    organizations benefit from having their board
    members serve as executives or directors of public
    companies. As such, they bring to their private and
    nonprofit organizations' boards the order, process,
    and discipline around regulatory compliance
    they expect in their public companies. After all, all
    board members in all companies have fiduciary
    responsibilities. They see the value of transparency
    and its importance to all stakeholders. They realize
    that public company requirements, like the SEC
    cyber disclosure requirements, may be a precursor
    for all organizations.

Conclusion

Some of the largest companies in the United States are private companies (by 2021 revenues, #1 Cargill $165 billion; #2 Koch $120 billion; #3 Publix Supermarkets $44.9 billion; #4 Mars $40 billion; #10 Fidelity Investments #21 billion).[67] Although they may not have SEC reporting and disclosure requirements, I fully expect that they are very proactive in their efforts to deepen trust with all their stakeholders. As a result, I would expect their digitization; Equity, Diversity, and Inclusion (ED&I); ESG; and enterprise cyber risk management programs, among others, to be world-class.

Private and nonprofit organizations should care about SEC cyber disclosure and other regulatory requirements as a means to an end …better safeguarding of their information assets and better outcomes for all stakeholders.

As I discussed in Chapter 1, using Uber Health as an example, complying with regulations is an opportunity your organization can seize to create business value. In Chapter 3, I discuss how the courts are joining legislators and regulators in raising the bar for C-suite and board engagement in leading and overseeing ECRM activities in your organization.

Questions Management and the Board Should Ask and Discuss

1. What team of executives should be assembled to examine these SEC and other regulatory requirements, monitor the changing regulations, and report to the board?

2. What standing board or ad hoc committee will oversee the work of this executive team? Or will it be the whole board?

3. What clarifications need to be made regarding the role of management vis-à-vis the board's role regarding these potential changes?

4. What is your ability today to meet these SEC cybersecurity disclosure requirements?

5. What is your risk appetite for managing these requirements?

6. What are your current risk and opportunity management policies, procedures, and practices? At first blush, how do they stand up to the SEC disclosure and other emerging requirements?

7. Do you have appropriate enterprise risk management and cybersecurity expertise on your management team and board?

8. What is the current state of your cyber incident response and reporting practices today? Do you have reasonable and appropriate policies, procedures, and forms to ensure documentation and follow-up?

9. Does your organization regularly and consistently conduct tabletop exercises to test your incident response program?

10. Do you include "materiality assessments" in your incident response, and are you prepared to identify "material cybersecurity incidents" according to the SEC's definitions?

11. Do your cyber incident response and reporting practices today capture and document all incidents so that you file timely Form 8-K amendments about incidents if key information was unavailable at the time of the initial required filing?

12. Are you prepared to provide regular updates regarding the previously reported incidents when and for so long as there are material changes, additions, or updates during a given reporting period?

13. Is your enterprise cyber risk management (ECRM) strategy formalized and documented? Are you comfortable disclosing your ECRM strategy to investors?

14. Would your organization's current risk assessment/
management work products meet national
or international standards promulgated by
NIST or ISO?

15. What is the level of cybersecurity expertise of your
management team and on your board today? Does
everyone on the board understand enterprise
cyber risk management (ECRM) issues? Are
you comfortable today disclosing your board's
cybersecurity expertise to investors?

16. Given your organization's current industry, "crown
jewels," attack surface, and ECRM strategy, would
your investors conclude that you have the correct
cybersecurity expertise on your management team
and board?

17. Does your current board skills matrix include
relevant attributes for cybersecurity expertise?

Endnotes

1. BrainyQuote. "If you have ten thousand regulations
you destroy all respect for the law." (n.d.)
Accessed June 29, 2023. Available at `https://
www.brainyquote.com/quotes/winston_
churchill_122577`

2. Augustinos, Theodore P. and Cox, Alexander
R. Locke Lord Privacy & Cybersecurity
Newsletter. "U.S. State Privacy Laws in 2023:
California, Colorado, Connecticut, Utah

and Virginia." December 2022. Available at
https://www.lockelord.com/newsandevents/
publications/2022/12/us-state-privacy-
laws-2023

3.   Geiger, Harley L. Venerable LLP. "Four
Cybersecurity Law Issues for Financial Services
to Track in 2023." February 16, 2023. Available
at https://www.venable.com/insights/
publications/2023/02/four-cybersecurity-law-
issues-for-financial-serv

4.   Block, Larry et al. Winston & Strawn. "Be
Prepared for CMMC Changes." October 16, 2023.
Accessed October 29, 2023. Available at https://
www.winston.com/en/blogs-and-podcasts/
investigations-enforcement-and-compliance-
alerts/be-prepared-for-cmmc-changes

5.   SysArc. "Final CMMC Rules Expected In June 2023."
May 3, 2023. Available at https://www.sysarc.com/
cmmc/final-cmmc-rules-expected-in-june-2023/

6.   Mitchell, Billy. Fedscoop. "New rule could impose
CMMC-like cyber requirements for civilian
agency contractors." April 5, 2023. Available at
https://fedscoop.com/new-rule-could-impose-
cyber-requirements-for-civilian-agency-
contractors/

7.   Acebo, Leslie. WSJ Pro Cybersecurity Research.
"Quarterly Cyber Regulations Update." June
15, 2023. Available at https://www.wsj.com/
articles/quarterly-cyber-regulations-update-
june-2023-c8f83dd1

8. Starks, Tim. Washington Post. "Cyber experts say regulators aren't going far enough with their rules." August 17, 2023. Accessed August 23, 2023. Available at https://www.washingtonpost.com/politics/2023/08/17/cyber-experts-say-regulators-arent-going-far-enough-with-their-rules/

9. Gensler, Gary. "Testimony Before the United States Senate Committee on Banking, Housing, and Urban Affairs." September 15, 2022. Available at https://www.sec.gov/news/testimony/gensler-testimony-housing-urban-affairs-091522

10. SEC. "Fact Sheet: Public Company Cybersecurity Disclosures; Final Rules." July 25, 2023. Accessed July 30, 2023. Available at https://www.sec.gov/files/33-11216-fact-sheet.pdf

11. SEC. "Comments on the Cybersecurity Risk Management, Strategy, Governance, and Incident Disclosure." Accessed October 21, 2022. Available at https://www.sec.gov/comments/s7-09-22/s70922.htm

12. Agency Rule List—Spring 2022. SEC. "Cyber Risk Governance." Accessed October 4, 2022. Available at https://www.reginfo.gov/public/do/eAgendaViewRule?pubId=202204&RIN=3235-AM89

13. Final Action. US GSA Office of Information and Regulatory Affairs. Accessed June 30, 2023. Available at https://www.reginfo.gov/public/do/eAgendaViewRule?pubId=202304&RIN=3235-AM89

14. SEC. "Final Rule: Cybersecurity Risk Management, Strategy, Governance, and Incident Disclosure." July 26, 2023. Accessed July 30, 2023. Available at https://www.sec.gov/files/rules/final/2023/33-11216.pdf

15. SEC. "Fact Sheet: Public Company Cybersecurity Disclosures; Final Rules." July 25, 2023. Accessed July 30, 2023. Available at https://www.sec.gov/files/33-11216-fact-sheet.pdf

16. SEC. "Final Rule: Cybersecurity Risk Management, Strategy, Governance, and Incident Disclosure." July 26, 2023. Accessed July 30, 2023. Available at https://www.sec.gov/files/rules/final/2023/33-11216.pdf

17. International Institute for Securities Market Development. SEC. "Overview of Enforcement." 2005. Available at https://www.sec.gov/about/offices/oia/oia_enforce/overviewenfor.pdf

18. Press Release. SEC. "SEC Announces Enforcement Results for FY22." November 15, 2022. Accessed September 11, 2023. Available at https://www.sec.gov/news/press-release/2022-206

19. Press Release. SEC. "SEC Announces Enforcement Results for FY22." November 15, 2022. Accessed September 11, 2023. Available at https://www.sec.gov/news/press-release/2022-206

20. SEC. "Office of the Whistleblower." (n.d.) Accessed September 11, 2023. Available at https://www.sec.gov/whistleblower

21. Needleman, Sarah E. WSJ. "Twitter's Ex-Security Head Files Whistleblower Complaint on Spam, Privacy Issues." Updated August 23, 2022. Available at https://www.wsj.com/articles/twitters-ex-security-head-files-whistleblower-complaint-11661263009

22. Dunn, Gibson. "2022 Year-End Securities Enforcement Update." February 2, 2023. Accessed July 30, 2023. Available at https://www.gibsondunn.com/2022-year-end-securities-enforcement-update/

23. Seets, Chuck and Niemann Pat, EY. Harvard Law School Forum on Corporate Governance. "How cyber governance and disclosures are closing the gaps in 2022." October 2, 2022. Available at https://corpgov.law.harvard.edu/2022/10/02/how-cyber-governance-and-disclosures-are-closing-the-gaps-in-2022/

24. SEC. "Final Rule: Cybersecurity Risk Management, Strategy, Governance, and Incident Disclosure." July 26, 2023. Accessed July 30, 2023. Available at https://www.sec.gov/files/rules/final/2023/33-11216.pdf

25. SEC. "Final Rule: Cybersecurity Risk Management, Strategy, Governance, and Incident Disclosure." July 26, 2023. Accessed July 30, 2023. Available at https://www.sec.gov/files/rules/final/2023/33-11216.pdf

26. Glossary. US Securities and Exchange Commission. "Form 8-K definition." Accessed October 15, 2022. Available at https://www.investor.gov/introduction-investing/investing-basics/glossary/form-8-k

27. SEC. "Final Rule: Cybersecurity Risk Management, Strategy, Governance, and Incident Disclosure." July 26, 2023. Accessed July 30, 2023. Available at https://www.sec.gov/files/rules/final/2023/33-11216.pdf

28. US Department of Health and Human Services. The HIPAA Breach Notification Rule. Accessed October 15, 2022. Available at https://www.hhs.gov/hipaa/for-professionals/breach-notification/index.html

29. Cybersecurity & Infrastructure Security Agency (CISA). "Cyber Incident Reporting for Critical Infrastructure Act of 2022 (CIRCIA)." March 2022. Available at https://www.cisa.gov/circia

30. Cybersecurity & Infrastructure Security Agency (CISA). "Cyber Incident Reporting for Critical Infrastructure Act of 2022 (CIRCIA)." March 2022. Available at https://www.cisa.gov/circia

31. Business Roundtable. "The Materiality Standard for Public Company Disclosure: Maintain What Works." 2015. Available at https://s3.amazonaws.com/brt.org/archive/reports/BRT.The%20Materiality%20Standard%20for%20Public%20Company%20Disclosure.2015.10.29.pdf

32.   SEC. "Proposed Rule Cybersecurity Risk Management, Strategy, Governance, and Incident Disclosure." March 9, 2022. Available at https://www.sec.gov/rules/proposed/2022/33-11038.pdf

33.   TSC Industries, Inc. et al., Petitioners, v. Northway, Inc. Cornell Law School. June 6, 1976. Available at https://www.law.cornell.edu/supremecourt/text/426/438

34.   ISS. "Cyber Risk Score." Accessed October 30, 2022. Available at https://www.issgovernance.com/esg/cyber-risk/

35.   Glass Lewis. "Cybersecurity Risk Evaluation Solution." Accessed October 30, 2022. Available at https://www.glasslewis.com/cybersecurity-risk-evaluation-solution/

36.   SEC. "Proposed Rule Cybersecurity Risk Management, Strategy, Governance, and Incident Disclosure." March 9, 2022. Available at https://www.sec.gov/rules/proposed/2022/33-11038.pdf

37.   SEC. "Final Rule. Cybersecurity Risk Management, Strategy, Governance, and Incident Disclosure." Jul. 26, 2023. Accessed Jul. 30, 2023. Available at https://www.sec.gov/files/rules/final/2023/33-11216.pdf

38.   Gensler, Gary. "Testimony Before the United States Senate Committee on Banking, Housing, and Urban Affairs." September 15, 2022. Available at https://www.sec.gov/news/testimony/gensler-testimony-housing-urban-affairs-091522

39. Inc Magazine. "SEC Disclosure Laws and
     Regulations." January 5, 2021. Available at `https://
     www.inc.com/encyclopedia/sec-disclosure-
     laws-and-regulations.html`

40. Regulation S-K, definition. Wex legal dictionary
     and encyclopedia. Legal Information Institute
     (LII). Cornell Law School. Accessed November
     7, 2022. `https://www.law.cornell.edu/wex/
     regulation_s-k`

41. SEC. "Final Rule: Cybersecurity Risk Management,
     Strategy, Governance, and Incident Disclosure."
     July 26, 2023. Accessed July 30, 2023. Available
     at `https://www.sec.gov/files/rules/
     final/2023/33-11216.pdf`

42. NACD. "Principles for Board Governance of
     Cyber Risk." March 2021. Available at `https://
     www.nacdonline.org/applications/
     secure/?FileID=319863`

43. Chaput, Bob. *Stop the Cyber Bleeding: What
     Healthcare Executives and Board Members Must
     Know About Enterprise Cyber Risk Management
     (ECRM)*. 2021. Clearwater. Available at `https://
     amzn.to/33qr17n`

44. SEC. "Proxy Disclosure Enhancements." February
     28, 2010. Available at `https://www.sec.gov/rules/
     final/2009/33-9089.pdf`

45. Section 303A, NYSE Listed Company Manual.
     Accessed November 7, 2022. Available at `https://
     nyseguide.srorules.com/listed-company-manual`

46.   Business Experience. 17 CFR §229.401(e) (Standard
       Instructions for Filing Forms Under Securities
       Act of 1933, Securities Exchange Act of 1934 and
       Energy Policy and Conservation Act of 1975—
       Regulation S-K). Available at `https://www.ecfr.`
       `gov/current/title-17/chapter-II/part-229/`
       `subpart-229.400/section-229.401`

47.   Board leadership structure and role in risk
       oversight. 17 CFR §229.407(h) (Standard
       Instructions for Filing Forms Under Securities
       Act of 1933, Securities Exchange Act of 1934 and
       Energy Policy and Conservation Act of 1975—
       Regulation S-K). Available at `https://www.ecfr.`
       `gov/current/title-17/chapter-II/part-229/`
       `subpart-229.400/section-229.407`

48.   Seets, Chuck and Niemann Pat, EY. Harvard Law
       School Forum on Corporate Governance. "How
       cyber governance and disclosures are closing
       the gaps in 2022." October 2, 2022. Available at
       `https://corpgov.law.harvard.edu/2022/10/02/`
       `how-cyber-governance-and-disclosures-are-`
       `closing-the-gaps-in-2022/`

49.   SEC. "Proposed Rule Cybersecurity Risk
       Management, Strategy, Governance, and Incident
       Disclosure." March 9, 2022. Available at `https://`
       `www.sec.gov/rules/proposed/2022/33-11038.pdf`

50.   Audit committee financial expert. 17 CFR
       § 229.407(d)(5) (Standard Instructions for
       Filing Forms Under Securities Act of 1933,
       Securities Exchange Act of 1934 and Energy

Policy and Conservation Act of 1975—
Regulation S-K). Available at https://
www.ecfr.gov/current/title-17/
chapter-II/part-229/subpart-229.400/
section-229.407#p-229.407(d)(5)

51.   Audit committee financial expert. 17 CFR
§ 229.407(d)(5) (Standard Instructions for
Filing Forms Under Securities Act of 1933,
Securities Exchange Act of 1934 and Energy
Policy and Conservation Act of 1975—
Regulation S-K). Available at https://
www.ecfr.gov/current/title-17/
chapter-II/part-229/subpart-229.400/
section-229.407#p-229.407(d)(5)

52.   Audit committee financial expert. 17 CFR
§ 229.407(d)(5) (Standard Instructions for
Filing Forms Under Securities Act of 1933,
Securities Exchange Act of 1934 and Energy
Policy and Conservation Act of 1975—
Regulation S-K). Available at https://
www.ecfr.gov/current/title-17/
chapter-II/part-229/subpart-229.400/
section-229.407#p-229.407(d)(5)

53.   SEC. "Proposed Rule Cybersecurity Risk
Management, Strategy, Governance, and Incident
Disclosure." March 9, 2022. Available at https://
www.sec.gov/rules/proposed/2022/33-11038.pdf

54. SEC. "Final Rule: Cybersecurity Risk Management,
     Strategy, Governance, and Incident Disclosure."
     July 26, 2023. Accessed July 30, 2023. Available
     at https://www.sec.gov/files/rules/
     final/2023/33-11216.pdf

55. Sloan, Rob. WSJ Pro Research. "Analyzing Board-
     Level Cybersecurity Experience." Updated
     November 29, 2022. Accessed October 28, 2023.
     Available at https://www.wsj.com/articles/
     analyzing-board-level-cybersecurity-
     experience-11669674866

56. Sloan, Rob. WSJ Pro Research. "Analyzing Board-
     Level Cybersecurity Experience." Updated
     November 29, 2022. Accessed October 28, 2023.
     Available at https://www.wsj.com/articles/
     analyzing-board-level-cybersecurity-
     experience-11669674866

57. CRISC. "Certified in Risk and Information Systems
     Controls." Accessed November 21, 2022. Available at
     https://www.isaca.org/credentialing/crisc

58. CISSP. "Certified Information Systems
     Security Professional." Accessed November
     21, 2022. Available at https://www.isc2.org/
     Certifications/CISSP#

59. Statista. "Comparison of the number of listed
     companies on the New York Stock Exchange (NYSE)
     and Nasdaq from 2018 to 3rd quarter 2022, by
     domicile". November 1, 2022. Available at https://
     www.statista.com/statistics/1277216/nyse-
     nasdaq-comparison-number-listed-companies/

60. Small Business and Entrepreneurship
     Council. "Facts & Data on Small Business and
     Entrepreneurship." Accessed November 21, 2022.
     Available at https://sbecouncil.org/about-us/
     facts-and-data/

61. Zippier. "25 Incredible Nonprofit Statistics [2022]:
     How Many Nonprofits Are in the US?" November
     13, 2022. Available at https://www.zippia.com/
     advice/nonprofit-statistics/

62. EY. "Economic contribution of the US private equity
     sector in 2020." May 2021. Available at https://www.
     investmentcouncil.org/wp-content/uploads/
     ey-aic-pe-economic-contribution-report-
     final-05-13-2021.pdf

63. WTW. "SEC enforcement is not just a public
     company concern: What private companies need
     to know." November 18, 2019. Available at https://
     www.wtwco.com/en-US/Insights/2019/11/sec-
     enforcement-is-not-just-a-public-company-
     concern-what-private-companies-need-to-know

64. Katz, David A. McIntosh, Laura A., and Lipton,
     Wachtell. Harvard Law School Forum on Corporate
     Governance. "The SEC Takes Aim at the Public-
     Private Disclosure Gap." January 28, 2022.
     Available at https://corpgov.law.harvard.
     edu/2022/01/28/the-sec-takes-aim-at-the-
     public-private-disclosure-gap/

65.   Forescout. "The role of Cybersecurity in M&A Diligence." 2019. Available at https://www.forescout.com/merger-and-acquisition-cybersecurity-report/

66.   US Department of Health and Human Services. Business Associate Contracts. Accessed November 21, 2022. Available at https://www.hhs.gov/hipaa/for-professionals/covered-entities/sample-business-associate-agreement-provisions/index.html

67.   Murphy, Andrea. Forbes. "America's Largest Private Companies." November 23, 2021. Available at https://www.forbes.com/largest-private-companies/list/

CHAPTER 3

The Courts Are Picking Up the Cyber Pace

There is a higher court than courts of justice and that is the court of conscience. It supersedes all other courts.

—Mahatma Gandhi[1]

There is an emergence of a de facto legal "standard of care" related to cyber risk management. This chapter highlights several foundational and recent privacy and cybersecurity legal cases that boards of directors should be mindful of, especially those of public companies. These cases may represent a trend toward expectations for greater board accountability for cyber risk management oversight.

All boards of directors have fiduciary responsibilities. A *fiduciary* is a person or business with "the power and obligation to act for another (often called the beneficiary) under circumstances which require total trust, good faith, and honesty."[2] While the legal duties of directors are covered by federal securities laws as well, fiduciary duties are spelled out in state corporation laws, usually based on the American Bar Association Model Business Corporation Act.[3]

© Bob Chaput 2024
B. Chaput, *Enterprise Cyber Risk Management as a Value Creator*,
https://doi.org/10.1007/979-8-8688-0094-8_3

Several of the cases discussed in this chapter are derivative lawsuits brought by shareholders of public companies who argued, some successfully, that specific boards of directors did not execute their fiduciary duties when providing oversight of cyber risk management. It is important to note that all board directors in private, not-for-profit, as well as public companies have legal fiduciary duties.

It may be these cyber-driven derivative and other suits that drive when the word "risk" becomes a four-letter harsh word for directors.

The Board and Risk Management Responsibilities

One of a board's top three critical responsibilities is providing risk oversight[4] (along with strategy planning oversight and executive leadership development). In *Governance, Risk Management, and Compliance*, Richard Steinberg cites Jim Kristie, editor and associate publisher of Directors & Boards, saying: ·

> *Frankly, boards have let down the nation and its capital markets. Boards have not had the right leaders in place; they have not adequately analyzed risk; they have not had the depth of knowledge of their company's operations that they should have had; they have not done a sufficient job of helping management see the big picture in front of them and in seeing around corners as to what lies ahead; and they have not acted smartly and speedily as conditions deteriorated and management faltered (emphasis added).*[5]

So where have board members let down investors regarding cyber risks, and how have they failed to analyze cyber risks adequately? Let's examine some cases.

Cyber Legal Cases

One of a board member's fiduciary responsibilities is the duty of care. Duty of care is

> *a requirement that a person acts toward others and the public with the watchfulness, attention, caution, and prudence that a reasonable person in the circumstances would use.*[6]

If a person's actions do not meet this standard of care, the acts may be considered negligent, and any damages resulting may be claimed in a lawsuit for negligence. For executives and board members, these fiduciary responsibilities demand paying much more attention to their organization's cyber risk management program.

Recent data breach litigation shows how corporate executives and board members can be at risk of personal liability when a cybersecurity incident occurs. For example, in 2013, cyberattackers infiltrated retailer Target and accessed the company's computer network via credentials stolen from a third-party vendor. The attackers installed malware and accessed 41 million customer payment card accounts.[7] As a result of this breach

> *[L]itigation was filed, regulatory and congressional investigations commenced, and heads rolled. Banks, shareholders, and customers all filed lawsuits against the company. Target's CEO was shown the door. And Target's directors and officers were caught in the crossfire. In a series of derivative lawsuits, shareholders claimed that the retailer's board and C-suite violated their fiduciary duties by not providing proper oversight for the company's information security program, not making prompt and accurate public disclosures about the breach, and ignoring red flags that Target's IT systems were vulnerable to attack.*[8]

In Target's case, the courts dismissed shareholder derivative lawsuits against the company's officers and directors. However, the severity of the case underscores "the critical oversight function played by corporate directors when it comes to keeping an organization's cyber defenses up to par."[9]

Shareholders also brought derivative litigation against Yahoo, Inc., for data breaches in 2014 and 2016. The $29 million settlement, approved in January 2019, "represents the first significant recovery in a data-breach-related derivative lawsuit targeting directors and officers for breach of fiduciary duty."[10] In an article reviewing the implications of the Yahoo case, Atty. Freya K. Bowen of the law firm Perkins Coie said:

> *[A] series of prominent and widely publicized data breaches, combined with the growth of a cybersecurity industry designed to assist corporations in protecting against cyber-attacks, may have created a corporate cybersecurity standard of care. ... In other words, the very development of stronger cybersecurity protections and controls may have created a known duty to act. The Yahoo data breach derivative litigation could be a harbinger of this trend. Many of the suit's allegations assert a bad-faith failure by the directors to adequately monitor the corporation's cybersecurity system, including through their failure to adequately fund the corporation's data-security infrastructure and through their refusal to approve necessary security updates.*[11]

Listed as the second most expensive data breach as of October 2022, the 2017 Equifax Inc. data breach, which impacted 147 million consumers, is estimated to have a total cost of $2 billion.[12] The lawsuits that followed the Equifax data breach also named certain officers and directors of the organization[13]:

Although the court granted the motion to dismiss with respect to most of the officers and directors, it denied it as to the Equifax's former CEO, who was alleged to have personal knowledge of the inadequacies in Equifax's cybersecurity system. This ruling makes Equifax the first major data-breach related claim against a corporate officer to survive a motion to dismiss. These cases, along with the increase in cybersecurity-related derivative and securities actions, indicate that directors and officers of major corporations may face an increased risk of personal liability in connection with data breaches.[14]

As an aside, your organization may benefit from studying the Equifax attack and derive some important lessons learned.[15]

The Caremark Standard and Recent Cyber Cases

In 1996, the Delaware Court of Chancery issued its seminal decision in *In re Caremark International Inc. Derivative Litigation*, establishing the conditions for director oversight liability under Delaware law.[16] Shareholders sued the board for breach of duty of care for allegedly failing to provide appropriate oversight of employee conduct, exposing the company to civil and criminal penalties. However, the board prevailed, and the court concluded that the board reasonably believed the practices were lawful and attempted to exercise employee oversight and monitoring responsibilities in good faith.

The case established the so-called Caremark standard, which imposes liability under the following two circumstances: where "(a) directors utterly failed to implement any reporting or information system or controls; or (b) having implemented such a system or controls, consciously failed to monitor or oversee its operations thus disabling themselves from being informed of risks or problems requiring their attention."[17]

A 2019 article examining *Marchand v. Barnhill*,[18] a subsequent case that affirmed and strengthened Caremark, stated, regarding derivative lawsuits:

> *Although Caremark claims will remain "the most difficult theory in corporation law upon which a plaintiff might hope to win a judgment," we expect an increase in attempted derivative litigation over a purported lack of board-level monitoring systems for specific risks as plaintiffs try to shoehorn as many standard business and non-business risks as possible into Marchand's "essential and mission critical" risk category.*[19]

So what does this mean for cybersecurity-related board liability? Assessing cyber risks is critical, if not essential, for most organizations. Are cyber risk oversight failures likely to be the cases that break the duty of care standard related to board liability? The following is a summary of two cases in 2021, where the Caremark standard intersected with cyber risk management claims:

- The first case involves two pension funds, which sued SolarWinds[20] when the company became a victim of a significant cyberattack and its stock dropped 40%. The lawsuits alleged the board did not receive relevant information from the committees responsible for cybersecurity, did not discuss cybersecurity at all in the two years leading up to the attack, and ignored warnings. Notwithstanding these allegations, in September 2022, the Delaware Court of Chancery found the plaintiffs "failed to plead specific facts to infer bad faith liability on the part of the directors." The court ruled that SolarWinds directors ensured that the company had at least a minimal reporting system about corporate risk, including cybersecurity, and further that the board was not alleged to have ignored sufficient red flags of cyber threats to imply a conscious disregard of a known duty.[21]

- The second case involves a lawsuit against the Marriott International, Inc. board of directors for breach of its fiduciary duties, ultimately dismissed by the Delaware Court of Chancery. In 2015, Marriott announced its intent to acquire Starwood Hotels and Resorts Worldwide. However, despite knowing cybersecurity is a significant risk, the Pre-Acquisition Board did not order any cybersecurity due diligence. Shortly after the acquisition, Starwood disclosed a malware infection, and Marriott subsequently found lapses in cybersecurity controls. Due to the timing of the acquisition and breach, shareholders brought a lawsuit alleging the board violated their fiduciary duties by (1) failing to undertake cybersecurity and technology due diligence before the acquisition, (2) failing to implement adequate internal controls post-acquisition, and (3) failing to publicly acknowledge the data breach until November 2018, two months after Marriott first learned of the issue. However, the court found that under the stringent *Caremark* standard, the plaintiff's allegations fell short, failing to demonstrate that the Marriott directors "completely failed to undertake their oversight responsibilities, turned a blind eye to known compliance violations, or consciously failed to remediate cybersecurity failures."[22] The court further indicated that as regulatory frameworks advance to address cybersecurity practices, corporate governance, and not the law, must evolve to address these risks.[23]

In both cases, the court did not find the directors liable, suggesting as stated previously Caremark claims will remain "the most difficult theory in corporation law upon which a plaintiff might hope to win a judgment."[24] Nevertheless, it is worth noting a few interesting points:

- In the SolarWinds case, the court observed:

- The directors did not act in violation of "positive law." It "remains an open question" whether the courts may impose Caremark liability for a board's failure to oversee business risk (such as cybersecurity risk unrelated to compliance with the law). How will this change when new cyber disclosure rules by the US Securities and Exchange Commission (SEC) and other "positive laws" exist?

- The growing and consequential risks posed by cybersecurity threats characterizing cybersecurity as a "mission-critical" risk for online providers.

- Bad cybersecurity practices alone may not constitute bad faith, a core requirement under the Caremark standard.[25]

- In the Marriott case, the court acknowledged:

  - "[T]he corporate harms presented by non-compliance with cybersecurity safeguards increasingly call upon directors to ensure that companies have appropriate oversight systems in place."

  - While Marriot could have done more to prevent the data breach, the court pronounced, "The difference between a flawed effort and a deliberate failure to act is one of extent and intent," and to adequately allege a *Caremark* claim, the plaintiff must demonstrate the latter.[26]

An Important Healthcare Case to Watch

In "Cyber Risk and Patient Safety: A Tragic Call to Arms,"[27] I wrote about a lawsuit against an Alabama medical center that experienced a ransomware attack. Subsequently, a challenging baby delivery occurred, and nine months later, the baby died. Patient safety is a theme in the lawsuit, with the plaintiffs asserting that "... *the cyberattack on the hospital's computer and network systems implicated, and placed at risk, patient safety.*"

Under multiple causes of action cited, the lawsuit asserts departures from "the accepted standard of care" by

> [F]ailing to have adequate rules, policies, procedures, and/or standards related to cyberattacks, including, but not limited to, specific standards associated with disclosure to the public, disclosure to physicians, appropriate assessment and risk analysis, training of hospital personnel, identification of potential hazards, and/or taking action regarding patients who are at risk when hospital electronic systems are not operational.[28]

The complaint names the hospital, a medical practice, a physician, and

> A, B, C, D, E, F and/or G, the persons, firms, or corporations responsible for delivery of medical care, nursing care, monitoring, diagnostics, and/or treatment of [baby's name] or [mother's name], at the times and places made the basis of this lawsuit; H, I, J, and/or K, the persons, firms and/or corporations who owned, operated and/or controlled the hospital known as Springhill Hospitals, Inc. d/b/a Springhill Memorial Hospital at the times and places made the basis of this lawsuit, all of whose true names and legal identities are otherwise unknown to Plaintiffs at this time, but who will be added by amendment when ascertained, individually and jointly" (emphasis added).[29]

Who are the unknown entities, H, I, J, and/or K? It's not a stretch to think that the plaintiffs named the C-suite and board as owners, operators, or controllers of the business.

Three Other Relevant Cybersecurity Cases

Three other recent cases of interest that potentially implicate boards and possible failures to provide adequate cybersecurity oversight are those involving T-Mobile US, Inc.; Twitter, Inc., now X; and Uber Technologies, Inc.

1. In November 2021, shareholders of T-Mobile filed a lawsuit alleging the board failed to "heed the red flags demonstrating the lack of cybersecurity over customer data."[30] The complaint focuses on the 2020 data breach, which affected 54 million customers, and the subsequent investigation by the Federal Communications Commission ("FCC"). Notably, the complaint alleges the board "utterly failed to fulfill its fiduciary duties to the Company and its stockholders":

[T]he Board was required to: (1) implement and maintain an effective system of internal controls to ensure that data breaches are prevented and that personal identifying information of its customers is safe and secure, as represented; (2) implement and maintain effective internal controls and corporate governance practices and procedures to monitor the material risks posed to the Company, its stockholders, and customers by the storage of customer data and the "target" such information posed to hackers and other malicious actors; and (3) take action when presented with red flags that internal controls over cybersecurity were inadequate and that bugs on the Company's website allowed hackers to access customers' personal identifying information.[31]

This complaint points to the FCC investigation and resulting fine levied on T-Mobile to allege that the board was "long aware of" yet "failed to heed … red flags" related to the company's cybersecurity inadequacies.[32] While it is unclear whether the court will find the plaintiffs allege valid Caremark claims, boards and their counsel should closely monitor this case.

2. As mentioned in Chapter 2, in August 2022, Peiter Zatko, Twitter's former head of security, filed whistleblower complaints with the US Securities and Exchange Commission (SEC), the Federal Trade Commission, and the Justice Department alleging "extreme, egregious deficiencies by Twitter in every area of his mandate, including privacy, digital and physical security, platform integrity and content moderation."[33] Twitter, now X, subsequently reached a $7 million settlement with Zatko, and a judge ruled that Elon Musk could discuss security problems raised by Zatko during an October trial then related to Musk's bid to buy Twitter. As for the executive team and board, it is yet to be determined whether there are governance and oversight implications and liability. As a recent SEC press release reminds us, whistleblower awards can range from 10% to 30% of the money collected when the monetary sanctions exceed $1 million and are regarded as a meaningful arrow in the SEC's enforcement quiver.[34] Will more CISOs come forward with similar allegations?

3. The October 2022 conviction of former Uber
    Chief Security Officer (CSO) Joe Sullivan has
    been characterized as "[T]he wrong result and a
    lost opportunity for the Federal Government to
    send a real message and set an example on cyber
    governance."[35] Sullivan was convicted of making
    payments to hackers in exchange for them signing
    non-disclosure agreements, which was seen as
    attempted concealment.[36] The complaint also
    alleged that Uber's then-CEO, Travis Kalanick,
    knew of the payments. If Kalanick did know
    of the payments, should the acronym CSO be
    redefined to mean "Chief Scapegoat Officer"?
    Shareholders might have raised the question of
    board oversight in the derivative lawsuits previously
    discussed; however, as Uber is private, there are no
    shareholders to file complaints against the board.
    Nevertheless, questions remain. How much did the
    board know? How would the Caremark standard
    have been applied in this case? We will never know.

At last, it seems the question of whether the SEC will order new
cyber disclosure rules and other "positive laws" has been answered. As
I discussed in Chapter 2, in July 2023, the SEC issued a final rule titled
"Cybersecurity Risk Management, Strategy, Governance, and Incident
Disclosure."[37]

Effective Compliance Programs: US Sentencing Guidelines and Federal Prosecution of Business Organizations

As boards think about complying with the SEC's new cybersecurity disclosure requirements, they should also prepare for and guard against the risk of enforcement action by the SEC or prosecution by the Department of Justice (DOJ).

In 1999, the DOJ issued the "Principles of Federal Prosecution of Business Organizations" (Principles) to articulate and standardize the factors to be considered by federal prosecutors in making charging decisions against corporations.[38] The DOJ announced that the existence and adequacy of an organization's compliance program and efforts to implement or improve an existing compliance program were among the factors that prosecutors would weigh when determining whether to prosecute an organization.[39] The advent of this new prosecutorial policy was based on the influence of Chapter Eight of the US Sentencing Commission's Sentencing Guidelines, titled "Sentencing of Organizations."[40] This chapter instructs courts to determine an organization's culpability by considering six factors.[41] There are four aggravating factors "that increase the ultimate punishment of an organization" and two mitigating factors:

1. The existence of an effective compliance and ethics program

2. Self-reporting, cooperation, or acceptance of responsibility[42]

The fact that federal prosecutors are advised to use these mitigating factors further encourages (1) boards to focus on creating effective cybersecurity risk management programs as part of their existing compliance and ethics programs and (2) boards to foster a system of

91

accountability for cybersecurity breaches or failures. Doing so may prevent or detect employee misconduct and better position the company for leniency under the Principles or the Sentencing of Organizations' guidelines in a DOJ criminal investigation.[43] It is worth noting that although the Principles share many factors with the Sentencing Guidelines, they differ from the Sentencing Guidelines in that they do not create a formulaic decision-making process for prosecutors.[44]

The Principles describe specific factors for prosecutors to consider in investigating a corporation, determining whether to bring charges, and negotiating a plea or other agreements.[45] There are three "fundamental questions" a prosecutor should ask when investigating a corporation's compliance program—boards should consider these questions while assessing their cybersecurity risk management programs:

1.   Is the corporation's compliance program well designed?

2.   Is the program being applied earnestly and in good faith? (In other words, is the program adequately resourced and empowered to function effectively?)

3.   Does the corporation's compliance program work in practice?[46]

Knowledge of these factors can help boards ensure that their compliance programs' cybersecurity risk management aspects are up to speed. Keeping these questions in mind as a board assesses its compliance program and cybersecurity risk management efforts could ensure a more favorable outcome if a board's company becomes subject to a federal enforcement action. Finally, boards should note that the DOJ, in its "Evaluation of Corporate Compliance Programs," made a point to state:

*The company's top leaders—the board of directors and execu-
tives—set the tone for the rest of the company. Prosecutors
should examine the extent to which senior management have
clearly articulated the company's ethical standards, conveyed
and disseminated them in clear and unambiguous terms, and
demonstrated rigorous adherence by example.*[47]

Based on this statement, the DOJ will look for evidence of board
leadership when evaluating a company's compliance program. The DOJ
may also look for the same evidence of board leadership when assessing a
company's cybersecurity risk management program.

Conclusion

All boards of all organizations need to increase their oversight of cyber risk
management. This increase should include assessing and managing cyber
opportunities. While the cases cited have primarily involved the boards
of public companies in the United States, others, such as private and
not-for-profit companies, are not immune. While the courts in many of
the foundational cases ultimately found in favor of the boards, these legal
cases and the board's general responsibilities for risk, directors' fiduciary
duty of care, emerging national and international regulations, and
enforcement should be seen as a precursor for increased board liabilities
in the courts.

As privacy, security, cyber risk management, and data breach laws
continue to develop, boards should act now to jump-start their enterprise
cyber risk management (ECRM) efforts to establish, implement, and
mature capabilities to manage these increased cyber risks and their
attendant organizational and personal liabilities.

With a foundational case for action established based on the opportunities associated with "managing the upside," the ongoing need to "manage the downside," and the legislators, courts, and regulators picking up the cyber pace, in Chapter 4, I begin the work of formulating a plan of action starting with the most critical cybersecurity decision your C-suite and board must make.

Questions Management and the Board Should Ask and Discuss

1. What sources are your C-suite and board using to keep abreast of relevant legal cases involving cyber risk management and cybersecurity?

2. Have your C-suite executives and board members discussed their *fiduciary responsibility* for managing cyber risk?

3. What is your C-suite's and board members' understanding of their *duty of care* concerning managing cyber risk?

4. Have your C-suite executives and board members received adequate enterprise cyber risk management (ECRM) training and education? If so, do they value the training received?

5. Would your organization benefit from a session reviewing these and related legal cases by competent outside counsel and cyber risk management experts?

6. What is the level of leadership by your executive team and degree of oversight by the board of your ECRM program?

7. As a public company, how strong a position does your organization currently have in defense against the two prongs of a Caremark-based lawsuit?

Endnotes

1. BrainyQuote. "There is a higher court than courts of justice and that is the court of conscience. It supersedes all other courts." (n.d.) Accessed June 30, 2023. Available at https://www.brainyquote.com/quotes/mahatma_gandhi_134775

2. Fiduciary. *The People's Law Dictionary*. 2002. Available at https://dictionary.law.com/Default.aspx?selected=744

3. American Bar Association. Model Business Corporation Act Annotated (fifth ed., 2020). Available at https://www.americanbar.org/products/inv/book/402676454/

4. Lipton, Martin et al. Harvard Law School Forum on Corporate Governance. "Risk Management and the Board of Directors." March 20, 2018. https://corpgov.law.harvard.edu/2018/03/20/risk-management-and-the-board-of-directors-5/

5. Steinberg, Richard M. *Governance, Risk Management, and Compliance*. 2011.

6. Duty of Care. *The People's Law Dictionary*. 2002.
    Available at https://dictionary.law.com/
    Default.aspx?selected=599

7. McCoy, Kevin. USA Today. "Target to pay
    $18.5M for 2013 data breach that affected 41
    million consumers." May 23, 2017. https://
    www.usatoday.com/story/money/2017/05/23/
    target-pay-185m-2013-data-breach-affected-
    consumers/102063932/

8. Newman, Craig. NACD BoardTalk. "Lessons from
    the War Over the Target Data Breach." July 27, 2016.
    https://blog.nacdonline.org/posts/lessons-
    from-the-war-over-the-target-data-breach

9. Newman, Craig. NACD BoardTalk. "Lessons from
    the War Over the Target Data Breach." July 27, 2016.
    https://blog.nacdonline.org/posts/lessons-
    from-the-war-over-the-target-data-breach

10. Bowen, Freya K. Perkins Coie Tech Risk Report.
    "Recent Developments in Yahoo and Equifax
    Data Breach Litigation." February 6, 2019.
    https://www.techriskreport.com/2019/02/
    recent-developments-yahoo-equifax-data-
    breach-litigation-suggest-increased-risk-
    personal-liability-directors-officers-
    cybersecurity-incidents/

11. Bowen, Freya K. Perkins Coie Tech Risk Report.
    "Recent Developments in Yahoo and Equifax
    Data Breach Litigation." February 6, 2019.

https://www.techriskreport.com/2019/02/
recent-developments-yahoo-equifax-data-
breach-litigation-suggest-increased-risk-
personal-liability-directors-officers-
cybersecurity-incidents/

12. Gold Sky Security. "The 5 Most Expensive Data
     Breaches of All Time." October 25, 2022. Accessed
     September 11, 2023. Available at https://www.
     goldskysecurity.com/the-5-most-expensive-
     data-breaches-of-all-time/

13. Bowen, Freya K. Perkins Coie Tech Risk Report.
     "Recent Developments in Yahoo and Equifax
     Data Breach Litigation." February 6, 2019.
     https://www.techriskreport.com/2019/02/
     recent-developments-yahoo-equifax-data-
     breach-litigation-suggest-increased-risk-
     personal-liability-directors-officers-
     cybersecurity-incidents/

14. Bowen, Freya K. Perkins Coie Tech Risk Report.
     "Recent Developments in Yahoo and Equifax
     Data Breach Litigation." February 6, 2019.
     https://www.techriskreport.com/2019/02/
     recent-developments-yahoo-equifax-data-
     breach-litigation-suggest-increased-risk-
     personal-liability-directors-officers-
     cybersecurity-incidents/

15. Barrett, Eamon. Fortune. "A hack at Equifax
     exposed the data of 147 million people. Here's what
     businesses can learn from the company's response."

August 18, 2023. Accessed August 27, 2023. Available at https://fortune.com/2023/08/18/lessons-from-equifax-security-breach/

16. Micheletti, Edward B. and Lindsay, Ryan M. Skadden, Arps, Slate, Meagher & Flom LLP. "The Risk of Overlooking Oversight: Recent Caremark Decisions From the Court of Chancery Indicate Closer Judicial Scrutiny and Potential Increased Traction for Oversight Claims." December 15, 2021. https://www.skadden.com/insights/publications/2021/12/insights-the-delaware-edition/the-risk-of-overlooking-oversight

17. Micheletti, Edward B. and Lindsay, Ryan M. Skadden, Arps, Slate, Meagher & Flom LLP. "The Risk of Overlooking Oversight: Recent Caremark Decisions From the Court of Chancery Indicate Closer Judicial Scrutiny and Potential Increased Traction for Oversight Claims." December 15, 2021. https://www.skadden.com/insights/publications/2021/12/insights-the-delaware-edition/the-risk-of-overlooking-oversight

18. Marchand v. Barnhill, 212 A.3d 805 (Del. 2019).

19. Mendro, Jason J., Tulumello, Andrew S., and Hilborn, Jason H. Harvard Law School Forum on Corporate Governance. "Recent Application of Caremark: Oversight Liability." August 16, 2019. https://corpgov.law.harvard.edu/2019/08/16/recent-application-of-caremark-oversight-liability/#more-120953

20. Constr. Indus. Laborers Pension Fund v. Bingle, C.A. No. 2021-0940-SG (Del. Ch. Sept. 6, 2022).

21. Fried, Frank, Harris, Shriver & Jacobson LLP. Lexology.com. "Court of Chancery Addresses Board Responsibility Under Caremark for Cybersecurity Risk—SolarWinds." October 21, 2022. https://www.lexology.com/library/detail. aspx?g=567d6aeb-c484-487a-9dbc-6cd397b02378

22. Troutman Pepper. jdsupra.com. "Delaware Court of Chancery Highlights Seriousness of Cybersecurity Concerns While Maintaining High Standard for Caremark Claims." October 14, 2021. https://www. jdsupra.com/legalnews/delaware-court-of-chancery-highlights-1691774

23. Strine, Leo E. Jr., Smith, Kirby M., and Steel, Reilly S. 106 Iowa L. Rev. 1885. "Caremark and ESG: Perfect Together: A Practical Approach to Implementing an Integrated, Efficient and Effective Caremark and EESG Strategy." 1893 (describing "the first principle of corporate law: corporations may only conduct lawful business by lawful means").

24. Mendro, Jason J., Tulumello, Andrew S., and Hilborn, Jason H. Harvard Law School Forum on Corporate Governance. "Recent Application of Caremark: Oversight Liability." August 16, 2019. https://corpgov.law.harvard.edu/2019/08/16/ recent-application-of-caremark-oversight-liability/#more-120953

25. Fried, Frank, Harris, Shriver & Jacobson
     LLP. Lexology.com. "Court of Chancery Addresses
     Board Responsibility Under Caremark for
     Cybersecurity Risk—SolarWinds." October 21, 2022.
     https://www.lexology.com/library/detail.
     aspx?g=567d6aeb-c484-487a-9dbc-6cd397b02378

26. Troutman Pepper. jdsupra.com. "Delaware Court of
     Chancery Highlights Seriousness of Cybersecurity
     Concerns While Maintaining High Standard for
     Caremark Claims." October 14, 2021. https://www.
     jdsupra.com/legalnews/delaware-court-of-
     chancery-highlights-1691774

27. Chaput, Bob. Clearwater Compliance. "Cyber Risk
     and Patient Safety: A Tragic Call to Arms." October
     6, 2021. https://clearwatercompliance.com/
     blog/cyber-risk-and-patient-safety-a-tragic-
     call-to-arms/

28. Complaint at 39, Kidd v. Springhill Hosp., 02-
     CV-2020-900171 (Jun. 4, 2020). Available at https://
     s3.documentcloud.org/documents/21072978/
     kidd-amended-complaint.pdf

29. Complaint at 1, Kidd v. Springhill Hosp., 02-
     CV-2020-900171 (Jun. 4, 2020). Available at https://
     s3.documentcloud.org/documents/21072978/
     kidd-amended-complaint.pdf

30. Litwin v. Sievert, 2:21-cv-01599 (W.D. Wash. Nov.
     29, 2021).

31. Litwin v. Sievert, 2:21-cv-01599 (W.D. Wash. Nov.
     29, 2021).

32. Velevis, Robert S. and Koenig, Christina C. Sidley. "Caremark's Comeback Includes Potential Director Liability in Connection With Data Breaches." January 26, 2022. https://datamatters.sidley. com/2022/01/26/caremarks-comeback-includes- potential-director-liability-in-connection- with-data-breaches/

33. Needleman, Sarah E. The Wall Street Journal. "Twitter's Ex-Security Head Files Whistleblower Complaint on Spam, Privacy Issues." Last updated August 23, 2022. https://www.wsj.com/ articles/twitters-ex-security-head-files- whistleblower-complaint-11661263009

34. US Securities and Exchange Commission. "SEC Awards $20 Million to Whistleblower." November 28, 2022. https://www.sec.gov/news/press- release/2022-211

35. Westby, Jody R. Forbes. "Uber Trial: A Lost Opportunity For Cyber Governance." October 8, 2022. https://www.forbes.com/sites/ jodywestby/2022/10/08/uber-trial-a-lost- opportunity-for-cyber-governance/

36. US Attorney's Office, Northern District of California. justice.gov. "Former Chief Security Officer Of Uber Convicted Of Federal Charges For Covering Up Data Breach Involving Millions Of Uber User Records." October 5, 2022. https://www.justice.gov/ usao-ndca/pr/former-chief-security-officer- uber-convicted-federal-charges-covering- data-breach

37.   SEC. "Final Rule: Cybersecurity Risk Management, Strategy, Governance, and Incident Disclosure." July 26, 2023. Accessed July 30, 2023. Available at https://www.sec.gov/files/rules/final/2023/33-11216.pdf

38.   Wilkinson, Beth A. and Oh, Alex Young K. Inside Newsletter. "The Principles of Federal Prosecution of Business Organizations: A Ten-Year Anniversary Perspective." 2009. Available at https://www.paulweiss.com/media/1497187/pw_nysba_oct09.pdf

39.   Grilli, Kathleen C., Maass, Kevin T., and Ray, Charles S. United States Sentencing Commission. The Organizational Sentencing Guidelines: Thirty Years of Innovation and Influence 48. 2022. Available at https://www.ussc.gov/sites/default/files/pdf/research-and-publications/research-publications/2022/20220829_Organizational-Guidelines.pdf

40.   Grilli, Kathleen C., Maass, Kevin T., and Ray, Charles S. United States Sentencing Commission. The Organizational Sentencing Guidelines: Thirty Years of Innovation and Influence 48. 2022. Available at https://www.ussc.gov/sites/default/files/pdf/research-and-publications/research-publications/2022/20220829_Organizational-Guidelines.pdf

41.   Grilli, Kathleen C., Maass, Kevin T., and Ray, Charles S. United States Sentencing Commission. The Organizational Sentencing Guidelines: Thirty Years of Innovation and Influence 48. 2022. Available at

https://www.ussc.gov/sites/default/files/
pdf/research-and-publications/research-
publications/2022/20220829_Organizational-
Guidelines.pdf

42. Grilli, Kathleen C., Maass, Kevin T., and Ray, Charles
    S. United States Sentencing Commission. The
    Organizational Sentencing Guidelines: Thirty Years
    of Innovation and Influence 48. 2022. Available at
    https://www.ussc.gov/sites/default/files/
    pdf/research-and-publications/research-
    publications/2022/20220829_Organizational-
    Guidelines.pdf

43. Wilkinson, Beth A. and Oh, Alex Young K. Inside
    Newsletter. "The Principles of Federal Prosecution
    of Business Organizations: A Ten-Year Anniversary
    Perspective." 2009. Available at https://www.
    paulweiss.com/media/1497187/pw_nysba_oct09.pdf

44. Wilkinson, Beth A. and Oh, Alex Young K. Inside
    Newsletter. "The Principles of Federal Prosecution
    of Business Organizations: A Ten-Year Anniversary
    Perspective." 2009. Available at https://www.
    paulweiss.com/media/1497187/pw_nysba_oct09.pdf

45. US Dep't of Justice, Criminal Division. "Evaluation
    of Corporate Compliance Programs." June 1, 2020.
    At 1, https://www.justice.gov/criminal-fraud/
    page/file/937501/download

46. US Dep't of Justice, Criminal Division. "Evaluation
    of Corporate Compliance Programs." June 1, 2020.
    At 2, https://www.justice.gov/criminal-fraud/
    page/file/937501/download

47.   US Dep't of Justice, Criminal Division. "Evaluation of Corporate Compliance Programs." June 1, 2020. At 10, https://www.justice.gov/criminal-fraud/page/file/937501/download

CHAPTER 4

The Most Critical Cybersecurity Decision

It is change, continuing change, inevitable change, that is the dominant factor in society today. No sensible decision can be made any longer without taking into account not only the world as it is, but the world as it will be.

—Isaac Asimov[1]

Enterprise cyber risk management (ECRM) is a mouthful and would naturally have different meanings for different individuals. From a C-suite and board perspective, your board's most crucial decision is HOW your organization will conduct ECRM. The decisions you make about HOW you will build your ECRM Program and Cybersecurity Strategy must consider how the cyber world is changing. In this chapter, I will unpack the term *ECRM* and discuss other foundational concepts to set the stage for making that HOW decision.

Developing and documenting your ECRM Program and Cybersecurity Strategy sets forth HOW your organization conducts ECRM and is essential to creating a solid defense and competitive advantage. HOW

© Bob Chaput 2024
B. Chaput, *Enterprise Cyber Risk Management as a Value Creator*,
https://doi.org/10.1007/979-8-8688-0094-8_4

you operationalize ECRM is the most important decision the board must oversee. It is about how you will identify and analyze your unique cyber risks and opportunities, set your cyber risk appetite and opportunity threshold, and manage your cyber risks and opportunities.

C-suite executives and board members must become ECRM enablers, not necessarily cybersecurity experts; overseeing the decision on HOW your organization will conduct ECRM is crucial and is part of enabling your organization to be successful. Execution of your program and strategy (including the WHAT, WHO, WHERE, and WHEN) should be left to the C-suite and their teams.

This HOW decision will create critical reporting for the board to be informed of cyber risks and opportunities and set the stage for ongoing monitoring and action on potential cyber events requiring the board's attention.

What Does "HOW Your Organization Will Conduct ECRM" Mean?

Deciding HOW your organization will conduct ECRM is about something other than your organization's firewalls, your spam/malware filtering service, your password policy, or whether to implement multifactor authentication. It is not about silly discussions about the threats, vulnerabilities, or controls du jour that have pulled too many executives and directors into the trees and weeds, losing sight of the forest. Yes, you must deal with the ravaging ransomware outbreak, but that's an operational and tactical matter. The board's cybersecurity responsibility is strategic and must transcend all the changes in your organization's vision, mission, strategy, values, and services over time. Your ECRM approach must also prepare you for continued high-speed technology changes.

It is not only about managing cybersecurity from a risk management or defensive perspective. It is about using ECRM to address cybersecurity as a business enabler and value driver and taking advantage of cybersecurity opportunities, as discussed in Chapter 1.

First, let's review some basic concepts.

Risk

The Committee of Sponsoring Organizations of the Treadway Commission (COSO) defines risk as "the possibility that events will occur and affect the achievement of strategy and business objectives."[2] Note that this definition does not focus on negative events or adverse effects. In other words, risk can have a positive outcome or be an opportunity.

The National Institute of Standards and Technology (NIST) defines risk as "A measure of the extent to which an entity is threatened by a potential circumstance or event, and typically a function of (i) the adverse impacts that would arise if the circumstance or event occurs, and (ii) the likelihood of occurrence."[3] Here the focus is on a threatening event creating adverse outcomes.

I like the enlightened treatment of risk that the National Association of Corporate Directors (NACD) presents in its Virtual Director Professionalism program.[4] In discussing treating risk by "managing the downside," "managing the expected," and "managing the upside," it takes the view that events may create opportunities like the COSO definition. NACD materials state that companies win because they do a better job of taking risks, not because they do a better job of avoiding them. A strong, proactive ECRM program facilitates taking suitable risks and leveraging certain opportunities.

In this book, consistent with the theme of creating business value and leveraging cybersecurity for competitive advantage, I will discuss risks and opportunities side-by-side. In certain circumstances, for example, when discussing ways to leverage readily available tools from NIST to build your program, I will take some license and expand that which is focused on "managing the downside" (i.e., cyber risks) and suggest adopting those tools in a manner that also facilitates "managing the upside" (i.e., cyber opportunities). For example, the key process step of conducting a risk assessment will be expanded to discuss risk and opportunity assessment. Risk response will become risk and opportunity response. And so on.

While there are other ways to define risk, cybersecurity risks emanating from various threat sources—accidental, adversarial, structural, and environmental—will occur. They will affect an organization's ability to deliver on its vision, mission, strategy, values, and services. As discussed in Chapter 1, cybersecurity strengths may be leveraged to improve competitive position and growth in your market, increase customer trust, facilitate M&A activities, and drive down insurance and capital costs.

Research sources, publications, surveys, and reports try to identify organizations' top risks. Choose your favorite expert resource on global risks, and you will find that cyber risk has worked its way into the top ten or top five of most top risk lists over the last five years. As an example, a recent Forbes article sums up an increase in attacks on accounting and finance data:

> According to a Deloitte Center for
> Controllership poll

> *During the past 12 months, 34.5% of polled executives report that their organizations' accounting and financial data were targeted by cyber adversaries. Within that group, 22% experienced at least one such cyber event and 12.5% experienced more than one.*

> and

> *Nearly half (48.8%) of C-suite and other executives expect the number and size of cyber events targeting their organizations' accounting and financial data to increase in the year ahead. And yet just 20.3% of those polled say their organizations' accounting and finance teams work closely and consistently with their peers in cybersecurity.*[5]

Google Research found, "We've seen an over 300% increase in Russian phishing campaigns directed against users in NATO countries in 2022 (compared to a 2020 baseline)."[6] The negative consequences of weak, poorly implemented, and misinformed ECRM programs and cybersecurity strategies keep piling up and can be found in numerous articles and sources such as Forbes' "Cybersecurity Trends & Statistics For 2023; What You Need To Know,"[7] "30 Sobering Cybersecurity Statistics for 2023,"[8] and "2023 Must-Know Cyber Attack Statistics and Trends."[9]

Risk Owner/Executive

Lack of clarity on who owns cyber risk and opportunity decision-making leads to many cyber risks going untreated and cyber opportunities being squandered. Often the lack of risk ownership goes hand-in-hand with the absence of clear ownership of information assets (i.e., data, system, and devices) that support business processes. I discuss this topic further in Chapter 7 under the assignment of ownership of information assets, risk, and opportunity to business owners. The punchline is that line-of-business, functional, and process owners must own their information assets and, therefore, associated cyber risks and opportunities.

Like many risk terms, there are several definitions of *risk owner*. NIST defines a risk executive (function) as

> *an individual or group within an organization that helps to ensure that: (i) security risk-related considerations for individual information systems, to include the authorization decisions for those systems, are viewed from an organization-wide perspective with regard to the overall strategic goals and objectives of the organization in carrying out its missions and business functions; and (ii) managing risk from individual information systems is consistent across the organization, reflects organizational risk tolerance, and is considered along with other organizational risks affecting mission/business success.*[10]

ISO 31000 more simply defines *risk owner* as a person or entity that has been given the authority to manage a particular risk and is accountable for doing so.[11] And finally, the Risk Management Society (RIMS) defines the risk owner as an individual accountable for the identification, assessment, treatment, and monitoring of risks in a specific environment.[12]

Too many organizations remain stuck with the concept that the IT department owns these information assets and worse yet that IT or the CISO owns all the cyber risks and opportunities. If this is the view in your organization, I encourage you to fix it now.

Risk Management

Many definitions exist for risk management. The Risk Management Society (RIMS) defines *risk management* as "... coordinated activities to plan, direct, control and make decisions concerning the effects of uncertainty on objectives. (Adapted from ISO Guide 31000:2018)."[13] Notice the phrase "the effects of uncertainty." It does not specify good or bad effects. That is, uncertainty may bring positive results.

Focusing on risk for a moment, anything threatening a company's ability to achieve its financial goals is considered a business risk. Many factors can converge to create business risks, including strategic, financial, regulatory, operational, and legal risks. Figure 4-1 illustrates the types of risks executives and boards typically consider.

Figure 4-1. *Mosaic of Business Risks the C-Suite, Boards, and Investors Must Consider*

In the context of cyber risks, according to the National Institute and Standards and Technology, risk management refers to the broader ongoing program and supporting processes deployed to manage risks to organizational operations (including mission, functions, image, and reputation), organizational assets, individuals, and other organizations.[14] Here again, you should include in your ongoing program and supporting processes management of cyber opportunities to organizational operations.

Enterprise Risk Management (ERM)

Enterprise risk management (ERM) is a company's holistic process of identifying, assessing, and managing risks that could interfere with achieving its corporate objectives. It is a systematic approach to dealing with all risks with a reasonable likelihood of significantly affecting a business.[15] Unfortunately, even though there are seemingly progressive definitions like those of COSO and NACD previously as well as the ISO 31000 guidelines mentioning the upside or opportunity, the focus of

ERM remains on "managing the downside," regulatory compliance, and implementing controls to mitigate risks—all important, but not innovative and value-generating.[16]

Perhaps this will change with book titles like *Enterprise Risk and Opportunity Management*[17] starting to appear. I have found few sources available commercially or in academic research. This simply means we have our work cut out for us to make the pivot to value creation. All risk discussions need to include a discussion about "managing the upside."

Enterprise Cyber Risk Management (ECRM)

Cyber risk management is an enterprise risk management issue with consequences that can impact every stakeholder in your organization, from individual consumers to vendors and business partners to advisors to employees to C-suite executives and board members. It is impossible to separate "cyber risk management" from your enterprise's overall risk management program. I always refer to cyber risk management as enterprise cyber risk management (ECRM).

ECRM tends to deal specifically with *cyber* risks that can result in loss or harm to your stakeholders and organization and affect your organization's ability to achieve its strategy and business objectives. Your ECRM program must also pursue opportunities to create business value.

Cybersecurity

Security is a condition resulting from establishing and maintaining protective measures that enable an organization to perform its mission or critical functions despite risks posed by threats to its use of systems.[18] Cybersecurity is the ability to protect or defend the use of cyberspace from cyberattacks.[19] Notice the emphasis on the threat source *cyber*, inferred to be adversarial and from cyber space. Cybersecurity describes the ability to safeguard, protect, and defend the confidentiality, integrity, and availability (CIA) of all your data, systems, and devices against all reasonably anticipated threats and vulnerabilities below your risk appetite.

Strategy

The board has three key responsibilities: (1) talent management, a.k.a., hiring/firing the CEO; (2) strategy oversight; and (3) risk management. Once again, there is a myriad of definitions of strategy. Since we're discussing cyber in the context of board risk management responsibilities and we're considering cyber opportunities as potential value drivers, I prefer the definition of *strategy* as "the means to create economic value by gaining competitive advantage through a unique value proposition"[20] used by the National Association of Corporate Directors (NACD). Creating economic value reminds us that our cybersecurity strategy must be business-enabling and value-driven, not just about warding off cyberattacks.

Cybersecurity Strategy

Your cybersecurity strategy must be driven by and aligned with your organization's unique vision, mission, strategy, values, and services and incorporate your cyber risk appetite and cyber opportunity threshold. In addition to implementing reasonable and appropriate security countermeasures, it will facilitate business enablement and growth opportunities. Your ECRM Program and Cybersecurity Strategy must be incorporated into your overall ERM program.

Your cybersecurity strategy must facilitate identifying and prioritizing all your organization's unique cyber risks and opportunities, followed by treatment by "managing the downside," "managing the expected," and "managing the upside." Figure 4-2 illustrates a model for creating this alignment and shows the relationship between ECRM, ERM, and your cybersecurity strategy.

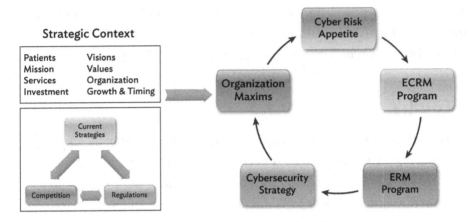

Figure 4-2. *Model for Driving Alignment in Your Cybersecurity Strategy*

The Board and Risk Management Responsibilities

A recent interview in an MIT Sloan Executive Education article stated:

> *Cyber risk is so significant that a responsible board can no longer ignore it or just delegate it to risk management experts. In fact, an organization's board of directors holds a uniquely vital role in safeguarding data and systems for the future because of their fiduciary responsibility to shareholders and their responsibility to oversee and mitigate business risk.*[21]

Whether your organization is a US public company, a PE- or VC-backed company, or a not-for-profit, your board must include cyber risk in its enterprise risk management (ERM) program. For US public companies, current risk-related requirements include but are not limited to all board members signing off on Management's Discussion and Analysis of Financial Condition and Results of Operations (MD&A), which describes any risk factors that could negatively impact company performance,[22] board disclosure of their role in risk oversight,[23] and, for some, NYSE requirements that audit committees discuss risk assessment and risk management policies.[24]

As I wrote in Chapter 3, several important, recent cyber legal cases indicate greater board accountability for cyber risk management oversight. I encourage you to reread that chapter in the context of the importance of your "HOW decision" regarding ECRM.

Regulatory and Enforcement Changes

As previously mentioned in Chapter 2, several new regulations are being introduced, such as the SEC's final rule, "Cybersecurity Risk Management, Strategy, Governance, and Incident Disclosure."[25]

President Biden signed the Cyber Incident Reporting for Critical Infrastructure Act of 2022 (CIRCIA)[26] into law in March 2022. CIRCIA will require, among other things, that organizations that are part of the national critical infrastructure sectors report covered cyber incidents within 72 hours of the organization's reasonable belief that a cyber incident has occurred and report ransom payments within 24 hours after a payment is made. The rulemaking process is underway and will likely take a couple of years.

A new "National Cybersecurity Strategy" has been published calling for mandatory regulations for most industries and aims to improve international collaboration.[27] Up to this point, the US approach has been sectoral and based on voluntary guidelines. Given the increasing number of significant attacks, the voluntary approach has not worked and must change.[28]

Regulators are raising the ante for global organizations. Enforcement agencies responsible for the General Data Protection Regulation (GDPR) received increased funding and staffing to enforce GDPR properly.[29]

GDPR became effective May 25, 2018,[30] and is designed to protect the data privacy of all EU citizens no matter where they are in the world; as such, compliance with the GDPR's data privacy regulations, which include cybersecurity implications, must be taken into account regardless of whether an organization maintains a physical presence in the EU or not.[31]

HOW your organization undertakes ECRM will significantly impact your success in complying with existing and new regulations.

Key Actions/Decisions to Facilitate Your Important "HOW Your Organization Will Conduct ECRM" Decision

Deciding HOW your organization will conduct ECRM requires thinking about a program as transformational as your ESG or digitization program or a significant M&A transaction. The following are essential ideas and concepts to consider as you decide HOW your organization will conduct ECRM:

1. Establish and formalize strong governance as the starting point for ECRM as you would for any transformational program. At the risk of grossly oversimplifying it, in practice, I've come to define governance as a set of interrelated questions: Who makes what decisions? How and when do they make those decisions? And what data and facts do they use to make those decisions? Formalizing and communicating ECRM governance are classic "set the tone at the top" moves that boards must undertake.

2. Critically evaluate your current ECRM situation. Would your current ECRM program pass a regulatory audit? Would your current ECRM posture stall or kill an M&A transaction? How would your disclosures under SEC cybersecurity reporting stand up to investor scrutiny? Is your organization currently completing comprehensive, enterprise-wide cybersecurity risk and opportunity assessments? Are you seizing cyber opportunities with as much zeal as you are mitigating cyber risks?

3. Decide if your organization's approach will be principle-based. I recommend that you adopt and communicate strong ECRM governance principles. This important step is also about "setting the tone at the top," a critical element of your organization's ECRM culture. I will cover these principles in Chapter 9. Keeping with the theme of this book, consider adopting a principle such as "ECRM is viewed as a business value creator and a means to create a competitive advantage. Business value is created from treating our cyber risks and leveraging our cyber opportunities."

4. Voltaire is attributed with saying, "If you wish to converse with me, define your terms."[32] It underscores the importance of shared understanding. I've used that Voltaire quote for 14+ years because of the constant miscommunication in so many inconsistent cyber risk management policies, procedures, and practices I have observed. It is not about precision or perfection. If your organization cannot come to a mutual

understanding of essential cyber risk management and cybersecurity terms and terminology, you will unlikely ever be effective at cyber risk and opportunity management.

5. Discuss, debate, and decide if you treat ECRM as an "IT problem," a business risk management issue, or a pathway to competitive advantage. Of course, I recommend treating it as the latter. Revisit Chapter 1 or see "Cyber Risk Management: A Business Enabler (Not an IT Issue)"[33] for additional insight. Yes, you must safeguard assets and "manage the downside." At the same time, there is an equally important, if not more significant, opportunity to "manage the upside." Settling the matter that ECRM is "not an IT problem" paves the way to assign ownership of information assets and their attendant cyber risks and cyber opportunities to business managers.

6. Discuss whether your organization treats cybersecurity as simply a matter of compliance with applicable regulations or as an existential business risk management issue. In healthcare, for example, cyber risk has also grown to encompass issues related to patient safety and medical professional liability far beyond the scope of HIPAA regulations. Boards need to think about their fiduciary responsibilities and attendant personal liabilities. Treat compliance as a byproduct of your strong ECRM program.

7. Realize that your role as a C-suite executive or
    board member is to become an ECRM *enabler*,
    not necessarily an ECRM *expert*. Seek outside help
    individually in the form of a cyber risk coach, a
    board advisor, or a board member. Remember, the
    SEC now requires, under governance, a disclosure
    of "whether and which management positions
    or committees are responsible for assessing and
    managing such risks, and the relevant expertise
    of such persons or members in such detail as
    necessary to fully describe the nature of the
    expertise."[34] Are you prepared for this disclosure?

8. Make ECRM a "team sport." Insist on cross-
    functional engagement and accountability by line-
    of-business, functional, and process owners. Do not
    delegate this foundational work to a single person or
    role in your organization—not the Chief Risk Officer,
    Chief Information Officer, or Chief Information
    Security Officer. All these individuals have a position
    on the team but are not solely responsible. Is your
    ECRM program broken into silos?

9. Decide on proven industry-standard, globally
    recognized methodologies. I highly recommend
    adopting a NIST approach to ECRM. In Appendix C,
    I provide an explanation of why implementing an
    ECRM program based on the NIST Cybersecurity
    Framework would be the optimal decision for your
    organization.

10. Decide upon and be creative in funding your ECRM program. Consider reductions in your cost of capital, insurance premium savings, and captive insurance grants as sources of funds. Consider the exposure consequences (e.g., financial, legal, regulatory, talent acquisition, operational, etc.) of not establishing, implementing, and maturing an ECRM program that results in a sound cybersecurity strategy for your organization. If cyber risks represent an existential risk to your organization, how can you not find funding to address it? See Chapter 5 for a deeper discussion of ECRM funding and budget philosophy.

11. Focus on your organization's unique assets and their exposures, not a third-party controls checklist. Insist on a risk-based approach to ECRM rather than a controls-checklist-based approach. Reasonable and appropriate controls are one factor in the risk equation, which first and foremost includes assets, threats, vulnerabilities, likelihood, and impact. Controls must not drive your ECRM program.

Once you have addressed the preceding items and followed the recommendations in the rest of this book, you will have effectively decided HOW your organization will conduct ECRM. The next critical step is to develop and document your organization's ECRM Program and Cybersecurity Strategy, which I will cover in Part 2.

Conclusion

The most crucial cybersecurity decision your board must oversee related to ECRM is HOW your organization will conduct ECRM. This book is designed to help you make that decision and develop and document your ECRM Program and Cybersecurity Strategy.

Several compelling reasons for board oversight over this critical HOW decision include the board's general responsibilities for risk, directors' fiduciary duty of care, emerging regulations and enforcement, and recent cyber legal cases.

In the next chapter, given the case to act and understanding the most critical decision to make, I discuss how to think differently about ECRM and cybersecurity funding in order to be able to jump-start your program.

Questions Management and the Board Should Ask and Discuss

1. How are you performing ECRM today? Is it formalized and documented?

2. Will a board committee or the entire board facilitate making this critical decision of HOW the organization will conduct ECRM?

3. What will be the respective roles and responsibilities of the C-suite and the board in HOW the organization will conduct ECRM?

4. How will ECRM be treated in your organization—as an "IT problem," a business risk management issue, or a value driver/business enabler?

5. Have you established a Cross-Functional Working Group to help ensure engagement and accountability by line-of-business, functional, and process owners?

6. On what proven industry-standard, globally recognized methodologies will you establish, implement, and mature your ECRM program?

7. Have you debated and decided whether your ECRM program will be risk-based or controls-checklist-based?

8. Have you assigned ownership of information assets and associated cyber risks and opportunities to line-of-business, functional, and process owners?

Endnotes

1. BrainyQuote. "It is change, continuing change, inevitable change, that is the dominant factor in society today. No sensible decision can be made any longer without taking into account not only the world as it is, but the world as it will be." (n.d.) Accessed July 1, 2023. Available at https://www.brainyquote.com/quotes/isaac_asimov_124394

2. COSO. "Compliance Risk Management: Applying the COSO ERM Framework." November 2020. Available at https://www.coso.org/Shared%20Documents/Compliance-Risk-Management-Applying-the-COSO-ERM-Framework.pdf

3. "Risk." Glossary. Computer Security Resource
    Center (CSRC). National Institute of Standards and
    Technology (NIST). Accessed January 13, 2023.
    Available at `https://csrc.nist.gov/glossary/`

4. Virtual Director Professionalism. National
    Association of Corporate Directors. (n.d.)
    Accessed January 25, 2023. Available at `https://`
    `www.nacdonline.org/events/detail.`
    `cfm?ItemNumber=74119`

5. Brooks, Chuck. "Cybersecurity Trends & Statistics
    For 2023; What You Need To Know." March 5, 2023.
    Available at `https://www.forbes.com/sites/`
    `chuckbrooks/2023/03/05/cybersecurity-trends-`
    `-statistics-for-2023-more-treachery-and-`
    `risk-ahead-as-attack-surface-and-hacker-`
    `capabilities-grow/`

6. Google. "Fog of War | How the Ukraine Conflict
    Transformed the Cyber Threat Landscape."
    February 14, 2023. Available at `https://services.`
    `google.com/fh/files/blogs/google_fog_of_war_`
    `research_report.pdf`

7. Brooks, Chuck. "Cybersecurity Trends & Statistics
    For 2023; What You Need To Know." March 5, 2023.
    Available at `https://www.forbes.com/sites/`
    `chuckbrooks/2023/03/05/cybersecurity-trends-`
    `-statistics-for-2023-more-treachery-and-`
    `risk-ahead-as-attack-surface-and-hacker-`
    `capabilities-grow/`

8.   Hewitt, Nik. TrueFort. "30 Sobering Cybersecurity Statistics for 2023." May 10, 2023. Available at https://truefort.com/2023-cybersecurity-statistics/

9.   Mclean, Mike. Embroider. "2023 Must-Know Cyber Attack Statistics and Trends." June 1, 2023. Available at https://www.embroker.com/blog/cyber-attack-statistics/

10. "Risk Executive (function)." Glossary. Computer Security Resource Center (CSRC). National Institute of Standards and Technology (NIST). Accessed August 31, 2023. Available at https://csrc.nist.gov/glossary/

11. "Risk owner." 2018 ISO 31000 Plain English Definitions. Accessed August 31, 2023. Available at https://www.praxiom.com/iso-31000-terms.htm

12. "Risk owner." RIMS Glossary. The Risk Management Society. Accessed August 31, 2023. Available at https://www.rims.org/other/rims-glossary

13. "Risk management." RIMS Glossary. The Risk Management Society. Accessed March 26, 2023. Available at https://www.rims.org/other/rims-glossary

14. "Risk Management." Glossary. Computer Security Resource Center (CSRC). National Institute of Standards and Technology (NIST). Accessed October 24, 2019. https://csrc.nist.gov/glossary/

15.   Steinberg, Richard M. *Governance, Risk Management, and Compliance.* Wiley. July 2011. Available at https://tinyurl.com/5n7vzf6y

16.   Hampton, John. *Fundamentals of Enterprise Risk Management: How Top Companies Assess Risk, Manage Exposure, and Seize Opportunity.* AMACOM. December 3, 2014. Accessed August 31, 2023. Available at https://a.co/d/1QxW8iv

17.   Benjamin, Allan S. Wiley Finance. "Enterprise Risk and Opportunity Management: Concepts and Step-by-Step Examples for Pioneering Scientific and Technical Organizations." February 6, 2017. Accessed August 31, 2023. Available at https://a.co/d/4d1975o

18.   "Security." Glossary. Computer Security Resource Center (CSRC). National Institute of Standards and Technology (NIST). Accessed March 25, 2023. https://csrc.nist.gov/glossary/

19.   "Cybersecurity." Glossary. Computer Security Resource Center (CSRC). National Institute of Standards and Technology (NIST). Accessed March 25, 2023. https://csrc.nist.gov/glossary/

20.   Blue Ribbon Commission Series. National Association of Corporate Directors (NACD). "Report of the NACD Blue Ribbon Commission on Strategy Development." October 13, 2014. Available at https://www.nacdonline.org/insights/publications.cfm?ItemNumber=12161&aitrk=nacd-1

21. MIT Sloan Executive Education. "3 Questions: Why cybersecurity is on the agenda for corporate boards of directors." November 30, 2022. Available at https://news.mit.edu/2022/cybersecurity-corporate-boards-directors-1130

22. NACD. Director Essentials Series. "Strengthening Risk Oversight Director Essentials." October 27, 2016. Available at https://www.nacdonline.org/insights/publications.cfm?ItemNumber=36685&aitrk=nacd-l

23. NACD. Director Essentials Series. "Strengthening Risk Oversight Director Essentials." October 27, 2016. Available at https://www.nacdonline.org/insights/publications.cfm?ItemNumber=36685&aitrk=nacd-l

24. NACD. Director Essentials Series. "Strengthening Risk Oversight Director Essentials." October 27, 2016. Available at https://www.nacdonline.org/insights/publications.cfm?ItemNumber=36685&aitrk=nacd-l

25. SEC. "Final Rule: Cybersecurity Risk Management, Strategy, Governance, and Incident Disclosure." July 26, 2023. Accessed July 30, 2023. Available at https://www.sec.gov/files/rules/final/2023/33-11216.pdf

26. Cybersecurity & Infrastructure Security Agency (CISA). "Cyber Incident Reporting for Critical Infrastructure Act of 2022 (CIRCIA)." March 2022. Available at https://www.cisa.gov/circia

27. Joshi, Akshay and Dobrygowski, Daniel. "The US has announced its National Cybersecurity Strategy: Here's what you need to know." March 9, 2023. Available at https://www.weforum.org/agenda/2023/03/us-national-cybersecurity-strategy/

28. Kaplan, Fred. Slate. "When It Comes to Cybersecurity, the Biden Administration Is Getting Much More Aggressive." January 17, 2023. Available at https://slate.com/news-and-politics/2023/01/biden-cybersecurity-inglis-neuberger.html

29. Stop, Catherine. WSJ Pro Cybersecurity. "European Privacy Regulators Step Up Scrutiny of Business Data Practices." January 18, 2023. Available at https://www.wsj.com/articles/european-privacy-regulators-step-up-scrutiny-of-business-data-practices-11674035444

30. GDPR FAQs. EU GDPR.org. Accessed March 6. 2023. Available at https://gdpr.eu/faq/

31. Dean, Una A. and Kiziltay Carter, Melis S. New York Law Journal. "New guidelines on GDPR's territorial scope confirm It reaches far beyond the EU." March 1, 2019. Accessed August 12, 2019. https://www.law.com/newyorklawjournal/2019/03/01/new-guidelines-on-gdprs-territorial-scope-confirm-it-reaches-far-beyond-the-eu/?slreturn=20190719160336

32.   Quotable quotes. Goodreads. "If you wish to converse with me, define your terms." Accessed December 21, 2022. Available at https://www. goodreads.com/quotes/7799868-if-you-wish-to-converse-with-me-define-your-terms

33.   Chaput, Bob. E-Briefings. The Governance Institute. "Cyber Risk Management: A Business Enabler (Not an IT Issue)." September 2019. Available at https:// www.governanceinstitute.com/page/EBriefings_ V16N5Sep2019#hide2

34.   SEC. "Final Rule: Cybersecurity Risk Management, Strategy, Governance, and Incident Disclosure." July 26, 2023. Accessed July 30, 2023. Available at https://www.sec.gov/files/rules/ final/2023/33-11216.pdf

CHAPTER 5

Justifying ECRM Funding

Alignment of business strategy and risk appetite should mini- mize the firm's exposure to large and unexpected losses. In addition, the firm's risk management capabilities need to be commensurate with the risks it expects to take.

—Jerome Powell[1]

Last spring, I read a *WSJ* article that quoted a CISO saying, "Even in a good economy, people are trying to grow the business, that's what they want to put their funds into. Security may be important, but security doesn't make revenue."[2] If you read Chapter 1, you know I disagree. Security can preserve and generate revenue and enable business growth in numerous ways. You can't afford to get stuck in a security-is-a-cost-center mindset.

Leaders and boards are dealing with a perfect storm, a confluence of forces. The world economy is wrestling with higher interest rates and a potential recession, putting pressure on all organizations to cut costs. Geopolitical tensions with Russia, China, North Korea, and Iran will likely increase the number of cyberattacks. Cyber liability insurance lines have been hardening—Mario Greco, chief executive at insurer Zurich, recently told the *Financial Times* that insurers could make cyberattacks uninsurable.[3] Combined with the SEC's final rule on Disclosure Regarding

© Bob Chaput 2024
B. Chaput, *Enterprise Cyber Risk Management as a Value Creator*,
https://doi.org/10.1007/979-8-8688-0094-8_5

the Board of Directors' Cybersecurity Expertise,[4] the Cyber Incident Reporting for Critical Infrastructure Act of 2022 (CIRCIA),[5] DFARS (Defense Federal Acquisition Regulation Supplement)[6] and the CMMC (Cybersecurity Maturity Model Certification) requirements,[7] and a new push for additional mandatory cyber security regulations,[8] protecting organizations' vital digital assets is more complicated than ever.

Good news, C-suites and boards are engaging in cybersecurity discussions and oversight. Ostensibly more good news, in June 2022, Gartner had forecasted "spending for the information security and risk management market would grow to $172.5 billion (current US dollars) in 2022, with a constant currency growth of 12.2%. The market will reach $267.3 billion in 2026, with a constant CAGR of 11.0% (2022 to 2026)."[9]

The bad news is that leaders continue to make suboptimal and fundamentally flawed decisions over how and where to spend even the most robust cybersecurity budgets. Something is not working: spending is up, and breaches of confidentiality, integrity, and availability of the data, systems, and devices are up even more!

In a survey conducted at the 2022 RSA Conference, 73.48% of organizations surveyed feel they have wasted most of their cybersecurity budget on failing to mitigate risks, despite having an overabundance of security tools at their disposal.[10] Only 13.81% of those surveyed indicated they wasted no money at all.[11]

Companies are squandering a large amount of cybersecurity funding; good news, you can address it. In this chapter, I discuss two important topics: 1) the need for a new ECRM Budget Philosophy and 2) the most critical cybersecurity question for executives and the board to ask about your organization's ECRM and cybersecurity expenditures. I present several practical, tangible actions the C-suite and board can take to manage ECRM and cybersecurity expenditures better.

The Challenge of Cybersecurity Investments Being Wasted

How and why is cybersecurity funding being wasted? You should investigate all the potential reasons to determine which apply to your organization. The following are four of the top reasons to consider:

1. Too many new shiny objects/tools can add to security teams' complexity. Organizations are investing in tools without appropriate prioritization. According to one study, mature security organizations have deployed, on average

   - In small businesses, 15 and 20 security tools

   - In medium-sized companies, 50–60 security tools

   In large enterprises, over 130 security tools[12]

   Does your organization have the talented individuals to master all these tools? Does your organization have the staff to respond to all the alerts/alarms generated by these tools? Alert fatigue is a real thing. Underutilized, excessive tools can waste both money and time. A Foundry Security Priorities Study found that the proliferation of security tools can increase risk and complexity without improving outcomes and ultimately reduce the return on investment.[13] Did anyone explicitly ask how these tools would reduce risks or create business value? Probably not.

2. Organizations are not conducting comprehensive, ongoing enterprise-wide risk and opportunity assessments. I regularly encounter organizations conducting good work in threat and vulnerability identification but not real risk and opportunity assessment work. Identifying threats and vulnerabilities is easy, especially with the overwhelming number of available tools. Unfortunately, these two factors are only two of five that must be considered in evaluating business risks emanating from cyber. Organizations must conduct risk and opportunity assessments starting with identifying their digital or information assets. Then, they must identify all reasonable anticipated threats and vulnerabilities. A risk exists only when a risk scenario or triple comprising an asset, a threat, and a vulnerability exists (think: server | hacker | unpatched operating system). Once you identify a triple, you need to evaluate it by considering the likelihood of that threat exploiting that vulnerability and the impact of that exploitation. From those values, risk can be rated and prioritized. Processes described in NIST SP 800-39 "Managing Information Security Risk" and NIST SP 800-30 "Guide for Conducting Risk Assessments"[14] cover risk assessment and management in detail. Most organizations do not come close to conducting a fundamental risk and opportunity assessment, considering all five factors—assets, threats, vulnerabilities, likelihood, and impact. How do you know if spending money on tools or controls without knowing your risks makes sense?

3. There is not enough emphasis on filling risk
    management positions and too much on security
    operations, architecture, and engineering jobs.
    Your organization must develop and execute a
    cybersecurity strategy. However, you can only
    set a reasonable and appropriate cybersecurity
    strategy once you understand your unique risks.
    Therefore, while security operations, architecture,
    and engineering are important, you must invest
    in cyber risk and opportunity management talent.
    Hiring individuals with risk and opportunity
    management skills enables establishment of a
    risk-based program, not one based on controls
    checklists, journalists' articles on trends, threats,
    vulnerabilities, controls du jour, or opinions and
    emotions.

4. Too much reliance is on controls checklists and the
    threats, vulnerabilities, and controls du jour. Cyber
    risk and opportunity management and, therefore,
    cybersecurity are not one-size-fits-all. You can't
    achieve a strong cybersecurity posture by engaging
    in a technical controls arms race and implementing
    someone else's controls checklist. These actions
    typically result in needless expenditures,
    duplication, and redundancy. Please do not
    misunderstand me—I understand the importance
    of controls. Your cybersecurity program aims to
    implement reasonable and appropriate controls
    to reduce risk ratings below your risk appetite.
    Controls (also called *safeguards* or *countermeasures*)
    are the tools your organization uses to mitigate risks

to an acceptable level. As I have written many times, the single biggest deficiency I have observed is the failure of organizations to invest in cybersecurity based on their unique risks. You must start with *your* unique vision, mission, strategy, values, and services; examine all *your* unique data, devices, and systems that support *your* unique business; and then identify all *your* unique cyber exposures across *your* entire enterprise. This failure to identify *your* unique risks usually leads to a one-size-fits-all, checklist-based approach to cybersecurity. The upshot is overspending to treat perceived risks and underspending on *your* real risks.[15] Ask the question every time: Will implementation of these controls reduce your risks or increase your opportunities?

A New ECRM Budget Philosophy Is Needed

So how much should your organization spend on the ECRM Program and Cybersecurity Strategy it produces? How must expenditures be justified? In whose budget should the ECRM and cybersecurity CapEx and OpEx funds reside? What are the assigned roles and responsibilities for the ECRM budgeting process? Should ECRM and cybersecurity costs be considered part of the IT budget? Should ECRM expenditures be regarded as an unusual bubble of expenditures that will ultimately be tamed and managed down as a percent of total OpEx, revenue, or some other denominator? How do you decide how much to spend on what? These are among the many ECRM budget and funding questions to consider.

Why Create an ECRM Budget Philosophy

Like other elements of your ECRM Program and Cybersecurity Strategy, increasing regulations and enforcement call for explicit transparency in how your organization funds and manages ECRM expenditures.

For example, consider the SEC's originally proposed Disclosure of a Registrant's Risk Management, Strategy, and Governance Regarding Cybersecurity Risks. Under risk management and strategy, specific suggested SEC disclosure items would have required disclosure of whether cybersecurity risks are considered part of *"the registrant's business strategy, financial planning, and capital allocation, and if so, how"*[16] and *"whether and how the board or board committee considers cybersecurity risks as part of its business strategy, risk management, and financial oversight."*[17] While the requirement was dropped from the final rule, it is illustrative of the importance of ECRM Program and Cybersecurity Strategy funding considerations.

As another example, both DFARS (Defense Federal Acquisition Regulation Supplement)[18] and the CMMC (Cybersecurity Maturity Model Certification) requirements[19] aim to enhance the cybersecurity of the Defense Industrial Base (DIB) and ensure that contractors and subcontractors meet minimum cybersecurity standards. DFARS and CMMC recognize that cybersecurity is not just a technical issue but also a business issue that requires proper investment and resource allocation. DFARS clause 252.204-7012[20] requires contractors to "provide adequate security" on covered defense information (CDI) by implementing the security controls specified in NIST SP 800-171.[21] Providing adequate security requires proper resource allocation, which includes budgeting and capital allocation, to ensure that the organization appropriately resources its information security program.

What drives you to create an ECRM Budget Philosophy should go beyond law, regulation, and enforcement. With the steady increase in cyberattacks and the reality that these adversarial and other threat sources may compromise your digital strategies, you must sure up your philosophy and processes around financial planning and capital allocation.

Boards are recognizing this requirement as part of an essential principled-based approach to ECRM as illustrated in the NACD publication "Cyber-Risk Oversight 2020: Key Principles and Practical Guidance for Corporate Boards,"[22] which includes Principle #4:

> *Directors should set the expectation that management will establish an enterprise-wide, cyber-risk management framework with **adequate staffing and budget**. [Emphasis added]*

NACD also reinforced this principle in its most recent 2021 "Principles for Board Governance of Cyber Risk," under Principle 2.4, Ensure organizational design supports cybersecurity:

> *Set expectations that cybersecurity and cyber-risk functions are to receive **adequate staffing and funding** and monitor the efficacy of these determinations. [Emphasis added]*

Cybersecurity spending has increased as organizations recognize the importance of protecting their digital assets from cyber threats. As discussed previously, last June, Gartner forecasted significant increases in expenditures for the information security and risk management market. Various factors drive this growth, including the increasing frequency and sophistication of cyber threats, the growing regulatory landscape, and the impact of digital transformation on organizational risk profiles.

While overall cybersecurity spending is on the rise, it is essential to allocate these resources effectively. Proper budgeting and capital allocation processes are critical to ensure that organizations appropriately invest in the areas that matter most for their risk profile.

It's time for all organizations to focus on what is likely to be an increasing outflow of cash.

Building Your ECRM Budget Philosophy

Creating your ECRM Budget Philosophy can be done by discussing and agreeing to a set of maxims that address questions like the ones initially posed in the preceding introduction. The following are several of these maxims to provoke your thinking about your ECRM Budget Philosophy:

1. *"Part of the ordinary course of doing business" maxim*

    Consider the words of Jamie Dimon, chairman and chief executive officer of JPMorgan Chase. In his April 2019 Letter to Shareholders on the topic of cybersecurity, Dimon wrote:

    *I have written in previous letters about the enormous effort and resources we dedicate to protect ourselves and our clients—we spend nearly $600 million a year on these efforts and have more than 3,000 employees deployed to this mission in some way. Indirectly, we also spend a lot of time and effort trying to protect our company in different ways **as part of the ordinary course of running the business.**[23] [Emphasis added]*

    Your organization does not need to match JPMorgan Chase's spending benchmark! The point is that Dimon understands that investing in ECRM and cybersecurity is "part of the ordinary course of running the business." This perspective is the same way all organizations should consider cybersecurity investments. Call this the "part of the ordinary course of doing business" maxim. As a reminder, a maxim is "an expression of a general truth or principle."[24]

2. *"Risk-based and opportunity-based expenditure" maxim*

One day, before he was made president, some
friends were discussing Lincoln and Douglas and
comparing their heights. When Lincoln entered
the room, someone asked him, "How long ought a
man's legs to be?" "Long enough to reach from his
body to the ground," said Lincoln coolly.[25] You can
say the same about funding your ECRM Program
and Cybersecurity Strategy. Your organization's
spending on cyber risk management should
reflect your organization's unique assets, threat
sources, threat events, likelihood, and other factors,
including your organization's specific risk appetite
and opportunity threshold. Furthermore, since
your expenditures should be all about mitigating
risks or leveraging opportunities, for every dollar
requested, the most crucial question that C-suite
executives and board members should ask is, "Will
this expenditure reduce our risks or create business
value?" Call this the "risk-based and opportunity-
based expenditure" maxim.

3. *"An ounce of prevention" maxim*

ECRM investment is often more about cost
avoidance and minimizing losses than revenue
generation. There are few visible business rewards
for stopping phishing or hacking attacks. At the
same time, experiencing a cyber event can severely
impact your organization's revenue and margin
and even put an organization out of business. The
American Medical Collection Agency (AMCA) case
illustrates the point. Between 2018 and 2019, AMCA
experienced a system hack that exposed the data of

up to 20 million patients.[26] In 2019, AMCA's parent company filed for Chapter 11 protection, noting in the court filing that the company had incurred "enormous expenses that were beyond the ability of the debtor to bear."[27]

The fact is that your organization will spend money on cybersecurity in one way or another. Would you instead make those spending and allocation decisions proactively, with your organization's best interests as the driver? Or will your spending occur reactively in response to a cybersecurity incident? In 1735, Benjamin Franklin famously wrote, "An ounce of prevention is worth a pound of cure." At the time, Franklin was writing about fire prevention, but his maxim applies equally to cyberattack prevention today. Call this the "ounce of prevention" maxim.

4. *"Business and risk ownership" maxim*

Who should own ECRM and cybersecurity expenditures? If not directly included in a business owner's budget currently, I would encourage the line-of-business, functional, and process owners to be held accountable and responsible for ECRM and cybersecurity expenditures. Business leaders' lack of accountability and engagement has perpetuated the idea that ECRM and cybersecurity are somehow an "IT problem." Assigning this cybersecurity budget ownership is all part of clarifying who owns information assets and their related cyber risks and cyber opportunities that I discussed in Chapter 4.

Once again, encouraging a principle-based approach, NACD publication "Cyber-Risk Oversight 2020: Key Principles and Practical Guidance for Corporate Boards"[28] includes as its Principle #1:

*Directors need to understand and approach cybersecurity as a strategic, enterprise risk—**not just as an IT risk.** [Emphasis added]*

This principle applies to senior management, lines of business, functional and process leaders, and everyone in the organization. Your company designs processes to produce and deliver your products, services, and solutions. Line-of-business, business function, and process leaders own these processes supported by underlying data, systems, and devices—information assets. The CIO, CTO, and CISO may be stewards and custodians of these information assets and their associated risks and opportunities. But they do not own the information assets or the risks and opportunities; the business owners do. With the assistance of the CIO, CTO, and CISO, line-of-business, functional, and process leaders must decide which risks to accept, avoid, mitigate, or transfer. They must also decide which cyber opportunities to seize. And they must own the budgets for their decisions. Call this the "business and risk ownership" maxim.

5. *"Security-by-design" maxim*

Organizations have, for decades, embarked on significant, transformational digitization and modernization programs, which means more data, systems, and devices to manage and safeguard effectively. Along with all the digitization, there has been a host of new regulations and compliance mandates to assure the confidentiality, integrity, and availability of these data, systems, and devices. Some organizations adopted security-by-design principles or built security into these new solutions. In "Tips to Effectively Fund Your Enterprise Cyber Risk Management (ECRM) Program,"[29] I defined the term "ECRM debt" to mean "... dollars that should have been spent on managing cyber risk while other dollars were rapidly being spent implementing yet again, more new digital solutions." "ECRM debt" accrued rapidly for many organizations. Said another way, managing cyber risks was, too often at best, an afterthought and not proactively considered as part of deploying the latest technologies.

I recommend that you force a security-by-design approach by adopting the concepts of "authorization to operate" and "authorization to use" before approving the deployment of any new technology solutions. Adopting these pre-authorization terms will help forge business ownership of risks and, therefore, ECRM and cybersecurity expenditures. To become familiar with these terms and processes, reference "Risk Management Framework for Information Systems and Organizations" NIST Special Publication 800-37, Revision 2.[30] Call this the "security-by-design" maxim.

6. *"Business enabler" maxim*

Creating an ECRM program requires the C-suite
executives' leadership and the board's oversight.
ECRM is not an "IT problem"; furthermore, if
handled properly, it can become a business enabler.
The C-suite and board must leverage ECRM
successfully as a business enabler. And this leverage
can be enhanced by an enlightened view that ECRM
is a growth driver and business enabler, as discussed
in Chapter 1. Effective ECRM enables organizations
to securely deploy consumer-centric, technology-
based innovations that build customer trust and
encourage customer confidence.

According to Deloitte's "2023 Global Future of Cyber
Survey"[31]

*Leaders are looking at cyber through a sharp, new lens—one
that reveals the inherent business value that can come by
embedding cyber. Not only across the enterprise, but as a crucial part of a powerful growth strategy.*

The survey identified three leading practices—
cyber planning, cyber activities and practices, and
board involvement—that hinge on stakeholders
recognizing the importance of cyber responsibility
and engagement across the organization. Budgeting,
financial planning, and capital allocation are
critical cyber planning practices. This maxim is the
"business enabler" maxim.

I recommend that you use these and other maxims relevant to your
organization to help shape your thinking about your ECRM budget
approach and philosophy.

ECRM Budget Philosophy

You should make your ECRM Budget Philosophy a formal policy statement. It should indicate what you plan to do with ECRM funding, why you plan to do it that way, the ECRM values of your organization, and what you expect of members of your workforce regarding ECRM Program and Cybersecurity Strategy budgeting, financial planning, and capital allocation. Policies are higher-level aspirational statements emphasizing "what" and "why"—that is, what your course of action will be and why you've chosen this course of action. Your policy statement also establishes your good faith intent.

Base your ECRM Budget Philosophy on how you formulate the budget maxims you develop. As your budgeting and capital allocation process matures, you may further codify it in explicit procedures and practices.

The Single Most Important Cybersecurity Question for the Board to Ask

A recent Harvard Business Review article summarized the power of asking questions this way:

Asking questions is a uniquely powerful tool for unlocking value in organizations: It spurs learning and the exchange of ideas, it fuels innovation and performance improvement, it builds rapport and trust among team members. And it can mitigate business risk by uncovering unforeseen pitfalls and hazards.[32]

Interestingly, the last sentence references mitigating business risk, a key focus of this book. Asking questions about cyber opportunities and emphasizing a focus on "managing the upside" sends a positive message to your organization.

143

C-suite executives and board members must ask essential questions about ECRM and cybersecurity. When it comes to ECRM and cybersecurity expenditures, the most critical cybersecurity question for the board to request and require management to ask is:

Will this expenditure reduce our risks or create business value?

In other words, base the focus and justification of ECRM and cybersecurity expenditures on both risk reduction and creating business value. Risk reduction comes from reducing a risk rating on a particular risk. Risk reduction presupposes several actions. You must have identified, analyzed, and rated your risks and opportunities. You must have established a risk appetite and defined what it means for a risk to be acceptable. To assess creating business value, you must also articulate your opportunity threshold and the rating at which you will invest to harvest your cybersecurity strengths.

Justify a risk reduction or opportunity leverage investment when and only when it provably moves the risk to an acceptable one in a reasonable time or further enables your business. As a risk example, investing in a multifactor authentication (MFA) solution may reduce the risk of unauthorized access into your financial systems from "high" to "low." As an opportunity example, advertising your strong *customer* cybersecurity awareness training program may generate new business.

Investments to create business may come in several forms, considering the topics covered in Chapter 1. They may be investments in your ECRM program or cybersecurity strategy to facilitate an accretive acquisition. You can invest in strengthening your cybersecurity posture, which could build customer trust and increase market share by promoting your progressive, comprehensive efforts to safeguard customer-sensitive information. I previously discussed reducing or preserving your cost of capital by suitable investments in ECRM and cybersecurity. The integration of cybersecurity metrics and indicators into established ESG reporting standards may help create a more comprehensive evaluation of your company's sustainability.[33]

The Solution: Overcoming ECRM and Cybersecurity Investment Challenges

Focusing on this critical question—Will this expenditure reduce our risks or create business value? —helps address numerous issues related to ECRM and cybersecurity funding challenges.

For example, many organizations need to see expenditures as part of the ordinary course of business to change their approach. Others are reluctant to allocate resources for something that may not happen. Many still think that ECRM and cybersecurity are IT problems, not enterprise risks and opportunities. While everyone has heard of the increase in the frequency and severity of data breaches and cyberattacks, there's too often a misunderstanding of your organization's actual cyber incident costs. And finally, a lack of understanding of where to start coupled with no perceived or actual ROI results in inaction.

What's great about this critical question—Will this expenditure reduce our risks or create new opportunities?—is that it will drive everything to enable a solid risk- and opportunity-based cybersecurity strategy. Sticking with risk reduction and competitive advantage/value creation questions creates an intense focus that allows the organization to act.

To answer that question means that you must identify your unique risks and opportunities. Knowing risks and opportunities means you must conduct risk and opportunity assessments (not new to the board!). Risk and opportunity assessments imply risk and opportunity ratings that lead to risk and opportunity management, forcing a discussion about your risk appetite and opportunity threshold.

To overcome ECRM and cybersecurity investment challenges does not mean to cut cybersecurity spending. That's not the solution. The following are five actions that boards should consider requiring management to undertake to improve the quality of funding decisions related to ECRM and cybersecurity:

1. Formalize governance. Establish a governance structure that clearly articulates *who* makes *what* cyber risk and opportunity management *funding* decisions and *how* and *when* using what data and facts. A critical part of governance is establishing how to undertake cyber risk and opportunity management. Formal governance includes deciding that your approach will be risk-based and not controls-checklist-based. See Chapter 8 for more information about the importance of governance and how to establish it.

   Reflecting substantial input in its process to create version 2.0 of the NIST Cybersecurity Framework, NIST plans to include a new "Govern" function that will help you formalize your approach to governance, to emphasize cybersecurity risk management governance outcomes.[34]

2. Develop a short game and long game. There are must-implement cyber security controls. For example, suppose it's time to renew your cyber liability policy. In that case, you may be faced with a list of must-implement safeguards like these: phishing-resistant multifactor authentication (MFA), expanded privileged access protections, frequent security awareness training, rapid patching for critical vulnerabilities, extended detection and response (XDR), 24/7/365 security monitoring, and isolated and immutable backups.[35] These controls must be part of your short game. Implement what you must implement at a level appropriate for your organization to ensure your insurance cyber

coverage is in good standing. Insurance companies are becoming more stringent as illustrated when UCLA sued several insurance firms for refusing to pay out on cyber policies from attacks in 2014. The insurers, members of Lloyd's syndicate, claim that UCLA Health failed to satisfy cybersecurity requirements under the contract terms.[36]

Your long game must take a more strategic view and focus on establishing your ECRM program as a transformational endeavor. This perspective involves developing and maturing strategic capabilities, including governance, people, process, technology, and engagement. In this strategic work, you designate and adopt an ECRM Framework, an ECRM Process, and an ECRM Maturity Model, among other tasks. In upcoming chapters, I will cover these and other actions critical to building your ECRM Program and Cybersecurity Strategy as part of your long game.

3. Prioritize expenditures by leveraging your comprehensive enterprise risk and opportunity assessment. If there was ever a time to prioritize your cyber risk and opportunity assessment processes, it would be now. The single best way to decide on your cybersecurity spending is to focus on those risks that are above your risk appetite and on those opportunities that are below your opportunity threshold. To identify those risks and opportunities, conduct a comprehensive, enterprise-wide risk and opportunity assessment. If that seems overwhelming, prioritize your assessment work by

starting with your "crown jewel" information assets. What are those information assets without which you could go out of business?

Simultaneously, stop implementing new systems and applications without formal "authorization to use/operate" as I discussed previously.

4. Converge/reduce the number of tools being used. For starters, issue a moratorium on non-strategic tools. Next, formalize processes to reassess the use of cybersecurity tools continuously. I have seen tools layered upon tools, layered upon tools. When CISOs and their staff change organizations, there can be a tendency to bring in tools from previous company assignments. Start today by requiring your team to inventory all the licensed and deployed tools. Too often, tools are acquired and become shelf-ware. Once you have a complete inventory, complete an assessment of the extent to which you are using each tool and the value, if any, you are receiving. Jettison the low-value, underutilized tools. And, of course, always ask how that next new tool will directly reduce your risks or increase your cyber opportunities. Invest your money elsewhere if the next tool doesn't deliver on either outcome.

What is most commonly missing is a tool to establish, implement, and mature your ECRM program. The right software can simplify and facilitate the task of conducting enterprise-wide risk and opportunity assessments and cyber risk management. The wrong software—or worse, no

cyber risk management software solution—makes
it nearly impossible to establish, implement,
and mature an effective ECRM program. Refer
to Appendix B to learn more about evaluating an
ECRMS tool.[37]

5. Call on cybersecurity and regulatory compliance
   experts. ECRM is a specialty area that requires
   expertise beyond what companies typically find in
   their IT, security, or risk management departments.
   Your IT and risk management departments may
   be excellent at meeting your organization's tactical
   and operational needs. Still, they may not have
   the time, independence, experience, or strategic
   expertise to evaluate your cybersecurity spending
   critically. If this is the case for your organization,
   you may consider hiring a third-party service
   provider to help build your organization's ECRM
   Program and Cybersecurity Strategy. But beware
   since ECRM consultants and service providers are
   not regulated or evaluated by a reliable, objective
   third party. Anyone can call themselves a "cyber risk
   and opportunity management expert." Therefore,
   it is incumbent on your organization to exercise
   due diligence before contracting with a cyber risk
   management consultant or service provider. Refer to
   Appendix A to learn more about how to evaluate an
   ECRM company.[38]

Conclusion

There is significant pressure from the increase in laws, regulations, enforcement, and court actions on how your organization addresses ECRM and cybersecurity budgeting, financial planning, and capital allocation. It should be a function of *your* unique vision, mission, strategy, values, and services; all *your* unique data, devices, and systems that support *your* unique business; and all *your* unique cyber exposures across *your* entire enterprise. Including a section in your ECRM Program and Cybersecurity Strategy document that covers ECRM Budget Philosophy is essential. The chief output of the work discussed in this chapter is your organization's ECRM Budget Philosophy based on the maxims that fit your organization.

As I mentioned in Chapter 2, the SEC has implemented a final rule that mandates registrants to disclose their cybersecurity risk management and strategy in a consistent and informative manner. Formalizing your ECRM Budget Philosophy will help meet this and other emerging disclosure requirements.

These times are difficult for businesses to balance pressures to manage or reduce costs in the face of increasing cyberattacks, a hardening cyber liability insurance market, and increased regulatory reporting requirements.

I would use these challenging times to ask if your requested cybersecurity expenditures will reduce your risks or create business value. The bigger ECRM and cybersecurity opportunity is to invest when and always when your organization can reduce risks, enable growth, or otherwise create value.

In this chapter, I presented recommended actions that executives and boards can take to improve their ECRM and cybersecurity spending decisions. The aim is to prevent any unnecessary waste of funds in cybersecurity spending within your organization. The key takeaway is always asking, "Will this expenditure reduce our risks or create business value?"

In Chapter 6, I discuss the critically important role of the C-suite and board of directors in providing the leadership and oversight necessary to leverage ECRM to create business value. While there appears to be solid progress around C-suite and board engagement in this subject matter, there is much room for improvement.

Questions Management and the Board Should Ask and Discuss

1. How are your organization's ECRM and cybersecurity budgeting, financial planning, and capital allocation conducted today? Is it facilitating good decision-making?

2. Which, if any, of these maxims can be adopted in your organization today—"part of the ordinary course of doing business," "risk-based expenditure," "an ounce of prevention," "business ownership," "security-by-design," and "business enabler"?

3. Has your organization agreed upon and documented an ECRM Budget Philosophy?

4. Does your organization have a good governance structure in place, one that clearly articulates and oversees your ECRM and cybersecurity budgeting, financial planning, and capital allocation?

5. Do you have the internal resources with the appropriate skills, knowledge, and experience to facilitate the development of your ECRM Budget Philosophy?

6. Would engaging an experienced, reputable ECRM partner be valuable to establishing, implementing, and maturing your organization's ECRM Budget Philosophy?

7. How does your organization prioritize cybersecurity spending?

8. Does your organization always ask if requested cybersecurity expenditures will reduce your risks or increase business value?

9. Are spending decisions based on comprehensive risk and opportunity assessment followed by informed risk and opportunity treatment decision-making using your organization's cyber risk appetite and opportunity threshold?

10. What is the most critical question your C-suite and board should ask about cybersecurity expenditures?

Endnotes

1. BrainyQuote. "Alignment of business strategy and risk appetite should minimize the firm's exposure to large and unexpected losses. In addition, the firm's risk management capabilities need to be commensurate with the risks it expects to take." (n.d.) Accessed July 2, 2023. Available at https://www.brainyquote.com/quotes/jerome_powell_857763?src=t_risk_management

2. Rundle, James and Nash, Kim S. WSJ Pro
    Cybersecurity. "Security Chiefs Trim the Fat as
    Budgets Bite." May 22, 2023. Available at https://
    www.wsj.com/articles/security-chiefs-trim-
    the-fat-as-budgets-bite-83c82f99

3. Smith, Ian. Financial Times. "Cyber attacks set to
    become 'uninsurable,' says Zurich chief." December
    26, 2022. Available at https://www.ft.com/
    content/63ea94fa-c6fc-449f-b2b8-ea29cc83637d

4. SEC. "Final Rule: Cybersecurity Risk Management,
    Strategy, Governance, and Incident Disclosure."
    July 26, 2023. Accessed July 30, 2023. Available
    at https://www.sec.gov/files/rules/
    final/2023/33-11216.pdf

5. CISA. "Cyber Incident Reporting for Critical
    Infrastructure Act of 2022 (CIRCIA)." March 2022.
    Available at https://www.cisa.gov/topics/
    cyber-threats-and-advisories/information-
    sharing/cyber-incident-reporting-critical-
    infrastructure-act-2022-circia

6. Defense Federal Acquisition Regulation Supplement
    (DFARS). Accessed March 9, 2023. Available at
    https://www.acquisition.gov/dfars

7. Cybersecurity Maturity Model Certification. CIO
    DoD. Accessed March 9, 2023. Available at https://
    dodcio.defense.gov/CMMC/

8. Nakashima, Ellen and Starks, Tim. Washington
    Post. "U.S. national cyber strategy to stress
    Biden push on regulation." January 5, 2022.
    Available at https://www.washingtonpost.com/
    national-security/2023/01/05/biden-cyber-
    strategy-hacking/

9. Gartner Research. "Forecast: Information Security
    and Risk Management, Worldwide, 2020–2026, 2Q22
    Update." June 30, 2022. Available at https://www.
    gartner.com/en/documents/4016190

10. Smythe, Zoe Deighton. Security on Screen | Security
    Industry Group (SOS|SIG). "70% of organisations
    feel they've wasted cybersecurity budget on
    failing to remediate threats, says Gurucul." July 19,
    2022. Available at https://securityonscreen.
    com/70-of-organisations-feel-theyve-wasted-
    cybersecurity-budget-on-failing-to-
    remediate-threats-says-gurucul/

11. Gurucul Research Report. "2022 Security Operations
    Efficiency Survey." July 15, 2022. Available at
    https://gurucul.com/resources/whitepapers/
    security-operations-efficiency-survey

12. Ariganello, Joe. Anomali Blog. "More Is Less: The
    Challenge of Utilizing Multiple Security Tools."
    April 14, 2022. Available at https://www.anomali.
    com/blog/more-is-less-the-challenge-of-
    utilizing-multiple-security-tools

13. Eaves, Sally. CIO. "Too Many Tools in the Security Box and What to Do About It." May 23, 2022. Available at https://www.cio.com/article/350333/too-many-tools-in-the-security-box-and-what-to-do-about-it.html

14. National Institute of Standards and Technology (NIST). NIST Special Publication 800-39. "Managing Information Security Risk." March 2011. Accessed November 11, 2019. https://nvlpubs.nist.gov/nistpubs/Legacy/SP/nistspecialpublication800-39.pdf and National Institute of Standards and Technology (NIST). NIST Special Publication 800-30, Revision 1. "Guide for Conducting Risk Assessments." September 2012. Accessed November 11, 2019. https://nvlpubs.nist.gov/nistpubs/Legacy/SP/nistspecialpublication800-30r1.pdf

15. Chaput, Bob. *Stop the Cyber Bleeding: What Healthcare Executives and Board Members Must Know About Enterprise Cyber Risk Management (ECRM)*. 2021. Clearwater. Available at https://amzn.to/33qr17n

16. SEC. "Proposed Rule Cybersecurity Risk Management, Strategy, Governance, and Incident Disclosure." March 9, 2022. Available at https://www.sec.gov/rules/proposed/2022/33-11038.pdf

17. SEC. "Proposed Rule Cybersecurity Risk Management, Strategy, Governance, and Incident Disclosure." March 9, 2022. Available at https://www.sec.gov/rules/proposed/2022/33-11038.pdf

18. Defense Federal Acquisition Regulation Supplement (DFARS). Accessed March 9, 2023. Available at https://www.acquisition.gov/dfars

19. Cybersecurity Maturity Model Certification. CIO DoD. Accessed March 9, 2023. Available at https://dodcio.defense.gov/CMMC/

20. 48 CFR 252.204-7012 Safeguarding Covered Defense Information and Cyber Incident Reporting. Available at https://www.ecfr.gov/current/title-48/chapter-2/subchapter-H/part-252/subpart-252.2/section-252.204-7012

21. National Institute of Standards and Technology (NIST). NIST Special Publication 800-171, Revision 2. "Protecting Controlled Unclassified Information in Nonfederal Systems and Organizations." February 2020. Available at https://nvlpubs.nist.gov/nistpubs/SpecialPublications/NIST.SP.800-171r2.pdf

22. Clinton, Larry, Higgins, Josh, and van der Oord, Friso. National Association of Corporate Directors (NACD). "Cyber-Risk Oversight 2020: Key Principles and Practical Guidance for Corporate Boards." Accessed March 4, 2020. https://nacdonline.org/insights/publications.cfm?ItemNumber=67298

23. Dimon, Jamie. JPMorgan Chase. "CEO Letter to Shareholders, 2018." April 4, 2019. Accessed January 8, 2020. https://www.jpmorganchase.com/corporate/investor-relations/document/ceo-letter-to-shareholders-2018.pdf

24. Maxim. Dictionary.com. (n.d.) Accessed March 6, 2023. Available at https://www.dictionary.com/browse/maxim

25. Hamilton, M.A., "Story of Abraham Lincoln." (n.d.). Accessed March 8, 2023. Available at https://www.heritage-history.com/index.php?c=read&author=hamilton&book=lincoln&story=captain

26. Davis, Jessica. Health IT Security. "AMCA files Chapter 11 after data breach impacting Quest, LabCorp." June 18, 2019. Accessed March 9, 2023. https://healthitsecurity.com/news/amca-files-chapter-11-after-data-breach-impacting-quest-labcorp

27. Davis, Jessica. Health IT Security. "AMCA files Chapter 11 after data breach impacting Quest, LabCorp." June 18, 2019. Accessed March 9, 2023. https://healthitsecurity.com/news/amca-files-chapter-11-after-data-breach-impacting-quest-labcorp

28. Clinton, Larry, Higgins, Josh, and van der Oord, Friso. National Association of Corporate Directors (NACD). "Cyber-Risk Oversight 2020: Key Principles and Practical Guidance for Corporate Boards." Accessed March 4, 2020. https://nacdonline.org/insights/publications.cfm?ItemNumber=67298

29. Chaput, Bob. Clearwater Blog Post. "Tips to Effectively Fund Your Enterprise Cyber Risk Management Program (ECRM)." April 29, 2022.

Available at https://clearwatercompliance.
com/blog/tips-to-effectively-fund-
your-enterprise-cyber-risk-management-
program-ecrm/

30. National Institute of Standards and Technology
(NIST). NIST Special Publication 800-37,
Revision 2. "Risk Management Framework
for Information Systems and Organizations."
December 2018. Accessed March 9, 2023. Available
at https://nvlpubs.nist.gov/nistpubs/
SpecialPublications/NIST.SP.800-37r2.pdf

31. Deloitte. "2023 Global Future of Cyber Survey."
January 27, 2023. Accessed March 9, 2023. Available
at https://www.deloitte.com/content/dam/
assets-shared/legacy/docs/analysis/2022/
deloitte_future_of_cyber_2023.pdf

32. Brooks, Alison Wood and John, Leslie K. Harvard
Business Review Magazine. "The Surprising Power
of Questions." May–June 2018. Available at https://
hbr.org/2018/05/the-surprising-power-of-
questions

33. Industry Insights. CFGI. "The Missing Link in
ESG Frameworks: Focus on Cybersecurity's Vital
Role in ESG Frameworks." July 31, 2023. Accessed
September 1, 2023. Available at https://www.cfgi.
com/blog/industry-insights/the-missing-link-
in-esg-frameworks/

34. National Institute of Standards and Technology
(NIST). "Discussion Draft of the NIST Cybersecurity
Framework 2.0 Core." April 24, 2023. Accessed July
16, 2023. Available at https://www.nist.gov/
system/files/documents/2023/04/24/NIST%20
Cybersecurity%20Framework%202.0%20Core%20
Discussion%20Draft%204-2023%20final.pdf

35. Quintana, Stephen and Sawyer, Woodruff. JDSupra.
"Cyber Insurance Requirements: The Next Frontier."
December 1, 2022. Available at https://www.
jdsupra.com/legalnews/cyber-insurance-
requirements-the-next-5944655/

36. Rundle, James. "University of California Sues Lloyd's
Syndicates Over Cyber Insurance." June 28, 2023.
Available at https://www.wsj.com/articles/
university-of-california-sues-lloyds-
syndicates-over-cyber-insurance-da4675f5

37. Chaput, Bob. *Stop the Cyber Bleeding: What
Healthcare Executives and Board Members Must
Know About Enterprise Cyber Risk Management
(ECRM)*. 2021. Clearwater. Available at https://
amzn.to/33qr17n

38. Chaput, Bob. *Stop the Cyber Bleeding: What
Healthcare Executives and Board Members Must
Know About Enterprise Cyber Risk Management
(ECRM)*. 2021. Clearwater. Available at https://
amzn.to/33qr17n

CHAPTER 6

The C-Suite and Board Role

Not only do I not know what's going on, I wouldn't know what to do about it if I did.

—George Carlin[1]

As with any transformational program, the C-suite and board have a significant role to play when it comes to establishing, implementing, and maturing your ECRM Program and Cybersecurity Strategy. In this chapter, I highlight several critical C-suite leadership and board oversight tasks that must be performed to make the pivot to creating business value and competitive advantage with ECRM:

1. Set the "tone at the top" with ECRM Guiding Principles.

2. Require ECRM to be formally established and documented.

3. Ensure equal focus on positive cyber opportunities.

According to an old adage, board oversight is "eyes open, noses in, fingers out."[2] You should apply this adage to your board members' involvement with your ECRM Program and Cybersecurity Strategy. "Eyes

© Bob Chaput 2024
B. Chaput, *Enterprise Cyber Risk Management as a Value Creator,*
https://doi.org/10.1007/979-8-8688-0094-8_6

open" means being informed and understanding what it means to have an effective ECRM Program and Cybersecurity Strategy. "Noses in" means understanding where your organization is concerning legal requirements, best practices, and standards related to cyber risk and opportunity management and providing leadership to close gaps between established ECRM best practices and your organization's approach. Finally, "fingers out" means leaving the details of the execution of your cybersecurity strategy to your organization's C-suite and appropriate team members, with you asking the right questions.

Set the "Tone at the Top" with Strong ECRM Guiding Principles

Good governance is the starting point for any transformational program. For most organizations, establishing, implementing, and maturing an ECRM program must be as transformational as their digitization or ESG programs. In my experience working with organizations to develop, implement, and mature ECRM programs, I have found that a three-tiered ECRM governance model is most effective. I will cover this model further in Chapter 9. For now, to illustrate how the three tiers would work, consider that an ECRM Cross-Functional Working Group would draft the ECRM Program and Cybersecurity Strategy document and an Executive Steering Committee would review and revise the document as needed and ultimately recommend it to the entire board or board committee approval to set the "tone at the top."

First and foremost, understand and communicate that cyber risk and opportunity management is a business issue and an opportunity to create a competitive advantage, not an "IT problem." Understand that "bad cyber things" related to cyber risks have happened to hundreds of organizations and will continue to happen. Help your organization embrace the reality that cyber risks have evolved. Cyber risk and opportunity management is no longer simply a matter of compliance or security. For example, recall that in healthcare, cyber risk has also grown to encompass issues related to patient safety and medical professional liability. Remember and remind your team that ECRM is a journey, not a destination, or as Sudhakar Ramakrishna, SolarWinds CEO, put it, this is a "forever project."[3] Act now! As of this writing, few organizations are conducting ECRM properly—now is the perfect time to correct that.

As a C-suite executive or board member, remember that your role is to become an ECRM and cybersecurity enabler, not necessarily a cybersecurity expert. Adopt and communicate strong governance principles. Emphasize the continuity of your ECRM program: your organization's vision, mission, strategy, values, and services should drive your ECRM program, which, in turn, feeds into your overall ERM program and determines your cybersecurity plan. Align your information assets and ECRM work with your business strategy and objectives; prioritize everything. Insist that ECRM is a "team sport"; insist on cross-functional engagement and accountability by line-of-business, functional, and process owners. Be creative in funding your ECRM program.

Critically evaluate your current ECRM situation. Would your current program pass a regulator's audit? Focus on your organization's unique assets and exposures, not a third-party controls checklist. Insist on a risk-based approach to ECRM vs. a controls-checklist-based system. Require industry-standard methodologies and techniques (such as NIST) rather than a closed or proprietary approach. Adopt the NIST Cybersecurity Framework. Implement the NIST ECRM Process.

Ensure that your ECRM program covers every information asset in every line of business, facility, and location. Assess the extent to which you have accrued "ECRM debt," and plan to prioritize any catch-up ECRM work you may have to undertake. Require a new approach to ECRM funding, including a new budgeting philosophy and practices (see Chapter 5).

Insist that all new projects involving data, systems, and devices include an ECRM budget line item before approval. Conduct ongoing risk and opportunity assessments and execute ongoing risk and opportunity management plans; remember that risk and opportunity assessment is not a once-and-done project. Monitor and measure your ECRM program maturity annually. Make sure that you integrate ECRM into your overall ERM program.

Require ECRM to Be Formally Established and Documented

In addition to setting the "tone at the top" by establishing strong governance, another critical step in establishing, implementing, and maturing an enterprise cyber risk management (ECRM) program is developing and documenting your ECRM Program and Cybersecurity Strategy.

Establishing and documenting an ECRM program requires the leadership of the C-suite executives and the board's oversight. The C-suite and board must engage in this process if ECRM will be leveraged for competitive advantage successfully. In Chapter 4, I described that the most critical decision the C-suite must make, and the board must oversee, is HOW your organization will undertake ECRM. Establishing and documenting your ECRM Program and Cybersecurity Strategy delivers on the HOW.

Part 2 of this book dives deeper into leading and overseeing that work. Through several chapters in Part 2, I will explain what constitutes an ECRM Program and Cybersecurity Strategy; who should be involved in its development; what you should include as content; why you must treat the document as a living, breathing, evolving document; and when you should update it.

In *Governance, Risk Management, and Compliance,* Richard Steinberg discusses ten potential pitfalls that directors must avoid, including two that are particularly relevant here:

- *Presuming top management knows what the critical risks are.*

- *Thinking you're apprised of critical risks when you're really told about problems.*[4]

Setting forth and agreeing upon HOW your organization will undertake ECRM will help avoid these two pitfalls. In Chapter 10, I will discuss three vital building blocks of your ECRM Program and Cybersecurity Strategy—a framework, a process, and a maturity model. All three call for C-suite and board engagement and help top management and the board understand critical cyber risks.

Your overall framework and the process of framing risk is the first building block, and its selection requires board involvement. The National Institute of Standards and Technology's Special Publication 800-39, "Managing Information Security Risk," describes NIST's recommended cyber risk management process—that is, risk framing, risk assessment, risk response, and risk monitoring.[5] The first step in this process is *Frame.* Think of this process step as creating your organization's ECRM Program and Cybersecurity Strategy and documenting it. NIST states:

> *The purpose of the risk framing component is to produce a risk management strategy that addresses how organizations intend to assess risk, respond to risk, and monitor risk—making explicit and transparent the risk perceptions that organizations routinely use in making both investment and operational decisions.*[6]

To maintain focus on value creation opportunities, you need to expand the risk framing step to consider cyber opportunities. That is, your framing work must also include how your organization will assess, respond to, and monitor your cybersecurity opportunities. Using NIST's language, address the opportunity perceptions that your organization uses to make investment and operational decisions.

Considering that a board's top responsibilities include strategy development and risk management, the C-suite and board must be heavily involved in this framing work and are uniquely positioned to do so. As another example of the need for C-suite and board engagement, the NIST Cybersecurity Framework[7] begins with two initial steps that align your ECRM Program and Cybersecurity Strategy with your business goals. These two steps, which easily incorporate cyber opportunities, are as follows:

> Step 1: Prioritize and scope. Identify business objectives and priorities to inform decision-making around cybersecurity implementation and scope.

> Step 2: Orient. Identify systems and assets, regulatory requirements, and overall risk approach.

In other words, the NIST Cybersecurity Framework suggests creating the context within which you should conduct ECRM at the onset. ECRM is about identifying and managing your *unique* cyber risks in the context of your organization's *unique* vision, mission, strategy, values, and services.

As its principal output, risk and opportunity framing produces a risk and opportunity management strategy that addresses how organizations intend to assess, respond to, and monitor risk. The strategy clarifies the assumptions, constraints, risk tolerances, and priorities/trade-offs organizations use to make investment and operational decisions.[8]

Without a well-articulated and agreed-upon ECRM Program and Cybersecurity Strategy, line-of-business, functional, and process owners will likely have divergent, if not conflicting, views on what constitutes cyber risk and how the enterprise will manage it. The C-suite and board can and must ensure consistency and alignment with your ECRM Program and Cybersecurity Strategy.

See Appendix E for a Pro Forma ECRM Program and Cybersecurity Strategy Table of Contents, which I cover in Part 2.

Ensure Equal Focus on Positive Cyber Opportunities

This task is the most important of the three leadership and board tasks covered in this chapter. As I discussed in Chapter 1, you must look for cyber opportunities to help drive growth, enable the business, and even create a competitive advantage. How's that song go? "*You've got to accentuate the positive, Eliminate the negative, Latch on to the affirmative, and Don't mess with Mister In Between.*" Humans tend to be more affected by or pay more attention to negative experiences than positive ones.[9] That's clearly been the case with our traditional "managing the downside" approaches to ECRM and cybersecurity and risk management in general.

In this section, I present several selective examples of positive cybersecurity opportunities that organizations are leveraging in addition to examples provided in Chapter 1.

Increasing Customer Trust and Brand Loyalty

In Chapter 1, I mentioned the Equifax Security Annual Report.[10] The Equifax breach and subsequent litigation are well documented. You can find several articles citing the many lessons learned from the Equifax breach. The transparency in this report is being used to rebuild the Equifax brand and customer trust. Similarly, in 2017, Slack started leveraging its strong cybersecurity program to build trust when it proactively published a white paper, "Slack's Approach to Security."[11] Apple and DuckDuckGo provide other examples of organizations connecting ECRM with their marketing efforts to increase customer trust and build their brand.[12]

Improving Social Responsibility

Once again, in Chapter 1, I discussed the relationship between compliance, cybersecurity, and privacy with core aspects of ESG, the environment, social issues, and corporate governance. According to Gartner, by 2026, 30% of large organizations will have publicly shared environmental, social, and governance (ESG) goals focused on cybersecurity, up from less than 2% in 2021.[13] According to NASDAQ, some of the most used rating agencies include Bloomberg, Institutional Shareholder Services (ISS), Moody's, MSCI, Refinitiv, Robeco, S&P Global, and Sustainalytics.[14] ESG ratings are regarded as a score of a company's commitment to ESG. Cybersecurity and privacy are becoming a more significant portion of ESG scores, with nearly a third (29%) of the ESG score for retail companies, 28% for telecom companies, and 20% for healthcare providers.

We're not quite there regarding seizing the opportunity to leverage ECRM to improve ESG ratings. Organizations are not yet fully connecting the dots between ECRM and ESG. Based on recent survey results, PwC observed that it is rare for cybersecurity, privacy, and ESG leaders to align their programs even though business leaders surveyed are simultaneously increasing investments in cybersecurity (49%) and ESG (45%).[15]

This failure to align ESG and ECRM may provide a first-mover advantage to your organization to make that linkage, improve your ESG scores, and leverage your cybersecurity program's strengths to demonstrate more social responsibility as more rating agencies integrate cybersecurity metrics into their ESG reporting standards.

Driving Revenue Growth

Over the years, the role of the Chief Information Officer has evolved from focusing on system uptime to driving efficiency to generating revenue.[16] You and your board should start to ask your Chief Information Security Officer to work on generating revenue.

Are there any ways in which you can directly generate new revenues from your ECRM program? Is there an innovative risk management or cybersecurity capability you have developed and implemented particularly well for which there is a market need? For example, if third-party risk management (TPRM) is a significant challenge in your industry and you have excelled at executing your TPRM program, you should ask three questions along these lines:

1. Does your TPRM capability provide a clear improvement over what is seen as current best practice?

2. Does your TPRM capability deliver tangible and measurable value?

3. Would a potential customer aware of current best practices consider your TPRM capability innovative?[17]

If so, you may create business value by generating incremental revenue for your organization, better protecting your supply chain, and facilitating your contract renewal process.

Indirectly, your cybersecurity posture affects your revenue in many ways. A recent Accenture Research Report highlighted the benefits of alignment between business objectives and ECRM:

> *Our latest cybersecurity research reveals some organizations are using cybersecurity as a differentiator to deliver better business outcomes. Those organizations that closely align their cybersecurity programs to business objectives are 18% more likely to increase their ability to drive revenue growth, increase market share and improve customer satisfaction, trust and employee productivity.*[18]

As a different practical example of an indirect effect on revenue, in transportation, consider the risks associated with attacks on fleets, whether ground, air, or shipping vehicles. Vehicles are connected to one another and to central dispatch, enabling an attack to propagate rapidly. Clearly, ECRM and cybersecurity solutions are required. These security solutions would provide security capabilities such as threat defense, risk assessment, compliance, and network segmentation, supporting ongoing revenue flows. What if, above and beyond their security functionality, these safeguards collected information that provided insight into better fleet asset and inventory management? Real-time utilization data may provide an opportunity for more optimal equipment utilization and, potentially, more revenue.

A strong ECRM and cybersecurity program can drive revenue growth, whether directly generating or indirectly facilitating revenue.

Facilitating Digital Transformation and Innovation

Organizations increasingly embrace digital transformation and innovation to remain competitive in today's rapidly evolving digital landscape. However, with these opportunities come significant cybersecurity challenges. Robust ECRM and cybersecurity should not be seen as a hindrance to innovation. In fact, you can foster a culture of innovation by providing a secure environment for experimentation. When employees feel confident that their innovative ideas won't compromise security, they are more likely to contribute to the organization's growth.

Siemens has incorporated cybersecurity into their innovative industrial products and services to protect critical infrastructure. Siemens' cybersecurity program supports digital transformation initiatives in industry sectors such as manufacturing, healthcare, and energy.[19]

Microsoft has been a leader in using cybersecurity to drive innovation. Their Azure cloud platform provides comprehensive security solutions that enable organizations to migrate to the cloud securely. Microsoft also invests heavily in AI and machine learning for threat detection and response, creating an environment where customers can innovate while being confident about their data security.[20]

Attracting and Retaining Talent

In Chapter 1, I made the point that companies with robust ECRM Programs and Cybersecurity Strategies are more likely to attract and retain top talent. Their intense focus on security and privacy makes them attractive to all employees, especially cybersecurity professionals.

Of course, technology companies will attract and retain top talent. Think: **Google,** known for its strong cybersecurity program; Microsoft, which invests heavily in security research and development and offers its employees a variety of training and development opportunities; Amazon, known for its innovative cybersecurity program, which includes a variety of initiatives, such as artificial intelligence–powered security tools and employee gamification programs; Apple, which designs its products and services with security in mind; and Cisco, a leading provider of cybersecurity solutions.

While your organization may be unable to keep up with these large technology companies, it's worth considering how it compares with your competitors.

Conclusion

There are numerous leadership and oversight responsibilities the C-suite and board might take on with respect to your ECRM Program and Cybersecurity Strategy. In keeping with "eyes open, noses in, fingers out,"

I recommend they focus on setting the "tone at the top," requiring formal development and documentation of your program, and ensuring your organization focuses an equal amount of time on cyber opportunities as it does on cyber risks.

No doubt, the elements of a well-designed ECRM Program and Cybersecurity Strategy are comprehensive and extensive. At the same time, agreeing on an approach before launching your ECRM program is essential. Realistically, I expect all organizations to have some cybersecurity activity underway; I hope so! Even if it turns out that you are retrofitting an ECRM Program and Cybersecurity Strategy into existing activities, it is still a fundamentally vital step to take. In Part 2, *I will cover one or more sections of the Table of Contents of your* ECRM Program and Cybersecurity Strategy document to give you a good head start on developing and documenting your approach.

The additional value creation examples provided are intended to stimulate asking the right questions in your organization and are not designed to come close to a comprehensive list. Use them to provide that equal focus on "managing the upside" as you do in "managing the downside."

In the next part and chapter, I begin to address specific steps to build and implement your ECRM Program and Cybersecurity Strategy. The key initial step, covered in Chapter 7, is to ensure the integration of ECRM into business strategy and plans.

Questions Management and the Board Should Ask and Discuss

1. Have you established a governance structure to develop your ECRM Program and Cybersecurity Strategy? Who oversees this work, the entire board or a board committee?

2. Have you clarified the ECRM roles and responsibilities of the C-suite and board?

3. To what degree has your ECRM Program and Cybersecurity Strategy been formally developed and documented?

4. Do you have the internal resources with the appropriate skills, knowledge, and experience to develop and document your ECRM Program and Cybersecurity Strategy?

5. On a continuum representing the extent to which an organization is "managing the upside" vs. "managing the downside," where would you place your organization?

6. What are your current risk and opportunity management policies, procedures, and practices? At first blush, how do they stand up to your applicable regulatory requirements? Do you meet all your cyber liability insurance requirements?

7. Do you have appropriate enterprise risk and opportunity management and cybersecurity expertise on your board?

Endnotes

1. BrainyQuote. *"Not only do I not know what's going on, I wouldn't know what to do about it if I did."* (n.d.) Accessed September 8, 2023. Available at https://www.brainyquote.com/quotes/george_carlin_385526

2. Bain, Belinda A. and Mastersmith, Loarraine. Lexology.com. Gowling WLG. "'Eyes open, nose in, fingers out': Understanding and managing the potential risks of signing on as a corporate director." September 19, 2017. Accessed March 27, 2023. https://www.lexology.com/library/detail. aspx?g=f670c6ea-23cf-4c96-bd5b-e6d1b75bfde9

3. Hill, Andrew. Financial Times. "'Attackers only have to get it right once': how cyber security burst into the boardroom." May 18, 2023. Available at https:// www.ft.com/content/a61fbda1-f956-498f-b88c-f0aaa55de4f0

4. Steinberg, Richard M. *Governance, Risk Management, and Compliance.* Wiley. July 2011. Available at https://tinyurl.com/5n7vzf6y

5. National Institute of Standards and Technology (NIST). NIST Special Publication 800-39. "Managing Information Security Risk." March 2011. Accessed December 17, 2019. https:// nvlpubs.nist.gov/nistpubs/Legacy/SP/ nistspecialpublication800-39.pdf

6. National Institute of Standards and Technology (NIST). NIST Special Publication 800-39. "Managing Information Security Risk." March 2011. Accessed December 17, 2019. https:// nvlpubs.nist.gov/nistpubs/Legacy/SP/ nistspecialpublication800-39.pdf

7. National Institute of Standards and Technology
    (NIST). "Framework for Improving Critical
    Infrastructure Cybersecurity, Version 1.1." April
    16, 2018. Accessed December 16, 2019. https://
    nvlpubs.nist.gov/nistpubs/CSWP/NIST.
    CSWP.04162018.pdf

8. National Institute of Standards and Technology
    (NIST). NIST Special Publication 800-39.
    "Managing Information Security Risk." March
    2011. Accessed December 17, 2019. https://
    nvlpubs.nist.gov/nistpubs/Legacy/SP/
    nistspecialpublication800-39.pdf

9. Drew, Chris, PhD. Helpful Professor. "25 Negativity
    Bias Examples." September 3, 2023. Accessed
    September 18, 2023. Available at https://
    helpfulprofessor.com/negativity-bias-
    examples/

10. Equifax. Investor Relations. "Equifax Releases
    2022 Security Annual Report." March 21, 2023.
    Available at https://investor.equifax.com/news-
    events/press-releases/detail/1283/equifax-
    releases-2022-security-annual-report

11. Slack. "Slack's approach to security." January 10,
    2017. Accessed September 15, 2023. Available at
    https://a.slack-edge.com/4c1ae/img/security_
    ent/Security_White_Paper.pdf

12. Kumar, Dhiraj. Forbes. "Cybersecurity And Branding: Building Brand Trust In A World Of Cyber Threats." June 3, 2022. Accessed September 1, 2023. Available at https://www.forbes.com/sites/forbescommunicationscouncil/2022/06/03/cybersecurity-and-branding-building-brand-trust-in-a-world-of-cyber-threats/

13. Industry Insights. CFGI. "The Missing Link in ESG Frameworks: Focus on Cybersecurity's Vital Role in ESG Frameworks." Jull 31, 2023. Accessed September 1, 2023. Available at https://www.cfgi.com/blog/industry-insights/the-missing-link-in-esg-frameworks/

14. NASDAQ. "ESG and Ratings: What Investors Need to Know." June 6, 2022. Accessed September 2, 2023. Available at https://www.nasdaq.com/articles/esg-and-ratings%3A-what-investors-need-to-know

15. Holcomb, Carolyn et al. PwC. "Want to advance on ESG? Cyber and privacy can help, while boosting trust in your brand." October 20, 2022. Accessed September 2, 2023. Available at https://www.pwc.com/us/en/tech-effect/cybersecurity/building-trust-with-esg-cybersecurity-and-privacy.html

16. Pratt, Mary K. CIO. "The rise of the revenue-generating CIO." October 24, 2022. Accessed September 17, 2023. Available at https://www.cio.com/article/410237/the-rise-of-the-revenue-generating-cio.html

17. Gupta, Ashutosh. "When and How to Turn Your Internal Capabilities Into Revenue-Generating Products." November 5, 2021. Accessed September 18, 2023. Available at https://www.gartner.com/en/articles/when-and-how-to-turn-your-internal-capabilities-into-revenue-generating-products

18. Dal Cin, Paolo et al. Accenture. Research Report. "State of Cybersecurity Resilience 2023." June 15, 2023. Accessed September 2, 2023. Available at https://www.accenture.com/content/dam/accenture/final/accenture-com/document/Accenture-State-Cybersecurity.pdf

19. Siemens. "Cybersecurity at Siemens." (n.d.) Accessed September 18, 2023. Available at https://www.siemens.com/global/en/company/digital-transformation/cybersecurity.html

20. Microsoft. "Microsoft Defender for Cloud." (n.d.) Accessed September 18, 2023. Available at https://azure.microsoft.com/en-us/products/defender-for-cloud/

PART II

Building and Implementing Your ECRM Program

CHAPTER 7

Integrating ECRM into Business Strategy

All men can see these tactics whereby I conquer, but what none can see is the strategy out of which victory is evolved.

—Sun Tzu[1]

The topic of the ECRM Program and Cybersecurity Strategy and related documentation covered in this chapter is about integrating ECRM into your business strategy, financial planning, and capital allocation processes.

In my work with CIOs and CISOs, I too often hear about efforts to build all or part of their ECRM program or strategy within their respective teams, then to be shared with the rest of their organization. It might be an ECRM sub-project effort to develop their identity and access management (IAM) standards, a program to stand up third-party risk management (TPRM), or even a tactical initiative to roll out a new multifactor authentication (MFA) solution. Sometimes, it is the primary strategic initiative of establishing, implementing, and maturing their overall ECRM program.

I always ask the same question: How and to what extent is the rest of the organization engaged? In all cases, if there is no organization-wide engagement, my recommendation is the same: STOP. As I wrote

© Bob Chaput 2024
B. Chaput, *Enterprise Cyber Risk Management as a Value Creator*, https://doi.org/10.1007/979-8-8688-0094-8_7

in previous chapters, you must require cross-functional engagement and accountability by line-of-business, functional, and process leaders. When and only when you have secured their attention and commitment, PROCEED.

Creating an ECRM program requires the C-suite executives' leadership and the board's oversight to ensure cross-functional engagement. You must be bored with or certainly tired of me saying that ECRM is not an "IT problem." Allowing the CISO or CIO to proceed alone in developing the entire ECRM Program and Cybersecurity Strategy or any part thereof perpetuates the misguided notion that it is an "IT problem." ECRM is not only not solely about IT, but also ECRM is not a problem! Properly managed, ECRM can be about creating value, driving growth, and enabling your business.

The proper management I call for begins with engagement, which is the starting point for successfully integrating ECRM into business strategy, financial planning, and capital allocation, the vital topic of this chapter.

The Challenge

By now, it should be clear that you must allocate resources to establish, implement, and mature your ECRM Program and Cybersecurity Strategy and to fund ongoing cybersecurity operational expenditures.

For most organizations, funding their ECRM program will require the pivot in thinking I discussed in Chapter 1—start to think about value creation, business enablement, and revenue growth. At the same time, some investing in ECRM is still about investing in preventing something terrible from happening. That aspect is a cost of doing business that you must take on, even though you don't know whether a cyberattack will hit your organization. Given the continued breaking pace at which attacks and breaches occur, the likelihood of your organization experiencing a cyberattack is substantial—increasing over time. In other words, investing in defensive ECRM is more about "when" than "if."

The fact is that your organization will spend money on cybersecurity in one way or another. Would you prefer instead to make those spending and allocation decisions proactively, with your organization's value-creating, business-enabling, and growth-driving best interests in mind? Or will your spending occur reactively in response to a cybersecurity incident? Integrating ECRM into business strategy, financial planning, and capital allocation will facilitate a proactive and progressive approach to ECRM.

The Case for Action

The NACD *2023 Director's Handbook on Cyber-Risk Oversight*, fourth edition, includes as one of its core principles (#4) that *"Directors should set the expectation that management will establish an enterprise-wide, cyber-risk management framework and reporting structure with **adequate staffing and budget**"*[2] [emphasis added].

The SEC had initially proposed to require disclosure of whether cybersecurity risks are considered part of the registrant's business strategy, financial planning, and capital allocation and, if so, how.[3] Under governance or, more precisely, the board's oversight, the disclosure required by Item 106(c)(1) would have been a disclosure, as applicable, of whether and how the board or board committee considers cybersecurity risks as part of its business strategy, risk management, and financial oversight.[4] While not adopted, these proposed requirements underscored the importance of setting realistic expectations around integrating ECRM into business planning. I mention them, even though not adopted, because they may be a harbinger of future regulations.

Another set of good reasons to invest includes the reality that legislatures, regulators, and the courts hold executives and directors responsible for ECRM failures, as discussed in Chapters 2 and 3.

I discussed how all boards have fiduciary responsibilities. Recall that a *fiduciary* is a person or business with "the power and obligation to act for another (often called the beneficiary) under circumstances which require total trust, good faith, and honesty."[5] Several cases discussed in Chapter 3 are derivative lawsuits brought by shareholders of public companies who argued, some successfully, that specific boards did not execute their fiduciary duties when providing oversight of cyber risk management. It is important to note that all board directors in private, not-for-profit, and public companies have legal fiduciary responsibilities.

It is essential for all organizations to adequately fund and integrate ECRM into business strategy, financial planning, and capital allocation. The question becomes, What is the best way to do so?

Actions to Take

The following are recommended actions to consider when integrating ECRM into your business strategy, financial planning, and capital allocation processes:

1. *Create a cyber risk and opportunity management culture.*

   In 2014, Deloitte published a paper entitled "Tone at the top: The first ingredient in a world-class ethics and compliance program."[6] Perfect! Today, swap out the "ethics and compliance program" and swap in the "ECRM Program and Cybersecurity Strategy." The tone at the top refers to a C-suite's and board's leadership and their honesty and ethical commitment. It sets forth a company's cultural environment and corporate values.[7] It drives the mood in the middle and the buzz at the bottom.

C-suite executives and board members are responsible for enabling and facilitating a strategic approach to ECRM at your organization and creating a cyber-risk-aware culture by showing their involvement in your program. An effective ECRM program begins by setting a tone that expects an intentionally designed, business-aligned, enterprise-wide strategic approach to cyber risk and opportunity management.

Line-of-business, process owners and functional leaders must also be responsible for creating a cyber-risk-aware culture. As is often quoted and attributed to Peter Drucker, *"Culture eats strategy for breakfast."*[8] You should derive your cyber-risk-aware culture from the principles, values, policies, and procedures outlined in your ECRM program documentation and, most importantly, how you act on those values.

2. *Break down the silos/establish risk governance.*

   ECRM is not a departmental issue: ECRM is an enterprise issue. But I repeatedly see ECRM relegated to some siloed section of an organization. Then, when an attack occurs, the response devolves into finger-pointing, blaming, and "not my job" defensiveness. The fact is that ECRM is everybody's responsibility. But without a C-suite-led, collaborative, and coordinated approach, your organization's ECRM program will be inefficient and ineffective.

This shared responsibility means that everyone—from board members to the Chief Human Resource Officer (CHRO) to the Chief Operating Officer (COO) to the Chief Financial Officer (CFO) to the Chief Information Officer (CIO) to the Chief Audit Executive (CAE) to the Chief Information Security Officer (CISO)—should be involved in your organization's ECRM program. ECRM must be a board-overseen and executive-led initiative, with engagement across and up and down your entire organization. Executive-level engagement helps drive engagement at all levels of your organization.

Part of this activity includes establishing governance. Governance is a system of processes and controls that ensures that stakeholder needs, conditions, and options are evaluated to determine balanced, agreed-upon enterprise objectives to be achieved, setting direction through prioritization and decision-making and monitoring performance and compliance against agreed-upon direction and goals.[9] Establishing a multi-tiered governance structure chartering teams and working groups to facilitate the development and documentation of your ECRM program and one that clearly articulates *who* makes *what* ECRM decisions and *how* and *when* using what data and facts is vital.

3. *Facilitate engagement in cyber risk and opportunity management throughout the organization.*

   In *Stop the Cyber Bleeding*,[10] I discussed extensively the importance of developing and improving five key capabilities to establish, implement, and mature your ECRM program: (1) *governance*, (2) *people*, (3) *process*, (4) *technology*, and (5) *engagement*. In that book, I discussed governance in the context of breaking down silos as earlier.

   I've advised numerous leaders on the importance of engagement. Without it, your program is doomed. As I have emphasized throughout this book, ECRM is not "just an IT problem." Nor is it "just a compliance problem" or "just a Chief Risk Officer problem." Cyber risk and opportunity management is an enterprise risk and opportunity management requirement with consequences that can impact your customers and every stakeholder in your organization. Everyone in your organization has a role to play in your ECRM program.

   Even if your C-suite and board provide appropriate leadership and oversight, if your organization's other executives, managers, and workforce members are not engaged, your ECRM program will fail. Without engagement and the ownership of risks by line-of-business, process, and functional leaders, people will make risk-related decisions without the whole strategic business view. This potential lack of a strategic perspective is why engagement is so critical. One way to assure executive engagement is to tie cybersecurity outcomes to executive pay. The $10 billion market-capitalized Australian health insurance firm Medibank Private Ltd. recently canceled $3.6 million of short-term bonuses for the chief executive officer, chief financial officer, and two other executives after Medibank was attacked and exposed the personal and health data of almost 10 million individuals.[11]

All organizations have (or should have) an enterprise-wide risk management plan that describes the broad, strategic objectives they will pursue. At the same time, requiring departments to develop their own ECRM plans (within the context of your organization's overall ECRM Program and Cybersecurity Strategy) can help enforce accountability for risk management throughout the organization.

4.   *Incorporate ECRM into strategic decision-making and ongoing business planning.*

The purpose of establishing, implementing, and maturing your ECRM program is to improve the quality of cyber risk and opportunity decision-making and, therefore, business decision-making. Recall the discussion about risk, risk management, and "managing the expected," "managing the upside," and "managing the downside." Make ECRM about managing risks and leveraging opportunities. Better decision-making improves the chance of achieving business goals and objectives and, ultimately, successfully executing your business strategy.

If ECRM rests solely in the hands of the CISO, CIO, or CRO, you are likely placing it in a silo. Individuals in these three positions have roles to play. You must engage line-of-business, process, and functional leaders in cyber risk and opportunity decision-making. Make ECRM part of business strategy and goal setting, financial planning, and capital allocation at this level of the organization.

Business plans and budgets must consider cyber risks, opportunities, and required staff resources, CapEx, and OpEx to manage cyber risks and leverage cyber opportunities to an acceptable level in the organization. Rather than treating ECRM as a line item in your CIO's or CISO's budget, I recommend viewing your ECRM spending as a percentage of *each* line-of-business, process, and functional leader's *revenue* or expense budget. Require that all operating budgets include these expenditures. Do not fund new programs, projects, or initiatives without associated ECRM CapEx, OpEx, and staff costs included.

5. *Assign ownership and risk of information assets to business owners.*

I'll refer to line-of-business, process, and functional leaders collectively as business owners. They have a mission to achieve. In today's digital era, they most undoubtedly rely upon information assets (think technology, data, systems or applications, and devices) to enable their business processes and achieve their mission. These information assets create, receive, maintain, and transmit sensitive information such as personally identifiable information (PII), protected health information (PHI), payment card information (PCI), controlled unclassified information (CUI), material non-public information (MNPI), trade secrets, business plans, software code, etc., all of which require safeguarding.

Too often, business owners do not take responsibility for these assets that enable the achievement of their respective missions. Therefore, they do not take responsibility for their risks and opportunities. They default to thinking that IT owns all the information assets, including all their unique cyber risks and opportunities. I run into this problem frequently in discussing the establishment of ECRM programs. How will you ensure your business owners take responsibility for their information assets' risks and opportunities if they don't take ownership of the assets? CISOs battle over the former, while CIOs battle over the latter.

When the OpEx and CapEx costs for those assets—systems, applications, data, devices—are in the IT budget, and there is no chargeback system, these leaders typically do not have rightful ownership. Here's a possible starter solution if your organization still has this asset ownership issue. I faced this situation as the CIO of a $750MM population health company while simultaneously hearing non-stop calls to cut the IT budget. The fix: zero-based budgeting during the next budget cycle. I submitted my first-round staffing, OpEx, and CapEx budget as all zeroes. Until or unless business owners came forward to own their information assets and jointly recommend their associated budget, I announced I would stop operating and supporting those assets (obviously a ridiculous and impractical possible outcome!). I identified and measured the number and percentage of information assets without assigned business owners. I made the point that the IT team would no longer support "orphaned" information assets AND that they were particularly vulnerable to exploitation because no single individual was accountable for the exposures and risks of those assets. That fix worked for my organization and is maybe something to consider in yours.

To successfully integrate ECRM into business strategy, financial planning, and capital allocation, business leaders must own 100% of their department's information assets.

6. *Require business ownership of risk through "authorization to operate/use."*

Adopting the "authorization to operate/use" concept, discussed in Chapter 5, is not only an effective way to encourage ownership of cyber risks by business owners, but it will also facilitate "security-by-design." To do so, as I pointed out previously, become familiar with the "authorization to operate/use" concept in NIST Special Publication 800-37, Revision 2, "Risk Management Framework for Information Systems and Organizations."[12] While NIST typically applies to government organizations subject to the Federal Information Security Management Act (FISMA), it's also terrific guidance applicable to any organization in any industry, regardless of federal information systems status.

I recommend that you stop the deployment of initiatives, projects, or programs involving technology, data, systems, or devices until or unless the responsible business leader grants formal authorization.

7. *Include specific ECRM performance goals in annual objectives.*

Leaders in goal-setting theory found that goals affect behavior and job performance and help mobilize energy, leading to a higher effort overall.[13] Include specific ECRM performance goals in all line-of-business, process, and functional leaders' annual objectives. Depending on the ECRM maturity of your organization, you might explicitly require that each leader has completed an inventory of all information assets for which they have responsibility. If your organization is mature, your objective for all line-of-business, process, and functional leaders might be to complete a comprehensive NIST-based risk assessment for *the most critical information assets* under their purview. The ultimate risk and opportunity assessment objective would be for all line-of-business, process, and functional leaders to conduct NIST-based risk assessments for *all the information assets* under their purview and update the analysis regularly (e.g., whenever changes in information assets, technology assets, or personnel occur).

Another performance goal would require adopting the "authorization to operate/use" discussed previously. Yet another might be to demonstrate how the responsible business leader incorporated ECRM into financial planning and capital allocation in their units' goals and objectives. For example, suppose a line-of-business executive has a post-merger integration project planned due to a recent transaction. In that case, they must include ECRM and cybersecurity costs in that project's budget. The ongoing management planning process needs to discuss cybersecurity and "managing the expected," "managing the downside," and "managing the upside"—that is, managing risks and leveraging opportunities.

8. *Require ECRM and cybersecurity budget line items in operational budgets.*

   As I discussed, considering ECRM expenditures as "part of the ordinary course of running the business" further affirms the need for business ownership of their information assets, associated risks, and business value-creating opportunities. That means budgeting appropriately for them. How much is enough, and how do you determine the right amount? It's simple: establish appropriate OpEx, CapEx, and human resource budgets in operational budgets to manage your organization's cyber risks to an acceptable level and leverage opportunities to drive growth.

Your organization's spending on cyber risk and opportunity management should reflect your organization's unique assets, threat sources, threat events, likelihood, and other factors, including your organization's specific risk appetite and opportunity threshold. You can't base your spending on somebody else's spending benchmarks any more than you can establish your ECRM program on somebody else's controls checklist.

Moving the ownership of ECRM budgets to business owners should facilitate better budget decision-making and overall cyber risk management.

9. *Proactively educate and train on your ECRM program and cybersecurity strategy.*

To truly leverage all the work put into establishing, implementing, and maturing your ECRM program, it is essential to get the word out. Most of Part 2 of this book is about developing and documenting your ECRM Program and Cybersecurity Strategy. If you go through all that effort, don't squander it by letting it become shelf- or SharePoint-ware. For your organization to be successful with ECRM, you must frequently and proactively educate everyone on the vision and principles of your program and train them on what the organization expects of them in their roles.

Education and training plans, policies, procedures, and materials must be prepared and shared. Education and training must be role-based and meaningful, not the too-often perfunctory annual security training some organizations still deliver. At the front line, the 2022 Global Risks Report released by the World Economic Forum[14] and the 2022 Data Breach Investigations Report (DBIR)[15] found, respectively, that 95% and 82% of breaches involved the human element, including social attacks, errors, and misuse. Exploiting human vulnerabilities traces back to inadequate cybersecurity education and training more times than not.

When I write about education and training, it is not about the annual, too often superficial, cybersecurity training. I am writing about the education and training required to implement your program. It is certainly not one-size-fits-all nor once-and-done. It should include all the program elements I will cover in the rest of this book and the topics I have covered thus far. Consistent with my call for solid governance and engagement, this training should include the board, executives, management, and workforce members at all levels. For most organizations, implementing an ECRM program will be transformational.

Conclusion

Integrating your ECRM Program and Cybersecurity Strategy goals into business planning is imperative. The failure to integrate will likely result in underspending on actual requirements and overspending in areas less critical to business growth.

In this chapter, I have provided numerous compelling reasons to undertake this integration work and nine specific actions you should consider completing this important integration and alignment work. In Chapter 8, I start discussing the detailed work involved in building and documenting your ECRM Program and Cybersecurity Strategy. In fact, Chapters 8–12 include discussions of essential elements of your ECRM and cybersecurity documentation.

Questions Management and the Board Should Ask and Discuss

1. Has your organization created a positive, forward-thinking cyber risk and opportunity management culture?

2. Does your organization have a formal ECRM governance structure in place? Are you comfortable disclosing your ECRM governance structure to investors and other stakeholders?

3. What is the level of commitment and engagement in cyber risk and opportunity management throughout the organization?

4. To what extent has your organization incorporated ECRM into strategic decision-making and ongoing business planning?

5. Has your organization assigned ownership and risk of information assets to business owners?

6. Has your organization adopted the "authorization to operate/use" concept?

7. Does your organization include specific ECRM
    performance goals in executives', leaders', and staff's
    annual objectives?

8. Do you require ECRM and cybersecurity budget line
    items in operational budgets rather than the CIO's
    or CISO's budget for CapEx, OpEx, and personnel?

9. Are you proactively educating and training
    your organization on your ECRM Program and
    Cybersecurity Strategy?

Endnotes

1. Sun Tzu. "All men can see these tactics whereby I
    conquer, but what none can see is the strategy out
    of which victory is evolved." (n.d.) Accessed July 4,
    2023. Available at `https://www.brainyquote.com/`
    `quotes/sun_tzu_155751`

2. National Association of Corporate Directors (NACD)
    and Internet Security Alliance (ISA). *2023 Director's
    Handbook on Cyber-Risk Oversight.* March 20,
    2023. Available at `https://www.nacdonline.org/`
    `insights/publications.cfm?ItemNumber=74777`

3. SEC. "Proposed Rule Cybersecurity Risk
    Management, Strategy, Governance, and Incident
    Disclosure." March 9, 2022. Available at `https://`
    `www.sec.gov/rules/proposed/2022/33-11038.pdf`

4. SEC. "Proposed Rule Cybersecurity Risk
    Management, Strategy, Governance, and Incident
    Disclosure." March 9, 2022. Available at `https://`
    `www.sec.gov/rules/proposed/2022/33-11038.pdf`

5. Fiduciary. *The People's Law Dictionary*. 2002. Available at `https://dictionary.law.com/Default.aspx?selected=744`

6. Deloitte. "Tone at the top: The first ingredient in a world-class ethics and compliance program." October 10, 2015. Available at `https://www2.deloitte.com/content/dam/Deloitte/us/Documents/risk/us-aers-tone-at-the-top-sept-2014.pdf`

7. CFI Team. Corporate Finance Institute. "Tone at the Top." December 15, 2022. Available at `https://corporatefinanceinstitute.com/resources/management/tone-at-the-top/`

8. Cave, Andrew. Forbes. "Culture eats strategy for breakfast. So what's for lunch?" November 9, 2017. Accessed April 13, 2023. `https://www.forbes.com/sites/andrewcave/2017/11/09/culture-eats-strategy-for-breakfast-so-whats-for-lunch/#78282ef27e0f`

9. Chaput, Bob. IT Toolbox Blog. "CEO-to-CEO: Top 5 questions CEOs should ask themselves & board about risk management." (n.d.) Accessed April 13, 2023. `https://it.toolbox.com/blogs/bobchaput/ceo-to-ceo-top-5-questions-ceos-should-ask-themselves-board-about-risk-management-111914`

10. Chaput, Bob. *Stop the Cyber Bleeding: What Healthcare Executives and Board Members Must Know About Enterprise Cyber Risk Management (ECRM)*. 2021. Clearwater. Available at `https://amzn.to/33qr17n`

11. Nash, Kim S. WSJ PRO. "Cybersecurity Enters Conversation About Executive Pay." August 30, 2023. Accessed September 2, 2023. Available at https://www.wsj.com/articles/cybersecurity-enters-conversation-about-executive-pay-488d702e

12. National Institute of Standards and Technology (NIST). NIST Special Publication 800-37, Revision 2. "Risk Management Framework for Information Systems and Organizations." December 2018. Accessed April 13, 2023. https://nvlpubs.nist.gov/nistpubs/SpecialPublications/NIST.SP.800-37r2.pdf

13. Locke, Edwin A. and Latham, Gary P. American Psychologist. "Building a Practically Useful Theory of Goal Setting and Task Motivation: A 35-Year Odyssey." September 2002. Available at https://med.stanford.edu/content/dam/sm/s-spire/documents/PD.locke-and-latham-retrospective_Paper.pdf

14. World Economic Forum. "The Global Risks Report 2022. 17th Edition." January 31, 2022. Available at https://www3.weforum.org/docs/WEF_The_Global_Risks_Report_2022.pdf

15. Verizon. "2022 Data Breach Investigations Report." May 25, 2022. Available at https://www.verizon.com/business/resources/reports/2022/dbir/2022-data-breach-investigations-report-dbir.pdf

CHAPTER 8

Getting Started

Change your thoughts and you change your world.

—Norman Vincent Peale[1]

Let's get started changing how we think about ECRM to include as much focus on cyber opportunity management as it does on cyber risk management. I will not repeat everything I've written up to this point about the importance of this pivot to "managing the upside" and "managing the downside." Chapter 7 reiterated the importance of integrating ECRM into business strategy, financial planning, and capital allocation by developing and documenting your ECRM Program and Cybersecurity Strategy. I've been asked often: What form might this documentation take?

This chapter will focus on several primary introductory sections of your ECRM Program and Cybersecurity Strategy documentation and the importance of establishing your glossary of ECRM terms. Referencing Appendix E for a Pro Forma ECRM Program and Cybersecurity Strategy Table of Contents, I will cover Document Management, Table of Contents, Executive Summary, Introduction, and Glossary. While the first four sections could be more exciting, they are essential in maintaining your ECRM Program and Cybersecurity Strategy as a living, breathing document. Remember, you will likely be required to submit this type of documentation to external auditors, regulators (e.g., NYDFS, SEC,

© Bob Chaput 2024
B. Chaput, *Enterprise Cyber Risk Management as a Value Creator*,
https://doi.org/10.1007/979-8-8688-0094-8_8

FFEIC, HHS/OCR, DFARS/CMMC, GDPR, etc.), or the courts, so good documentation management is essential. Most of my focus will be on your ECRM Glossary.

Document Management

Every organization has its approach to document management. If you do not, consider including these elements in your ECRM Program and Cybersecurity Strategy document management section: History, Location, Revision History, Authorization, Distribution, and Related Documents. The following are descriptions of what form these elements may take.

History

Include a brief chronology of events with statements as to what prompted the creation of the ECRM Program and Cybersecurity Strategy document, when it was first published, where it was first written, how it was written, and who is the intended audience.

Location

Clarify where the document will be stored, by whom, and how your workforce members can access it. For example, "This document is stored in the following location:"

Filename	COMPANY ECRM Program and Cybersecurity Strategy
Location	{URL}

Revision History

Maintain a running log of revisions, including a summary of changes made. For example, "This document has been through the following revisions:"

Version No.	Revision Date	Filename/Location	Brief Summary of Changes
V1.11	03/18/2023	{URL}	Incorporated edits from initial review by ECRM Working Group
V1.13	4/10/2023	{URL}	1. Section 5—Information asset definition updated 2. Section 7—Risk appetite/ threshold settings have been captured 3. Updated definition of "ECRM board members" throughout the document
V1.14	11/10/2023	{URL}	1. Updated Group Advisory Board definition throughout the document 2. Updated the terms "alternative" and "perspective" where required

Authorization

Describe the final approval and authority under which your ECRM Program and Cybersecurity Strategy has been developed and documented, for example:

AUTHORIZATION	Name	Signature	Date
Company ECRM Board Committee (e.g., audit or risk committee)	XXXXXXXXXX		
Company ECRM Executive Committee	XXXXXXXXXX		
Company ECRM Working Group	XXXXXXXXXX		

Distribution

Indicate how, when, and to whom you can distribute the document, including any specific restrictions. Of course, your ECRM Program and Cybersecurity Strategy documents contain sensitive and confidential information, and you must mark them as such.

"This document may be distributed to the following:"

Name	Version Issued	Date of Issue
Executive Leadership Team (line-of-business, process leaders, functional leaders)	V1.14	11/10/2023
ECRM Working Group members	V1.14	11/10/2023
Full Governance, Risk Management, and Compliance (GRC) Team	V1.14	11/10/2023
Full Internal Audit Team	V1.14	11/10/2023
Others	V1.14	11/10/2023

Related Documents

Indicate relevant internal and external references.

Document Type	Filename/ Location
ECRM Privacy Policies and Procedures	{URL}
ECRM Security Policies and Procedures	{URL}
ECRM Working Group Charter	{URL}
COMPANY Compliance Committee of the Board of Directors Charter	{URL}
COMPANY Audit Committee of the Board of Directors Charter	{URL}
Enterprise Risk Management (ERM) Strategy	{URL}
Risk and Opportunity Register Template	{URL}
Risk and Opportunity Response Template	{URL}

Table of Contents

Because your ECRM Program and Cybersecurity Strategy document will likely be lengthy—perhaps dozens of pages or even a hundred pages long—it is essential to insert a table of contents, making it easy to organize and navigate your document.

Executive Summary

An executive summary includes the critical points of your ECRM Program and Cybersecurity Strategy. It should restate the document's purpose, highlight its major points, and provide an overview of what material will be covered. It should include enough information so the reader can understand what the full document covers without reading it. You might include a high-level graphic highlighting your ECRM Process, roles, and responsibilities. Figure 8-1 is an example of information flows and duties from the NIST Cybersecurity Framework.[2]

Figure 8-1. *ECRM Roles and Responsibilities*

Source: Bob Chaput, Executive Chairman, Clearwater. Adapted from "Framework for Improving Critical Infrastructure Cybersecurity, Version 1.1." National Institute of Standards and Technology (NIST). April 16, 2018. Accessed July 10, 2023. *https://nvlpubs.nist.gov/ nistpubs/CSWP/NIST.CSWP.04162018.pdf*

Mention the standards upon which you are building your ECRM Program and Cybersecurity Strategy and how your organization developed and documented your ECRM Program and Cybersecurity Strategy—governance, people, process, etc.

Introduction

Think of the introduction as a deeper dive into the document's content and an orientation of what will be covered. Describe the major sections and appendices and the recommended approach for reading the document. You should mention how different readers could approach your documentation differently. For example, how would the C-suite executives or board members gain the most value? As Francis Bacon said:

> *Some books are to be tasted, others to be swallowed, and some few to be chewed and digested; that is, some books are to be read only in parts; others to be read, but not curiously; and some few are to be read wholly, and with diligence and attention.*[3]

Help your readers decide their best approach to derive the most significant value.

Glossary

The philosopher Ludwig Wittgenstein said, *"The limits of my language means the limits of my world."*[4] Language is vital in establishing, implementing, and maturing an ECRM and cybersecurity program.

Why bother to include a glossary? What's the problem? Recent conversations with Fortune 500 CISOs, CIOs, C-suite executives, and board members remind me of the importance of words and their definitions. Perhaps the relative immaturity of the cyber risk and opportunity management field and, possibly, to some extent, the relative immaturity of the broader field of risk and opportunity management underscores the importance of shared understanding. Remember what Voltaire said, "If you wish to converse with me, define your terms."[5]

Before an initial consultation, I typically ask clients to define seemingly obvious terms like governance, risk management, and compliance. The responses vary widely from organization to organization and person to person in the same organization! Variation explodes when I ask for definitions of "trickier" terms like assets, threats, vulnerabilities, controls, likelihood, and impact. I'm sure you've heard the line: ask *five* experts to define X, and you'll listen to *nine* different answers. That always happens when it comes to cyber risk and opportunity management terms. The problem is that cyber risk and opportunity management is ripe with misunderstanding and terrible communication due to a lack of mutually agreed-upon definitions of key terms and concepts.

ECRM fluency must come on par with financial fluency. Not all executives and board members are Certified Public Accountants, nor must they become Certified Information Systems Security Professionals (CISSPs). However, all board members understand enough to discuss your organization's P&L, balance sheet, and cash-flow statement. Similarly, they must understand enough to discuss your risk and opportunity register, risk appetite, opportunity threshold, and risk and opportunity treatment plan.

When you first engage in conversations about your organization's cyber risks and cybersecurity, you may feel like you are trying to speak in a foreign language. ECRM can seem quite technical and complex, but it is understandable once you have good working definitions of some fundamentals. To have a meaningful and productive conversation about cyber risk and cybersecurity, everyone at the table needs to speak with precision and understand the differences between, for example, a risk, a vulnerability, and a threat, among other terms.

I encourage you to develop an ECRM Program and Cybersecurity Strategy document with an essential glossary of cyber risk and opportunity management terms as one of its first sections. Circulate and socialize this glossary and agree on critical cyber risk and opportunity management terms and concepts.

In Appendix D, I define 25 essential terms for your ECRM Glossary. That content will help you build your glossary. One of the best references on cybersecurity terminology—and my primary resource in writing that appendix—is the glossary compiled by the Computer Security Resource Center (CSRC) at NIST.[6]

To illustrate the importance of a mutually agreed-upon vocabulary, consider that your C-suite executives and board members must provide the leadership and oversight to ensure the execution of four essential cyber risk and opportunity management steps:

(1) Identify and prioritize your organization's unique cyber risks and opportunities.

(2) Discuss, debate, and settle on your appetite for cyber risk, that is, determine what level of risk your organization will accept.

(3) Discuss, debate, and settle on your threshold for identifying cyber opportunities, that is, determine how low a level of risk is necessary to highlight a cyber opportunity for your organization.

(4) Treat each risk and leverage each opportunity, making informed decisions about how you will treat each risk (accept, avoid, mitigate, or transfer) and how you will leverage each opportunity (improve customer trust, drive revenue growth, lower cost of capital, etc.), and then execute on that plan.

How can your C-suite executives and board members possibly provide leadership and oversight of these four steps with a mutually agreed-upon understanding of cyber risk, risk appetite, cyber opportunity, opportunity threshold, risk treatment, and opportunity leverage? And these terms are just starters. Again, I define these terms and others in Appendix D, which I encourage you to use to create your ECRM Program and Cybersecurity Strategy Glossary.

Cyber Risk and Cyber Opportunity Notional Equations

Having covered five initial sections of your ECRM Program and Cybersecurity Strategy documentation (i.e., Document Management, Table of Contents, Executive Summary, Introduction, and Glossary) and keeping my focus on the glossary and critical concepts, I will end the chapter with two ideas and notional equations to help frame your thinking about cyber risk and cyber opportunities.

Cyber Risk Notional Equation

As you may recall, the National Institute of Standards and Technology (NIST) defines *risk* as "A measure of the extent to which an entity is threatened by a potential circumstance or event, and typically a function of (i) the adverse impacts that would arise if the circumstance or event occurs, and (ii) the likelihood of occurrence."[7]

Given this definition, consider this notional representation of risk in Figure 8-2.

$$Risk = f\left(\frac{[Asset * Threat * Vulnerability]}{Controls} * [Likelihood * Impact]\right)$$

Figure 8-2. *Cyber Risk Notional Equation*

Described in this way, risk is a function of three factors (assets, threats, and vulnerabilities) divided by the controls or measures put in place to mitigate that risk and then multiplied by two variables (likelihood and impact). Think of dividing by controls; you reduce the quotient when you divide. The more controls, typically, the lower the possibility of the threat exploiting a vulnerability and causing loss or harm to an asset.

Cyber Opportunity Notional Equation

Similarly, we can conceptualize an equation for cyber opportunity. NIST defines an *opportunity* as "A condition that may result in a beneficial outcome."[8] Consider this notional representation of opportunity in Figure 8-3.

$$\text{Opportunity} = f\left(\frac{[\text{Asset} * \text{Lever} * \text{Strength}]}{\text{Organizational Constraints}} * [\text{Likelihood} * \text{Impact}]\right)$$

Figure 8-3. *Cyber Opportunity Notional Equation*

Opportunity, then, can be thought of as a function of leveraging the strengths of your cybersecurity program to create a positive outcome. Dividing by organizational constraints such as old ways of thinking, non-ECRM-aware-culture, resources, etc. will reduce the opportunity.

Conclusion

Documenting the five essential elements of your ECRM Program and Cybersecurity Strategy discussed in this chapter will help ensure good hygiene in keeping your documentation current. Version control is vital for, among other good reasons, knowing what policies, procedures, and practices were in place at a particular time—perhaps, for example, at the time a cyber incident occurred.

It is vital to agree upon basic ECRM terminology at the outset when developing your ECRM Program and Cybersecurity Strategy. My Stop the Cyber Bleeding | Putting ECRM Into Action[9] YouTube channel includes brief video clips covering many ECRM terms that should be in your glossary. Appendix D should help you get off to a running start with your glossary.

The brief discussion of notional equations for cyber risk and cyber opportunity was presented to reinforce the importance of thinking of both and was designed to provide a working conceptual framework within which you may think about both.

Continuing with the establishment and implementation of your ECRM Program and Cybersecurity Strategy, in Chapter 9, I discuss several additional sections of your ECRM documentation with a focus on important work by the C-suite and board to establish guiding principles and to assure the alignment of ECRM strategy with business strategy.

Questions Management and the Board Should Ask and Discuss

1. Is there solid alignment between the executive team and the board on the value and importance of developing and documenting an ECRM Program and Cybersecurity Strategy?

2. What business value will your organization derive from developing and documenting an ECRM Program and Cybersecurity Strategy? Is it worth the effort?

3. Has your organization formed a governance structure and teams to initiate work on your ECRM Program and Cybersecurity Strategy documentation?

4. What individuals will comprise your ECRM Working Group (EWG) to start drafting your ECRM Program and Cybersecurity Strategy documentation?

5. Have your organization's C-suite and board discussed and agreed upon a standard set of definitions related to cyber risk and opportunity management?

6. Have these definitions been documented in your organization's ECRM Program and Cybersecurity Strategy documents and communicated via ECRM training?

7. As a basic example, does your organization understand that risk exists when and only when there is an asset, a specific threat, and a particular vulnerability?

8. Have you discussed, debated, and established your cyber risk appetite as C-suite executives and board members?

9. Equally essential but too often ignored, have you discussed, debated, and established your cyber opportunity threshold as C-suite executives and board members?

10. Do you believe your C-suite and board are fully exercising their leadership, oversight, and fiduciary responsibilities concerning ECRM?

11. Would engaging an experienced, reputable ECRM partner be valuable to establishing, implementing, and maturing your organization's ECRM program?

12. Can you meet the documentation requirements of the SEC's Cybersecurity Risk Management, Strategy, Governance, and Incident Disclosure final rule today?

13. Does your organization already conduct ongoing, rigorous, comprehensive, enterprise-wide risk and opportunity assessments that would meet regulatory requirements applicable to your industry?

Endnotes

1. Peale, Norman Vincent. "Change your thoughts and you change your world." (n.d.) Accessed September 20, 2023. Available at https://www.brainyquote.com/quotes/norman_vincent_peale_130593

2. National Institute of Standards and Technology (NIST). "Framework for Improving Critical Infrastructure Cybersecurity, Version 1.1." April 16, 2018. Accessed July 10, 2023. Available at https://nvlpubs.nist.gov/nistpubs/CSWP/NIST.CSWP.04162018.pdf

3. Francis Bacon Quotes. GoodReads. (n.d.) Accessed January 13, 2023. Available at https://www.goodreads.com/quotes/1242120-some-books-are-to-be-tasted-others-to-be-swallowed

4. Ludwig Wittgenstein Quotes. GoodReads. (n.d.) Accessed April 17, 2023. Available at https://www.goodreads.com/quotes/12577-the-limits-of-my-language-means-the-limits-of-my

5. Quotable quotes. Goodreads. "If you wish to converse with me, define your terms." Accessed December 21, 2022. Available at `https://www.goodreads.com/quotes/7799868-if-you-wish-to-converse-with-me-define-your-terms`

6. Glossary. Computer Security Resource Center (CSRC). National Institute of Standards and Technology (NIST). Accessed December 21, 2022. Available at `https://csrc.nist.gov/glossary/`

7. "Risk." Glossary. Computer Security Resource Center (CSRC). National Institute of Standards and Technology (NIST). Accessed January 13, 2023. Available at `https://csrc.nist.gov/glossary/`

8. "Opportunity." Glossary. Computer Security Resource Center (CSRC). National Institute of Standards and Technology (NIST). Accessed August 3, 2023. `https://csrc.nist.gov/glossary/`

9. Chaput, Bob. Stop the Cyber Bleeding | Putting ECRM into Action YouTube Channel. February 2022. Available at `https://www.youtube.com/@stopthecyberbleeding/videos`

CHAPTER 9

ECRM Guiding Principles and Business Alignment

There is no security on this earth; there is only opportunity.

—Douglas MacArthur[1]

In this chapter, I cover the following topics and sections of your ECRM Program and Cybersecurity Strategy and related documentation: ECRM Guiding Principles, Scope of the ECRM Strategy, Business Strategic Objectives, ECRM Strategic Objectives, and Responsibility for and Governance of the ECRM Program. Refer to Appendix E for the complete Pro Forma ECRM Program and Cybersecurity Strategy Table of Contents.

ECRM Guiding Principles

Setting forth and documenting the guiding principles by which your organization will undertake ECRM is a critical job of the board of directors. Principles provide guardrails and, importantly, set the tone at the top. The following are examples of principles to consider as you develop your ECRM Guiding Principles.

© Bob Chaput 2024

B. Chaput, *Enterprise Cyber Risk Management as a Value Creator*,
https://doi.org/10.1007/979-8-8688-0094-8_9

217

The NACD publication "Cyber-Risk Oversight 2020: Key Principles and Practical Guidance for Corporate Boards" suggested five core principles[2]:

1. Cybersecurity as a Strategic Risk: Directors need to understand and approach cybersecurity as a strategic enterprise risk—not just as an IT risk.

2. Legal and Disclosure Implications: Directors should understand the legal implications of cyber risks as they relate to their company's specific circumstances.

3. Board Oversight Structure and Access to Expertise: Boards should have adequate access to cybersecurity expertise, and discussions about cyber risk management should be given regular and adequate time on board meeting agendas.

4. An Enterprise Framework for Managing Cyber Risk: Directors should set the expectation that management will establish an enterprise-wide, cyber risk management framework with adequate staffing and budget.

5. Cybersecurity Measurement and Reporting: Board-management discussions about cyber risk should include identifying and quantifying financial exposure to cyber risks and which risks to accept, mitigate, or transfer, such as through insurance, and specific plans associated with each approach.

In a March 2021 update, in collaboration with the Internet Security Alliance, PwC, and the World Economic Forum, NACD published "Principles for Board Governance of Cyber Risk" and included these six globally applicable principles to aid board directors in governing cyber risk[3]:

1. Cybersecurity is a strategic business enabler: Cybersecurity is more than just an IT issue.

2. Understand the economic drivers and impact of cyber risk: Enterprise decision-making requires analysis of the economics of cyber risk.

3. Align cyber risk management with business needs: Boards should understand and assess how to effectively manage cyber risks in the pursuit of business objectives.

4. Ensure organizational design supports cybersecurity: Organizational structure should integrate and support security and strategic goals.

5. Incorporate cybersecurity expertise into board governance: Boards need diverse sources of cybersecurity expertise.

6. Encourage systemic resilience and collaboration: Effective cyber risk strategy includes improving the cyber resilience of industries and sectors.

The wording of the first NACD principle in the 2020 publication ("Cybersecurity as a Strategic Risk") changed positively to the language in the 2021 version ("Cybersecurity is a strategic business enabler"). "Business enabler" is a move in the right direction. I encourage you to insist on including a guiding principle that emphasizes your pivot from thinking about cybersecurity only in the context of risks and "managing the downside" to including opportunities and "managing the upside," perhaps something like the following: "ECRM is viewed as a business value creator, a means to create a competitive advantage. Business value is created from treating our cyber risks and leveraging our cyber opportunities."

I do not recommend a wholesale adoption of any one set of principles. Take the time to discuss these and other principles and use them to create the foundation of your principle-based approach to ECRM. Importantly, whatever principles you adopt, document and communicate your ECRM Guiding Principles.

Scope of the ECRM Strategy

Defining the scope of your ECRM program is about setting boundaries around what will be included and excluded from your program. Developing a realistic and reasonably sized scope is essential as it will enable your team to earn some ECRM wins.

The first question in setting scope is: In which organizational entities will you undertake ECRM at the outset? Will your scope initially include the entire enterprise or organization? Will you limit it to business units within a specific geography? Will you limit it to specific business functions and their underlying processes (e.g., HR, finance, or manufacturing)? Will you focus on business units or activities with a history of intrinsic risk? Will you focus on highly regulated business units?

Once you set your organizational scope, you should refine it based on mission-essential functions (MEFs) within that organization. You derive your MEFs by completing a business impact analysis (BIA). A BIA facilitates prioritizing those business functions and processes most critical to the ongoing execution of your mission.[4]

Some organizations, perhaps motivated by a recent security incident, may set their scope based on critical information assets or so-called crown jewels. This asset-centric approach has merit and is usually most appropriate for organizations.

Others may take a threat-centric, controls-centric, or even people-centric approach to setting the scope of their ECRM program. I am less favorably disposed to these approaches because they ignore the complete components of risk—an asset, a threat, a vulnerability, controls, likelihood, and impact.

And finally, it is essential to include both cyber risks and opportunities in your scope. When you communicate the scope of your ECRM strategy, the organization must know that you intend to identify and leverage your ECRM strengths to create business value whenever possible. Otherwise, individuals and organizations will focus on the negative by default.

Business Strategic Objectives

In the NIST Cybersecurity Framework, the recommended first step in adopting the framework includes the important scoping discussed previously and setting forth business objectives:

> *Step 1: Prioritize and Scope. The organization identifies its business/mission objectives and high-level organizational priorities. With this information, the organization makes strategic decisions regarding cybersecurity implementations and determines the scope of systems and assets that support the selected business line or process.*[5]

Your unique vision, mission, strategy, values, and services are achieved year after year by setting strategic, tactical, and operational objectives. These objectives, especially strategic objectives, must be clearly articulated and become the basis of your ECRM strategic objectives.

Covering strategy development is well beyond this book's scope, but starting your ECRM journey based on your current strategic objectives is vital.

NIST emphasizes creating your ECRM Program and Cybersecurity Strategy in the context of your organization's unique mission and business strategic objectives by creating a new function, Govern, in version 2.0 of the NIST Cybersecurity Framework. The function includes, among others, a category called Organizational Context that provides for business focus at the onset:

The organization's risk context, including mission, mission priorities, stakeholders, objectives, and direction, is understood.

- *Organizational mission is understood in order to prioritize cybersecurity risk management.*

- *Internal and external stakeholders, and their expectations regarding cybersecurity risk management, are determined.*

- *Legal, regulatory, and contractual requirements regarding cybersecurity, including privacy and civil liberties obligations, are understood and managed.*

- *Critical objectives, capabilities, and services that stakeholders expect are determined and communicated.*

- *Critical outcomes, capabilities, and services that the organization relies on are determined and communicated.*[6]

ECRM Strategic Objectives

In Chapter 4, Figure 4-2, I presented a model for aligning your ECRM strategic objectives with business objectives. The flow in that model illustrates that your strategic objectives inform organization maxims, which help derive your cyber risk appetite and opportunity threshold, which drives your ECRM program.

The CEO of a large national healthcare organization once told me, "Taking care of our patient's information is just as important as taking care of our patients." That objective, or organizational maxim, served as a touchstone for his organization as it built its ECRM program. Using this company as an example, an ECRM objective of performing a comprehensive risk assessment of their electronic health records system to understand all the possible ways in which there could be a compromise of confidentiality, integrity, and availability of patient information would probably trump an objective of implementing security auditing and logging of the payroll system.

As another example of business objectives driving ECRM objectives, consider Equifax's remarkable recovery from its 2017 breach. CEO Mark Begor made a personal commitment to make Equifax an industry leader in data security. Equifax's CISO, Jamil Farshchi, built a strategy focused on both "managing the downside" and "managing the upside," which he called the "MinMax strategy"—minimizing cyber risks while maximizing business growth.

Responsibility for and Governance of the ECRM Program

Your ECRM Program and Cybersecurity Strategy documentation should clarify roles and responsibilities for how you will complete this work, approve it by the C-suite, and oversee it by the board. In Chapter 6, I mentioned a three-tiered ECRM governance model that I found practical and compelling. The three tiers in this governance model include

> *Tier 1: The entire board or designated board committee (e.g., audit committee, risk committee, or a specific ECRM Oversight Committee) sets direction, articulates principles, and provides oversight.*

> *Tier 2: An ECRM Executive Steering Committee*
> (including the CEO and their entire team) ensures
> the execution of the ECRM program and approves
> program priorities and work products.

> *Tier 3: An ECRM Cross-Functional Working Group*
> (depending on your organization, should include
> representatives from legal, risk management,
> finance, HR, audit, compliance, privacy, IT,
> clinical engineering, security, quality, and others
> as appropriate) executes the steps to establish,
> implement, and mature the ECRM program.

The model will vary by the size and resources of each organization. In all cases, each of the three tiers should have a formal, written charter delineating the group's decision-making authority, structure, scope of responsibilities, work processes to be followed, etc. For example, a small organization might use a simplified version of this model by combining Tier 2, the ECRM Executive Steering Committee, with Tier 3, the Cross-Functional Working Group. On the other hand, a large, complex organization with multiple lines of business might add additional tiers or establish a three-tiered model within each line of business. Assigning your internal audit organization with overall assurance responsibility is also essential to provide an independent opinion on the ECRM Program and Cybersecurity Strategy to the board. Figure 9-1 illustrates how the three-tiered ECRM governance model might work in a large organization.

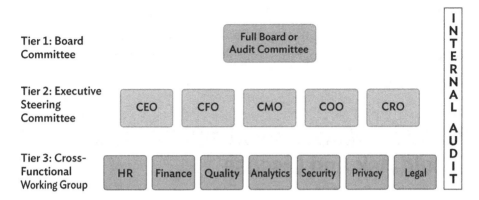

Figure 9-1. *Example of the Three-Tiered ECRM Governance Structure*

As I emphasized in Chapter 6, good governance is critical for any transformational program. ECRM is undoubtedly such a program for most organizations.

Conclusion

Sticking with the theme that C-suite executives or board members must become ECRM enablers, not necessarily ECRM experts, overseeing the completion of the parts of your ECRM Program and Cybersecurity Strategy detailed in this Chapter— ECRM Guiding Principles, Scope of the ECRM Strategy, Business Strategic Objectives, ECRM Strategic Objectives, and Responsibility for and Governance of the ECRM Program—is essential executive leadership and board-level oversight work.

You may wish to view the short video clip on my YouTube channel, "Episode 23: Principles for C-Suite & Board to Adopt | Putting ECRM Into Action,"[7] which discusses adopting guiding principles. Other videos in the Stop the Cyber Bleeding | Putting ECRM Into Action channel may further drive the development of your ECRM Program and Cybersecurity Strategy. They can be accessed and subscribed to at www.youtube.com/ @stopthecyberbleeding/videos.

Chapter 10 continues the work of establishing and documenting your ECRM Program and Strategy. I discuss three building blocks that are vital to your overall program—your ECRM Framework, Process, and Maturity Model.

Questions Management and the Board Should Ask and Discuss

1. Considering the sections of the ECRM Program and Cybersecurity Strategy covered in this chapter, to what degree has this documentation of your ECRM Program and Cybersecurity Strategy been created?

2. Do the sample guiding principles align with your views on how you should oversee ECRM? What others are you considering?

3. Do your ECRM Guiding Principles address "managing the upside" and leveraging your cyber opportunities?

4. Can you provide an ECRM Working Group with a clear articulation of strategic business objectives to serve as the basis for creating the scope of your ECRM program?

5. Can you currently meet the documentation requirements of the SEC's Cybersecurity Risk Management, Strategy, Governance, and Incident Disclosure final rule today?

6. Do you have the internal resources with the appropriate skills, knowledge, and experience to undertake this work?

7. Would your organization benefit from a session reviewing these documentation requirements and related ECRM Program and Cybersecurity Strategy by competent outside counsel and cyber risk and opportunity management experts?

Endnotes

1. BrainyQuote. "There is no security on this earth; there is only opportunity." (n.d.) Accessed May 2, 2023. Available at www.brainyquote.com/quotes/ douglas_macarthur_141016

2. Clinton, Larry, Higgins, Josh, and van der Oord, Friso. National Association of Corporate Directors (NACD). "Cyber-Risk Oversight 2020: Key Principles and Practical Guidance for Corporate Boards." February 2022. https://nacdonline.org/ insights/publications.cfm?ItemNumber=67298

3. NACD. "Principles for Board Governance of Cyber Risk." March 2021. Available at www.nacdonline. org/applications/secure/?FileID=319863

4. Clearwater. White Paper. "Business Impact Analysis (BIA): Key to Organizational Resiliency." Accessed January 27, 2023. Available at https:// clearwatercompliance.com/bia-key-to- organizational-resiliency/

5. Cybersecurity Framework. NIST. April 16, 2018. Available at www.nist.gov/cyberframework

6. Discussion Draft of the NIST Cybersecurity Framework 2.0 Core. National Institute of Standards and Technology (NIST). April 24, 2023. Accessed July 16, 2023. Available at www.nist.gov/system/files/documents/2023/04/24/NIST%20Cybersecurity%20Framework%202.0%20Core%20Discussion%20Draft%204-2023%20final.pdf

7. Chaput, Bob. Stop the Cyber Bleeding | Putting ECRM into Action YouTube Channel. "Episode 23: Principles for C-Suite & Board to Adopt | Putting ECRM Into Action." Accessed May 2, 2023. February 7, 2022. Available at www.youtube.com/watch?v=ypfPJiv4IZ8

CHAPTER 10

Three Vital ECRM Building Blocks

If we guard our toothbrushes and diamonds with equal zeal,
we will lose fewer toothbrushes and more diamonds.

—McGeorge Bundy[1]

In this chapter, I cover the following topics and sections of your ECRM Program and Cybersecurity Strategy and related documentation: ECRM Framework, ECRM Process, and ECRM Maturity Model. Please refer to Appendix E for the complete Pro Forma ECRM Program and Cybersecurity Strategy Table of Contents.

A framework, a process, and a maturity model are three essential building blocks of your approach to ECRM. Establishing the framework, process, and maturity model by which your organization will conduct its ECRM work enables the incorporation of ECRM into ongoing strategic decision-making and business planning. You will use your chosen framework to help document your ECRM objectives. Your ECRM Process will detail how you conduct ECRM work; recall the four-step NIST process comprising Frame, Assess, Respond, and Monitor. Your ECRM Maturity Model will assist with continuously improving your ECRM Program and Cybersecurity Strategy. Figure 10-1 illustrates the high-level relationship between the three.

© Bob Chaput 2024
B. Chaput, *Enterprise Cyber Risk Management as a Value Creator*,
https://doi.org/10.1007/979-8-8688-0094-8_10

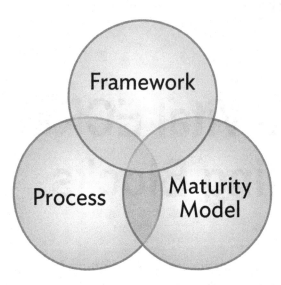

Figure 10-1. *Relationship Between Your ECRM Framework, Process, and Maturity Model*

ECRM Framework

Think of an ECRM Framework as a tool—an architectural blueprint, as it were—that will facilitate developing your desired cybersecurity outcomes. In this context, it will help you document what you must achieve to manage your cyber risks and leverage your cybersecurity strategy to create business value. Your ECRM Framework is the tool that will help you set "what" ECRM outcomes or goals your organization must achieve.

Like many terms in cybersecurity and cyber risk and opportunity management, there needs to be clarity over what constitutes a framework and what may be available for your use. Items often cited as frameworks are not existing frameworks. One resource listed these seven: NIST Cybersecurity Framework, ISO 27001 and 27002, SOC2, NERC-CIP, HIPAA, GDPR, and FISMA.[2] Yet, NERC-CIP requirements are not a cybersecurity framework. The Critical Infrastructure Protection (CIP) Standards are a set of mandatory requirements for owners and operators of electric utilities to protect bulk electric systems from physical and cyber threats. The North American Electric Reliability Corporation (NERC), an international regulatory authority, developed the standards to promote the reliability and adequacy of bulk power transmission in the electric utility systems of North America.[3] HIPAA, GDPR, and FISMA are regulations, not cybersecurity frameworks. Another article listed 25 frameworks, including a mixed bag of controls checklists, security standards, security R&D centers, and maturity models.[4] Yikes! Seriously?

The framework that I recommend is the Cybersecurity Framework developed by NIST.[5] A colleague who worked on the task force that produced the "Report on Improving Cybersecurity in the Health Care Industry"[6] once described the NIST Cybersecurity Framework to me:

> *The NIST Cybersecurity Framework provides a template for your organization's cybersecurity framework. The rest is up to you. It's like having a palette of colors to paint a canvas. The colors are what you combine to create your painting; your painting will be what cybersecurity looks like for your specific organization. The NIST Cybersecurity Framework gives you that palette to start with.*[7]

As you may know from my writings, I advocate the NIST approach to cyber risk management. Among the numerous features and benefits of leveraging these free resources is that they, including the Cybersecurity Framework, are industry agnostic. In Appendix C, I describe the many specific benefits of a NIST-based approach to ECRM. Figure 10-2 illustrates the NIST Cybersecurity Framework's so-called functions—Govern, Identify, Protect, Detect, Respond, and Recover.

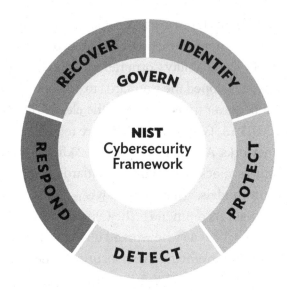

Figure 10-2. *The NIST Cybersecurity Framework Functions*

Source: Bob Chaput, Executive Chairman, Clearwater. Adapted from "Public Draft: The NIST Cybersecurity Framework 2.0." National Institute of Standards and Technology (NIST). August 8, 2023. Accessed September 30, 2023. *https://nvlpubs.nist.gov/nistpubs/CSWP/NIST.CSWP.29.ipd.pdf*

Importantly, in developing version 2.0 of the NIST Cybersecurity Framework, NIST has decided to include a new "Govern" function to emphasize the importance of articulating ECRM governance outcomes. This new crosscutting function consists of categories and subcategories that include organizational context, risk management strategy, policies and procedures, and roles and responsibilities.[8]

The critical takeaway is that selecting and adopting an ECRM Framework is essential. It facilitates setting your unique desired ECRM and cybersecurity outcomes. I recommend adopting the NIST Cybersecurity Framework to help align and articulate your desired ECRM program outcomes with your organization's vision, mission, strategy, values, and services. And be sure when you adopt the NIST Cybersecurity Framework, you consider cyber opportunities in your policies, procedures, and practices as you establish your framework.

ECRM Process

If your ECRM Framework details "what" cyber risk and opportunity management outcomes you must achieve, your ECRM Process describes "how" you will achieve them. It describes specific, repeatable steps your organization will take to conduct ECRM.

The cyber risk management process I recommend is based on "Managing Information Security Risk" (NIST Special Publication 800-39)[9] and is composed of four basic steps, each of which informs the other steps in the process:

1. *Frame risk.* That is, establish the context for risk-based decisions and your overall approach to and your desired outcomes of your ECRM program discussed previously. Adopting and implementing your ECRM Framework is completing this framing step. I also recommended you expand your scope to establish the context for opportunity-based decisions.

2. *Assess risk.* In other words, identify your exposures via an enterprise-wide, comprehensive risk assessment. NIST has published a separate guide for risk assessments, NIST SP 800-30 "Guide for Conducting Risk Assessments."[10] Keeping with our theme of value creation, you must identify and assess your cyber opportunities.

3. *Respond to risk.* In this step, your organization focuses on making risk treatment decisions and executing risk treatment actions. As I will discuss further, this step involves deciding whether to accept, avoid, mitigate, or transfer risk. As a reminder, you must also treat or manage the cyber opportunities you identify.

4. *Monitor risk on an ongoing basis.* Risk management is more than just a once-and-done proposition. It is a continuous process, which includes a feedback loop for process improvement and consideration of internal and external changes. The feedback loop must also monitor your cyber opportunities.

This second building block of your ECRM program, and an essential part of your ECRM Program and Cybersecurity Strategy, is your ECRM Process. I recommend adopting NIST-based ECRM processes (as described in NIST SP 800-39 "Managing Information Security Risk" and NIST SP 800-30 "Guide for Conducting Risk Assessments"),[11] for example.

Because your ECRM Process is at the heart of your ECRM program and how you execute your cybersecurity strategy, I provide much more coverage of the ECRM Process in Chapter 11. As I mentioned, you need to expand the NIST definition of risk to include applying the NIST risk management process to manage your cyber opportunities.

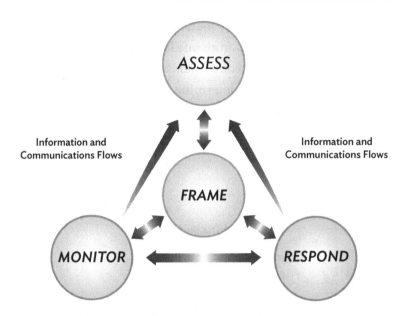

Figure 10-3. *The NIST Risk Management Process*

Source: Bob Chaput, Executive Chairman, Clearwater. Adapted from "Managing Information Security Risk." NIST Special Publication 800-39. National Institute of Standards and Technology (NIST). March 2011. Accessed July 10, 2023. *https://nvlpubs.nist.gov/ nistpubs/Legacy/SP/nistspecialpublication800-39.pdf*

ECRM Maturity Model

A capability maturity model is a *"tool that helps people assess the current effectiveness of a person or group and supports figuring out what capabilities they need to acquire next in order to improve their performance."*[12]

As it relates to ECRM, a capability maturity model helps your organization identify your current cyber risk and opportunity management maturity level about specific capabilities, facilitates the establishment of goals for performance improvement, and allows your organization to set priorities for improvements to achieve your desired maturity level.

Figure 10-4 illustrates the capability maturity model concept and the idea of progressive improvement from one level to the next. The idea is to decide at what level of maturity your organization needs to operate to meet your ECRM program objectives, determine your current maturity level, and close gaps to reach your target level of maturity.

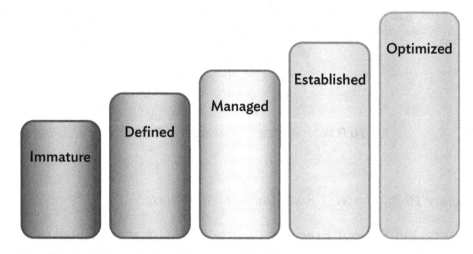

Figure 10-4. *Capability Maturity Model Concept*

Again, there are multiple points of view on what constitutes a maturity model. The same resource that cited the seven cybersecurity frameworks I discussed earlier then published another article that listed two of those seven frameworks—NIST Cybersecurity Framework and ISO 27000—as maturity models.[13] While some will disagree, the so-called tiers detailed in the NIST Cybersecurity Framework are not intended for maturity modeling; according to NIST, *"... Tiers do not represent maturity levels."*[14]

What's important is that your organization chooses a maturity model focusing on continuous process improvement. Recent research by Deloitte underscored the importance of having a maturity model in place.[15] Deloitte interviewed 18 CISOs, CIOs, and C-suite executives from biopharma companies, medical device manufacturers, health plans, and

health systems involved in cybersecurity decisions.[16] All interviewees—
without exception—use maturity models in their presentations to boards
and leadership.[17]

The maturity model provides a mechanism for determining whether
your ECRM program is improving over time. Based on my work with
organizations in several industries, I recommend focusing your ECRM
Maturity Model on improving five key capabilities:

1. *Governance*

2. *People*

3. *Process*

4. *Technology*

5. *Engagement*

I describe this maturity model I created in detail in *Stop the Cyber
Bleeding*.[18] Figure 10-5 shows a sample capability maturity model with the
five critical capabilities mentioned previously.

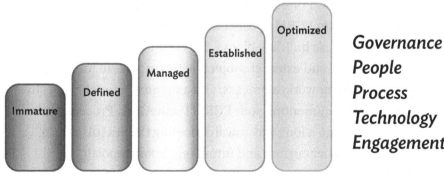

Figure 10-5. *Sample Capability Maturity Model*

Others will take a different approach. Some organizations have successfully adopted and adapted the Capability Maturity Model Integration (CMMI) developed by the Software Engineering Institute at Carnegie Mellon University as their cyber risk management maturity model.[19] With the so-called Cybersecurity Maturity Model Certification (CMMC 2.0)[20] becoming mandatory for defense contractors and subcontractors expected to start in 2024, many organizations will adopt CMMC 2.0. However, it falls short of meeting all the attributes of an actual maturity model.

What is important is that you focus on improving your ECRM effectiveness. Think about the four-step management model called the Deming Cycle. The four steps in this model are Plan, Do, Check, and Act.[21] Your maturity model must be designed to keep you in the Deming continuous process improvement mode.

Conclusion

Establishing the ECRM Framework, Process, and Maturity Model that you will use to perform ECRM consistently throughout your organization is essential. To set these building blocks, the C-suite and board should consult with internal and external subject matter experts to understand the alternatives for a framework, a process, and a maturity model, respectively.

Selecting and documenting your ECRM Framework, Process, and Maturity Model will go a long way toward meeting the SEC disclosure requirements and other current and future regulatory reporting requirements.

My Stop the Cyber Bleeding | Putting ECRM Into Action YouTube channel includes brief video clips covering many of the topics in this book and may help guide the development of your ECRM Program and Cybersecurity Strategy. It can be accessed and subscribed to at www. youtube.com/@stopthecyberbleeding/videos.

With most common approaches to ECRM, including the NIST approach, focused on risks or "managing the downside," in Chapter 11, I discuss how you can readily adapt the NIST ECRM Process to include the consideration of your cyber opportunities. As I will address, it is important to include your consideration of cyber opportunities or positive risks in your ECRM Program and Cybersecurity Strategy documentation.

Questions Management and the Board Should Ask and Discuss

1. Has your organization chosen an ECRM Framework? Is it working effectively?

2. Has your organization chosen an ECRM Process? Is it working effectively?

3. Has your organization chosen an ECRM Maturity Model? Is the effectiveness of your ECRM program improving?

4. Considering topics covered in this chapter—ECRM Framework, ECRM Process, and ECRM Maturity Model—to what degree has this content of your ECRM Program and Cybersecurity Strategy been documented?

5. Do you have the internal resources with the appropriate skills, knowledge, and experience to establish your ECRM Framework, ECRM Process, and ECRM Maturity Model?

6. Would engaging an experienced, reputable ECRM partner be valuable to establishing, implementing, and maturing your organization's ECRM program?

7. Can you meet the documentation requirements of the SEC's Disclosure of a Registrant's Risk Management, Strategy, and Governance Regarding Cybersecurity Risks[22] today?

Endnotes

1. Quote.org. "If we guard our toothbrushes and diamonds with equal zeal, we will lose fewer toothbrushes and more diamonds." Accessed May 2, 2023. Available at https://quote.org/quote/if-we-guard-our-toothbrushes-and-diamonds-596140

2. Cisternelli, Eric. Bitsight. "7 Cybersecurity Frameworks That Help Reduce Cyber Risk." August 15, 2022. Available at www.bitsight.com/blog/7-cybersecurity-frameworks-to-reduce-cyber-risk

3. Scott Madden Management Consultants. "What is NERC CIP Compliance and why is it important?" (n.d.) Accessed July 10, 2023. Available at www.scottmadden.com/insight/what-is-nerc-cip-compliance/

4. SecurityScorecard. "Top 25 Cybersecurity Frameworks to Consider." March 23, 2021. Available at https://securityscorecard.com/blog/top-cybersecurity-frameworks-to-consider

5. National Institute of Standards and Technology
    (NIST). "Framework for Improving Critical
    Infrastructure Cybersecurity, Version 1.1." April
    16, 2018. Accessed July 10, 2023. Available at
    https://nvlpubs.nist.gov/nistpubs/CSWP/NIST.
    CSWP.04162018.pdf

6. Health Care Industry Cybersecurity Task Force.
    "Report on Improving Cybersecurity in the Health
    Care Industry." June 2017. Available at www.phe.
    gov/preparedness/planning/cybertf/documents/
    report2017.pdf

7. Rob Suárez, CISO, BD (Becton, Dickinson, and
    Company), quoted in "Choosing an Information
    Risk Management Framework: The Case for the
    NIST Cybersecurity Framework in Healthcare
    Organizations." Clearwater. October 10, 2017.
    Available at https://clearwatercompliance.
    com/wp-content/uploads/2017/10/Choosing-
    an-IRM-Framework_The-Case-for-the-NIST-
    CSF-in-Healthcare_Clearwater-White-Paper.
    pdf?utm_campaign=White%20Paper%3A%20NIST%20
    Cybersecurity%20Framework

8. National Institute of Standards and Technology
    (NIST). "Discussion Draft of the NIST Cybersecurity
    Framework 2.0 Core." April 24, 2023. Accessed July
    16, 2023. Available at www.nist.gov/system/files/
    documents/2023/04/24/NIST%20Cybersecurity%20
    Framework%202.0%20Core%20Discussion%20
    Draft%204-2023%20final.pdf

9. National Institute of Standards and Technology (NIST). NIST Special Publication 800-39. "Managing Information Security Risk." March 2011. Available at https://nvlpubs.nist.gov/nistpubs/Legacy/SP/nistspecialpublication800-39.pdf

10. National Institute of Standards and Technology (NIST). NIST Special Publication 800-30, Revision 1. "Guide for Conducting Risk Assessments." September 2012. Available at https://nvlpubs.nist.gov/nistpubs/Legacy/SP/nistspecialpublication800-30r1.pdf

11. National Institute of Standards and Technology (NIST). NIST Special Publication 800-39. "Managing Information Security Risk." March 2011. Available at https://nvlpubs.nist.gov/nistpubs/Legacy/SP/nistspecialpublication800-39.pdf; and National Institute of Standards and Technology (NIST). NIST Special Publication 800-30, Revision 1. "Guide for Conducting Risk Assessments." September 2012. Available at https://nvlpubs.nist.gov/nistpubs/Legacy/SP/nistspecialpublication800-30r1.pdf

12. Fowler, Martin. MaturityModel. August 26, 2014. Available at https://martinfowler.com/bliki/MaturityModel.html#targetText=A%20maturity%20model%20is%20a,order%20to%20improve%20their%20performance.

13. Bitsight. "Cybersecurity maturity model." n.d. Accessed January 28, 2023. Available at www.bitsight.com/glossary/cybersecurity-maturity-model

14. National Institute of Standards and Technology
    (NIST). "Framework for Improving Critical
    Infrastructure Cybersecurity, Version 1.1." April
    16, 2018. Accessed July 10, 2023. Available at
    https://nvlpubs.nist.gov/nistpubs/CSWP/NIST.
    CSWP.04162018.pdf

15. Deloitte Insights. "Communicating the value
    of cybersecurity to boards and leadership:
    Seven strategies for life sciences and health care
    organizations. A report by the Deloitte Center for
    Health Solutions." 2019. Available at https://s3-
    prod.modernhealthcare.com/2019-05/DI_Value-
    of-cyber-investments.pdf

16. Deloitte Insights. "Communicating the value
    of cybersecurity to boards and leadership:
    Seven strategies for life sciences and health care
    organizations. A report by the Deloitte Center for
    Health Solutions." 2019. Available at https://s3-
    prod.modernhealthcare.com/2019-05/DI_Value-
    of-cyber-investments.pdf

17. Deloitte Insights. "Communicating the value
    of cybersecurity to boards and leadership:
    Seven strategies for life sciences and health care
    organizations. A report by the Deloitte Center for
    Health Solutions." 2019. *Available at* https://s3-
    prod.modernhealthcare.com/2019-05/DI_Value-
    of-cyber-investments.pdf

18. Chaput, Bob. *Stop the Cyber Bleeding: What Healthcare Executives and Board Members Must Know About Enterprise Cyber Risk Management (ECRM).* 2021. Clearwater. Available at https://amzn.to/33qr17n

19. Software Engineering Institute. Carnegie Mellon University. "CMMI for Development, Version 1.3." November 2010. Available at https://resources.sei.cmu.edu/library/asset-view.cfm?assetid=9661

20. Office of the CIO. Department of Defense. "Cybersecurity Maturity Model Certification." Accessed January 28, 2023. Available at https://dodcio.defense.gov/CMMC/

21. US Department of Health and Human Services, Agency for Healthcare Research and Quality, Health Information Technology. "Plan-Do-Check-Act Cycle." (n.d.) Accessed October 24, 2019. https://healthit.ahrq.gov/health-it-tools-and-resources/evaluation-resources/workflow-assessment-health-it-toolkit/all-workflow-tools/plan-do-check-act-cycle

22. Chaput, Bob. Enabling Cyber Risk Oversight Blog. "Disclosure of a Registrant's Risk Management, Strategy, and Governance Regarding Cybersecurity Risks." November 21, 2022. Available at https://bobchaput.com/disclosure-of-a-registrants-risk-management-strategy-and-governance-regarding-cybersecurity-risks/

CHAPTER 11

Adapting Your Process to Include Cyber Opportunities

If you can't describe what you are doing as a process, you don't know what you're doing.

—W. Edwards Deming[1]

In Chapter 10, I introduced the ECRM Process based on "Managing Information Security Risk" (NIST Special Publication 800-39)[2] and the four basic steps, each informing the other steps. To summarize, they are frame risk, assess risk, respond to risk, and monitor risk.

The NIST approach to ECRM focuses heavily on "managing the downside" with a focus on risk. I will not attempt to rewrite NIST Special Publication 800-39 in this chapter, but I will suggest handling both risks and opportunities in the process steps as much as possible. I will discuss each step in more detail and cover the importance of documenting respective standards, policies, and procedures covering both risks and opportunities for each of these four process steps in your ECRM Program and Cybersecurity Strategy documentation. This ECRM Process will create the mechanism by which you will execute your ECRM Program and Cybersecurity Strategy.

© Bob Chaput 2024
B. Chaput, *Enterprise Cyber Risk Management as a Value Creator*,
https://doi.org/10.1007/979-8-8688-0094-8_11

I draw heavily on "Managing Information Security Risk" (NIST Special Publication (SP) 800-39) but avoid repeating what is already well documented and readily accessible in that document. NIST states, *"the steps in the risk management process are not inherently sequential in nature"* and portrays the overall process in this way. Thank you, NIST, for allowing the process to be adaptable to manage both risks and opportunities. As a reminder, NIST depicts the risk management process as shown in Figure 11-1.

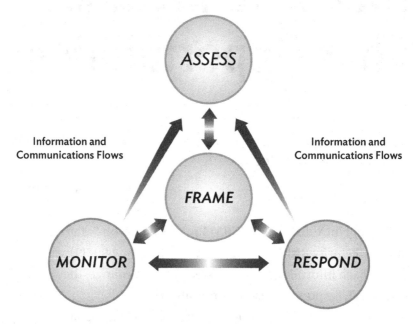

Figure 11-1.   *NIST Risk Management Process*

Source: Bob Chaput, Executive Chairman, Clearwater. Adapted from "Managing Information Security Risk" (NIST Special Publication 800-39). March 2011. Accessed September 14, 2023. *https://nvlpubs.nist.gov/nistpubs/Legacy/SP/ nistspecialpublication800-39.pdf*

NIST SP 800-39 guides that *"Organizations have significant flexibility in how the risk management steps are performed (e.g., sequence, degree of rigor, formality, and thoroughness of application) and in how the results of each step are captured and shared—both internally and externally."* This flexibility enables my coverage to include cyber opportunities.

As a reminder, I recommend leveraging all the standards and guidance from NIST applicable to your environment and requirements. In Appendix C, I explain why a NIST-based ECRM program may be a terrific choice for your organization. Also, you may wish to view my short YouTube video, "Why You Should Base Your Program on NIST | Putting ECRM Into Action,"[3] for more information about the benefits of a NIST-based approach. You can access and subscribe to my YouTube channel at https://www.youtube.com/@stopthecyberbleeding/videos.

Risk and Opportunity Framing

According to NIST and adding consideration of cyber opportunities, significant elements of this section of your ECRM Program and Cybersecurity Strategy document should include and not be limited to ECRM Key Inputs and Preconditions, ECRM Risk and Opportunity Assumptions, ECRM Risk and Opportunity Constraints, ECRM Risk Appetite and Opportunity Threshold, and ECRM Priorities and Trade-Offs. I expand on several of these elements in the following.

ECRM Key Inputs and Preconditions

Many factors inform risk and opportunity framing. For example, your organization's vision, mission, strategy, values, and services should drive your ECRM program. Additionally, your risk governance structure, financial posture, legal/regulatory environment, investment strategy, culture, security track record, and trust relationships established within and among organizations are all inputs that you must consider. At a strategic level, perhaps the most critical precondition for risk and opportunity framing is the level of engagement and support from your C-suite and board of directors. An operational risk precondition might be your geographic location, especially if your data center is close to the San Andreas fault. An operational opportunity precondition would be the strength of your regulatory compliance program.

ECRM Assumptions | Information Asset Assumptions

The assumptions you make and document affect how you conduct risk and opportunity assessments, responses, and ongoing monitoring. In the case of information asset assumptions, you will identify which assets are in scope and which are not in scope. You may choose, for example, to conduct a business impact assessment (BIA) and include only your so-called Tier 1 and Tier 2 assets, your "crown jewels," in scope.

Consider which, if any, already highly secured information assets can be leveraged to create business value.

ECRM Assumptions | Vulnerability and Strength Assumptions

Vulnerability assumptions would include consideration of the types of weaknesses or deficiencies on which your organization must focus. These may be people, process, or technology vulnerabilities. Your organization may be more susceptible to external vulnerabilities than internal ones. You should also document the level of granularity at which you will consider vulnerabilities and your source of vulnerability information—for example, your internal vulnerability scans, external third-party scans, sector Information Sharing and Analysis Centers (ISACs), and Common Vulnerability Enumeration (CVE) identifiers.

Opposite your vulnerabilities, your strengths must be understood and highlighted as these may present an opportunity to create business value. You may determine strengths from your risk assessment, compliance gap analysis, threat identification work, or in other ways.

ECRM Risk Appetite and Opportunity Threshold

See Chapter 9 and Appendix D for coverage and more information on *risk and opportunity ratings, risk appetite, and opportunity threshold.*

ECRM Constraints I Legal, Regulatory, and Contractual Constraints

As one final example, depending on your industry, whether you operate in the United States only or internationally, you will likely be obliged to comply with various privacy, security, and breach notification regulations. You should enumerate these requirements in your ECRM Program and Cybersecurity Strategy document. For organizations considered operating in one of the 16 national critical infrastructure sectors (e.g., chemical, commercial facilities, communications, etc.), new regulatory reporting requirements will become a regulatory constraint when rulemaking is completed.[4]

You should expand and elaborate on these elements and steps such that a workforce member will successfully conduct risk and opportunity framing if they follow all your process steps in your documented procedures. NIST Special Publication 800-39 provides additional discussion and examples to consider. Remember, a key point throughout the NIST guidance is that it is flexible and not a one-size-fits-all process.

Outputs from the risk and opportunity framing step are inputs to the other three steps in the overall process—assessment, response, and monitoring—and are discussed further in this chapter and "Managing

Information Security Risk" (NIST Special Publication 800-39).[5] Framing is critical for establishing your ECRM Program and Cybersecurity Strategy. It produces a set of organizational policies, procedures, standards, guidance, and resources covering the following sections:

- Scope of the organizational risk and opportunity management

- Risk and opportunity assessment assumptions and guidance covering assets, threats, vulnerabilities, etc.

- Risk and opportunity response guidance, including risk appetite and opportunity threshold

- Risk and opportunity monitoring guidance, monitored risk factors to determine changes in risk

- Risk constraints on executing risk and opportunity management activities

There are tools to assist with all NIST process steps. Just as most organizations would not consider writing their enterprise resource planning (ERP) software, ECRM is an instance where specialized software can make the execution of the NIST four-step process easier to conduct, document, implement, and maintain. In Appendix B, I provide more detail about the value of using specialized software.

The following are several risk and opportunity framing fundamentals to consider:

- Executives and the board must be engaged, minimally, on core principles.

- Framing sets the stage for the overall ECRM Program and Cybersecurity Strategy.

- Basic assumptions must be made and documented: scope, information assets, threats, vulnerabilities, likelihood, and impact.

- Business, risk, and opportunity management constraints must be defined.

- Risk appetite and opportunity threshold must be set.

- Five key capabilities should be considered— governance, people, process, technology, and engagement.

- Risk and opportunity management strategy must be documented and refined.

- Risk and opportunity framing informs all other steps.

- Critical output: the core of risk and opportunity management strategy.

In Chapter 2, I discussed the SEC's rulemaking that mandates registrants to offer more uniform and informative disclosure regarding their cybersecurity risk management and strategy. Your risk and opportunity management plan, which includes the framing stage, is crucial to fulfilling this disclosure requirement and other regulatory requirements.

Risk and Opportunity Assessment

The risk and opportunity assessment step identifies, estimates, and prioritizes risks and opportunities to organizational data, systems, and devices. In my experience, the most significant issue facing organizations today is their inability or unwillingness to identify all their unique risks and opportunities, that is, the failure to complete a comprehensive risk and opportunity assessment work.

This deficiency results in the failure of organizations to invest in cybersecurity based on their unique risks and opportunities. You must start with *your* unique vision, mission, strategy, values, and services;

examine all *your* unique data, devices, and systems that support *your* unique business; and then identify all *your* unique cyber exposures and opportunities across *your* entire enterprise. This failure to identify *your* unique risks and opportunities usually leads to a one-size-fits-all, checklist-based approach to cybersecurity. The upshot is likely overspending to treat perceived risks and underspending on *your* most severe risks. Similarly, underspending on your most promising opportunities results. How can you treat your *unique* risks and opportunities if you do not know what they are?

Depending on your industry, you may have additional guidance, requirements, or standards you must follow. For example, the New York Department of Financial Services (NYDFS) requires organizations that operate under its Banking Law, the Insurance Law, or the Financial Services Law to complete a risk assessment following specific language in Section 500.9 Risk Assessment of New York State Department of Financial Services 23 NYCRR 500, Cybersecurity Requirements for Financial Services Companies.[6] The NYDFS risk assessment requirement is explicit.

As another example of a specific requirement, in healthcare, the Department of Health and Human Services Office for Civil Rights has published HHS/OCR "Guidance on Risk Analysis Requirements under the HIPAA Security Rule,"[7] which references the NIST special publications I cited previously. Unfortunately, although the HIPAA Security Rule has been enforceable since April 2005, OCR enforcement only increased significantly starting in 2011. Current OCR enforcement data shows that approximately 90% of healthcare entities fail to conduct comprehensive, enterprise-wide risk assessments.[8]

The risk assessment process documented in NIST SP 800-30, Revision 1, "Guide for Conducting Risk Assessments,"[9] provides a solid starting point for your risk and opportunity assessment work and, at a high level, is depicted in Figure 11-2. Of course, you must amend the process and wording in the steps to consider opportunities.

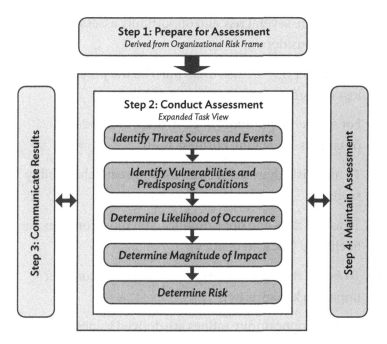

Figure 11-2. *NIST Risk Assessment Process*

Source: Bob Chaput, Executive Chairman, Clearwater. Adapted
from "Guide for Conducting Risk Assessments" (NIST Special
Publication 800-30, Revision 1). September 2012. Accessed October
2, 2023. *https://nvlpubs.nist.gov/nistpubs/Legacy/SP/*
nistspecialpublication800-39.pdf

NIST Special Publication 800-30 provides greater detail about the risk
assessment process, including examples of threat sources, threat actions,
vulnerabilities, predisposing conditions, the likelihood of occurrence,
impact, risk determination, and reports in the appendixes.

Outputs from the risk and opportunity assessment step are inputs
to the other three steps in the overall process—framing, response, and
monitoring—and are discussed in "Managing Information Security Risk"
(NIST Special Publication 800-39).[10] However, the most critical output
of the risk and opportunity assessment step is the risk and opportunity
register, which feeds directly into the risk and opportunity response step.

The following are several risk and opportunity assessment fundamentals to consider:

- For a cyber risk to exist, there must be the possibility of loss or harm.

- For a cyber opportunity to exist, there must be the possibility of creating business value.

- To have risk, there must be an asset-threat-vulnerability scenario.

- To assess risks and opportunities, you must consider likelihood (a.k.a. frequency).

- To assess risks and opportunities, you must consider impact (a.k.a. severity).

- Risk and opportunity ratings are derived values, like speed is a derived value = distance/time.

- The critical output of a risk and opportunity assessment is the risk and opportunity register.

Risk and Opportunity Response

As I discussed previously in section "Risk and Opportunity Assessment," once your organization has identified all the possible ways in which there can be a risk to the confidentiality, integrity, or availability of your assets or an opportunity to create business value, you need to rate each risk and opportunity by considering the likelihood and impact of each risk or opportunity scenario. In the case of risk, this means assessing the likelihood of a bad thing happening and, were it to happen, the loss or harm to your organization. For an opportunity scenario, this means assessing the likelihood of the organization investing to leverage that opportunity and, were it to be successful, the business value or benefit to your organization. The rating of each risk or opportunity scenario ultimately produces your risk and opportunity register.

The risk response process documented in NIST Special Publication 800-39 "Managing Information Security Risk"[11] is Step 1: Risk Response Identification, Step 2: Evaluate Alternatives, Step 3: Risk Response Decision, and Step 4: Risk Response Implementation.

You can quickly adopt this approach to opportunity response as you consider your alternatives, the pros/cons/costs of various responses, decide whether to leverage that opportunity, and, if so, execute the plans to leverage the opportunity. To pivot to a greater value creation focus, you need to flex a bit and figuratively and literally change "risk response" to "risk and opportunity response."

You should expand and elaborate on the preceding steps such that a workforce member will successfully conduct risk and opportunity response if they follow all your process steps in your documented procedures.

The following are several risk and opportunity response fundamentals to consider:

- All risks need a response.

- All opportunities need to be considered.

- Not all risks must be mitigated.

- Not all opportunities must be leveraged.

- Risk response choices are to accept, avoid, mitigate, transfer, or some combination.

- Opportunity response choices are to leverage or not leverage.

- Risk and opportunity response should be based on analysis and ratings, not checklists.

- A thoughtful evaluation of response alternatives is a critical part of the process.

- Business partners should own risk and opportunity response decisions, investments, residual risk, and opportunity gains.

- Use good project management and software to make sure plans get implemented.

- The critical output is a Plan of Action and Milestones (POAM) or Risk and Opportunity Response Plan.

Risk and Opportunity Monitoring

Let's face it. Most likely, everything will be different one year from now, if not sooner. Your vision, mission, strategy, values, and services may change, driving your business processes and information assets to change. This likely means new assets, threats, vulnerabilities, and risks that require a response. Externally, as discussed in Chapters 2 and 3, court cases, legislation, standards, guidance, and regulations will continue to change how cyber risks must be managed.

All these changes drive the requirement for ongoing risk and opportunity monitoring, which should be periodic and increasingly continuous. According to NIST, continuous risk monitoring "... *gives organizations the capability to maintain awareness of the risk being incurred, highlight the need to revisit other steps in the risk management process, and initiate process improvement activities as needed.*"[12] I suggest that continuous opportunity monitoring similarly allows organizations to maintain awareness of the opportunities being leveraged, get some early wins on the table, refine other steps in their risk and opportunity management process, and initiate process improvement activities as needed.

Important risk and opportunity monitoring goals include the following:

- Verify compliance (compliance monitoring).

- Determine ongoing effectiveness (effectiveness monitoring).

- Identify risk-impacting or opportunity-impacting changes (change monitoring).

Risk and opportunity monitoring requires as much automated data collection and reporting as possible and thoughtful and deliberate manual reviews. Monitoring should be architected into control and reporting solutions vs. "bolting them on" after the fact. To the extent possible, make it continuous monitoring where *"Information security continuous monitoring (ISCM) is defined as maintaining ongoing awareness of information security, vulnerabilities, and threats to support organizational risk management decisions."*[13]

Decide and document if your organization will use NIST's concept of Information Security Continuous Monitoring (ISCM) as one of your standards, referencing relevant documents as resources. Another standard you may adopt is "Assessing Security and Privacy Controls in Federal Information Systems and Organizations: Building Effective Assessment Plans" (NIST Special Publication 800-53A, Revision 4)[14] as a standard for monitoring the effectiveness of controls. Whatever monitoring approach you choose, adapt it to include monitoring your efforts to leverage cyber opportunities.

If you are subject to NYDFS, HIPAA, or any other regulatory requirements around monitoring, cite them in your documentation. These requirements may include auditing, compliance gap assessments, and technical testing. For example, consider the NYDFS requirements: *"The cybersecurity program for each Covered Entity shall include monitoring and testing, developed per the Covered Entity's Risk Assessment, designed to assess the effectiveness of the Covered Entity's cybersecurity program. The monitoring and testing shall include continuous monitoring or periodic Penetration Testing and vulnerability assessments.*"[15]

This requirement is a subset of the broader compliance monitoring, effectiveness monitoring, and change monitoring goals NIST calls for but still underscores the importance of effectiveness monitoring.

The risk monitoring process documented in "Managing Information Security Risk" (NIST Special Publication 800-39)[16] on the surface is surprisingly simple, so I recommend expanding your process to cover the following topics:

1. Verify compliance with internal policies and procedures and external requirements.

2. Determine the ongoing effectiveness of risk response measures and opportunity leverage actions.

3. Identify risk-impacting or opportunity-impacting changes to organizational information systems and environments of operation.

4. Validate that the security controls development life cycle (SCDLC) is working.

5. Determine the efficiency of risk response measures and opportunity leverage actions.

6. Specify how risk and opportunity monitoring is conducted (e.g., automated or manual).

7. Schedule the frequency of monitoring activities (e.g., periodic or continuous).

The preceding first three items represent the critical risk and opportunity monitoring goals. Compliance monitoring asks: Are you doing what is required? Effectiveness monitoring asks: Is what you've implemented working? Change monitoring asks: Are you staying on top of things?

Outputs from the risk and opportunity monitoring step are inputs to the other three steps in the overall process—framing, response, and assessment—and are discussed in "Managing Information Security Risk" (NIST Special Publication 800-39).[17] The most critical output of the risk and opportunity monitoring step is a regularly published and reviewed report that includes a critical review of compliance, effectiveness, and change monitoring.

The following are several risk and opportunity monitoring fundamentals to consider:

- Include opportunities, in addition to risk, in your monitoring activities.

- Cover three key considerations, which are compliance, effectiveness, and change.

- Base monitoring on learnings from all other process steps: Frame, Assess, and Respond.

- Balance risk and opportunity monitoring investment with value derived, of course.

- Monitor at all governance tiers: board, executive team, working groups, and systems owners.

- Think plan-do-check-act.

- Produce essential, tangible output: risk and opportunity monitoring report.

It is essential to include a section in your ECRM Program and Cybersecurity Strategy document that covers the preceding risk and opportunity monitoring elements and how you will conduct your monitoring.

ECRM Process Standards, Policies, and Procedures

Your ECRM Process standards, policies, and procedures should specify that you will conduct risk and opportunity framing, assessment, response, and monitoring. Detail when this work is undertaken, by whom it is performed, and the methodologies you will use.

For your standard for each step, decide and document that your organization will use COSO, NIST, ISO, or another alternative as your standard, referencing relevant documents as resources.

Your policy statements should indicate what you plan to do, why you plan to do so, and what you expect of members of your workforce. Remember, policies are higher-level aspirational statements emphasizing "what" and "why."

If policies state what your organization is going to do and why it is taking that approach, procedures provide the much-needed detail as to "how," "by whom," "when," etc. the policy will be implemented. You should expand and elaborate on these elements and steps such that a workforce member will successfully conduct risk and opportunity framing, assessment, response, and monitoring if they follow all your process steps in your documented procedures.

Your procedures must detail how to conduct each step effectively and efficiently. See NIST Special Publication 800-39 "Managing Information Security Risk" for additional information on the risk framing, risk assessment, risk response, and risk monitoring process steps.[18] Remember, NIST Special Publication 800-30 provides a deep dive into the risk assessment process. Adapt your procedures to include opportunities.

Your procedures should also include examples and illustrations. For example, you may evaluate the likelihood of a particular threat exploiting a vulnerability using the type of scale shown in Table D-1 in Appendix D. Include it as an example. Similarly, you would include your scale for assessing impact in the case of a threat exploiting a vulnerability. Table D-2 in Appendix D illustrates a risk impact scale. To tie these concepts together, you might also include an example of a risk and opportunity register, as shown in Table D-3 in Appendix D.

Conclusion

It is essential to include sections in your ECRM Program and Cybersecurity Strategy documentation that cover the framing, assessment, response, and monitoring steps discussed previously. And ensure that your policies, procedures, and practices consider both risks and opportunities. Do not lose focus on creating business value by "managing the upside." The four steps comprise an interrelated, closed-loop set of tasks to implement your ECRM Process.

The ECRM Process becomes the execution core of your ECRM program. In Chapter 2, I discussed the SEC rulemaking requiring registrants to provide more consistent and informative disclosure regarding their cybersecurity risk management and strategy. Your ECRM Process is a critical component of this disclosure requirement.

In Chapter 12, I complete the coverage of the essential elements of your ECRM Program and Cybersecurity Strategy documentation. Do not minimize their importance because I treat them last. ECRM education, consideration of supporting tools, third-party risk management, and ECRM recordkeeping are all key ECRM considerations.

Questions Management and the Board Should Ask and Discuss

1. Has your organization agreed upon and documented your framing standards, policies, and procedures?

2. Has your organization agreed upon and documented your assessment standards, policies, and procedures?

3. Has your organization agreed upon and documented your response standards, policies, and procedures?

4. Has your organization agreed upon and documented your monitoring standards, policies, and procedures?

5. Do you have the internal talent with the appropriate skills, knowledge, and experience to facilitate the development of your ECRM Process standards, policies, and procedures?

6. Would engaging an experienced, reputable ECRM partner be valuable to establishing, implementing, and maturing your organization's ECRM program?

7. Do your ECRM Process standards, policies, and procedures meet all the regulatory requirements your organization must comply with?

Endnotes

1. BrainyQuote. "If you can't describe what you are doing as a process, you don't know what you're doing." Accessed April 14, 2023. Available at `https://www.brainyquote.com/quotes/w_edwards_deming_133510?src=t_process`

2. National Institute of Standards and Technology (NIST). NIST Special Publication 800-39. "Managing Information Security Risk." March 2011. Available at `https://nvlpubs.nist.gov/nistpubs/Legacy/SP/nistspecialpublication800-39.pdf`

3. Chaput, Bob. Stop the Cyber Bleeding | Putting ECRM into Action YouTube Channel. "Episode 27: Why You Should Base Your Program on NIST." February 21, 2022. Available at `https://www.youtube.com/watch?v=ozDDKlmOVkQ&t=19s`

4. Cybersecurity & Infrastructure Security Agency (CISA). "Cyber Incident Reporting for Critical Infrastructure Act of 2022 (CIRCIA)." March 2022. Available at `https://www.cisa.gov/circia`

5. National Institute of Standards and Technology (NIST). NIST Special Publication 800-39. "Managing Information Security Risk." March 2011. Available at `https://nvlpubs.nist.gov/nistpubs/Legacy/SP/nistspecialpublication800-39.pdf`

6. New York State Department of Financial Services. "New York State Department of Financial Services 23 NYCRR 500, Cybersecurity Requirements

for Financial Services Companies." March
8, 2023. Accessed July 10, 2023. Available at
https://www.dfs.ny.gov/system/files/
documents/2023/03/23NYCRR500_0.pdf

7. OCR/HHS. "Guidance on Risk Analysis
    Requirements under the HIPAA Security Rule." July
    14, 2010. https://www.hhs.gov/sites/default/
    files/ocr/privacy/hipaa/administrative/
    securityrule/rafinalguidancepdf.pdf

8. Clearwater analysis of data publicly available at:
    Resolution Agreements and Civil Money Penalties.
    Health Information Privacy. U.S. Department
    of Health and Human Services. (n.d.) Accessed
    February 28, 2023. https://www.hhs.gov/hipaa/
    for-professionals/compliance-enforcement/
    agreements/index.html

9. National Institute of Standards and Technology
    (NIST). NIST Special Publication 800-30, Revision
    1. "Guide for Conducting Risk Assessments."
    September 2012. Available at https://
    nvlpubs.nist.gov/nistpubs/Legacy/SP/
    nistspecialpublication800-30r1.pdf

10. National Institute of Standards and Technology
    (NIST). NIST Special Publication 800-39. "Managing
    Information Security Risk." March 2011. Available at
    https://nvlpubs.nist.gov/nistpubs/Legacy/SP/
    nistspecialpublication800-39.pdf

11. National Institute of Standards and Technology (NIST). NIST Special Publication 800-39. "Managing Information Security Risk." March 2011. Available at https://nvlpubs.nist.gov/nistpubs/Legacy/SP/nistspecialpublication800-39.pdf

12. National Institute of Standards and Technology (NIST). NIST Special Publication 800-39. "Managing Information Security Risk." March 2011. Available at https://nvlpubs.nist.gov/nistpubs/Legacy/SP/nistspecialpublication800-39.pdf

13. National Institute of Standards and Technology (NIST). NIST Special Publication 800-137. "Information Security Continuous Monitoring (ISCM) for Federal Information Systems and Organizations." September 2011. Available at https://nvlpubs.nist.gov/nistpubs/legacy/sp/nistspecialpublication800-137.pdf

14. National Institute of Standards and Technology (NIST). NIST Special Publication 800-53A, Revision 4. "Assessing Security and Privacy Controls in Federal Information Systems and Organizations: Building Effective Assessment Plans." Available at https://www.nist.gov/privacy-framework/nist-sp-800-53a

15. New York State Department of Financial Services. "New York State Department of Financial Services 23 NYCRR 500, Cybersecurity Requirements for Financial Services Companies." March 8, 2023. Accessed July 10, 2023. Available at https://www.dfs.ny.gov/system/files/documents/2023/03/23NYCRR500_0.pdf

16. National Institute of Standards and Technology
     (NIST). NIST Special Publication 800-39. "Managing
     Information Security Risk." March 2011. Available at
     https://nvlpubs.nist.gov/nistpubs/Legacy/SP/
     nistspecialpublication800-39.pdf

17. National Institute of Standards and Technology
     (NIST). NIST Special Publication 800-39. "Managing
     Information Security Risk." March 2011. Available at
     https://nvlpubs.nist.gov/nistpubs/Legacy/SP/
     nistspecialpublication800-39.pdf

18. National Institute of Standards and Technology
     (NIST). NIST Special Publication 800-39. "Managing
     Information Security Risk." March 2011. Available at
     https://nvlpubs.nist.gov/nistpubs/Legacy/SP/
     nistspecialpublication800-39.pdf

CHAPTER 12

Additional Essential ECRM Program Elements

The way to secure peace is to be prepared for war. They that are on their guard, and appear ready to receive their adversaries, are in much less danger of being attacked, than the supine, secure, and negligent.

—Benjamin Franklin[1]

The ECRM Program and Cybersecurity Strategy topics and related documentation covered in this chapter are education and training, automation and technology tools, third-party risk management, and recordkeeping and reporting. As with other key program elements and related documentation, these are not insignificant topics and will strengthen your ECRM Program and Cybersecurity Strategy. As I have discussed and will mention again, you must include standards, plans, policies, and procedures in your ECRM program documentation.

© Bob Chaput 2024
B. Chaput, *Enterprise Cyber Risk Management as a Value Creator*,
https://doi.org/10.1007/979-8-8688-0094-8_12

ECRM Education and Training

Completing the work outlined throughout Part 2 of this book positions your organization to establish, implement, and mature your ECRM program. For many organizations, doing so represents a transformational program. Any significant business transformation is about behavior change, which usually begins with C-suite leaders and the board, who must provide the leadership and oversight to complete work on these essential items.

In previous chapters, I discussed five critical core capabilities—governance, people, processes, technology, and engagement—that you must develop to ensure your successful ECRM transformation. Education and training are relevant to establishing all these capabilities.

The standards, policies, and procedures developed in your ECRM Program and Cybersecurity Strategy require the appropriate amount of education and training across and up and down the organization to equip your organization to execute. Education and training are essential to any change management program, such as implementing a new ECRM program.

To educate means *"to develop the faculties and powers of (a person) by teaching, instruction, or schooling."*[2] To train means *"to give the discipline and instruction, drill, practice, etc., designed to impart proficiency or efficiency."*[3] Education is more about knowledge; training is more about task skills and abilities. You *educate* your C-suite and board on ECRM. You *train* frontline workforce members and managers on ECRM. Groups in between will likely receive a mix of education and training. In all cases, education and training ensure everyone understands and buys into what you expect of them.

Your ECRM education and training plans, policies, and procedures focus on enterprise cyber risk management and what is needed to implement and sustain your program and execute your strategy. It is not the same as, nor a replacement for, security awareness training.

In terms of content, all the topics in your ECRM Program and Cybersecurity Strategy documentation are candidates for various education and training plans. For example, providing *education* sessions on all the topics I covered in this book would be relevant for all workforce members to provide awareness of what the program entails. While understanding all the subjects would be essential for all workforce members, skills *training* would be more appropriate, for example, for those responsible for completing the specific ECRM Process steps such as risk and opportunity framing, assessment, response, and monitoring.

ECRM education and training are critical, regardless of the organization's size. The education and training amount and type will depend on the robustness of your ECRM program and possibly regulatory requirements. Your education and training program provides an excellent opportunity to reinforce the focus on creating business value through your ECRM program.

Education and training are not one-time activities but require ongoing, evolving content as your organization's needs, standards, policies, and procedures change. Education and training should be tailored to job needs. It must be customized and based on job responsibilities. Training must be focused on the successful establishment, implementation, and maturation of your ECRM program.

ECRM education and training plans should vary by audience, be refreshed with different frequencies, and be reinforced with reminders and regular updates. For example, ongoing board of directors' education may include both an examination of relevant current events and educational activities and subjects such as the following: hiring outside experts to brief the board on ECRM 101; having internal advisors such as your chief audit executive provide in-depth briefings; engaging outside counsel to discuss the legal implications of a breach; engaging your organization's executive risk insurance broker to discuss potential gaps, clashes, and redundancies in your liability policy portfolio; conducting desktop exercises on incident response and business continuity; etc.

What materials you use to conduct your education and training will vary. There may be certain off-the-shelf content that you can use. You may wish to develop your own. You may deliver content live and in person, virtually, or both. I encourage engagement and discussion as much as possible.

You must include a section in your ECRM Program and Cybersecurity Strategy document that covers ECRM education and training standards, policies, and procedures. A well-documented education and training program that routinely keeps the workforce trained and updated based on the organization's cyber risk and opportunity management efforts can be the best way to leverage ECRM. The chief output of the work discussed in this section is your organization's ECRM education and training standards, plans, policies, and procedures.

ECRM Automation and Technology Tools

Your organization must develop core ECRM capabilities such as governance, people, processes, technology, and engagement to ensure your ECRM transformation is successful. Adopting the appropriate technology tools and solutions is critical to success. For example, you can use tools and automation judicially across all four steps in the ECRM Process (frame, assess, respond, and monitor risk and opportunity).

For example, comprehensive, enterprise-wide risk and opportunity assessment, a foundational step in developing a sound cybersecurity and cyber risk and opportunity management strategy, cannot be conducted, documented, or maintained using a simple Excel spreadsheet. Risk and opportunity assessment, as a part of ECRM, is a complicated enough task that it is worth considering using specialized software to facilitate and document your ECRM program.

Ultimately, the technology and automation tools you use to support your ECRM program will range from strategic-level solutions (such as a GRC or an ECRMS solution) to operational-level solutions (such as a security information and event management [SIEM] system). Additional tool examples include asset and configuration management solutions, identity management and authentication, incident response and reporting, malware detection and eradication, automation solutions or service providers for technical testing, etc.

The technology with the most significant relevance to the C-suite and board is the ECRMS solution. The ECRMS solution provides the foundation for the ECRM program. It should include appropriate C-suite and board-level dashboards and reports that give the C-suite and board the information they need to execute their ECRM leadership and oversight responsibilities.

Cyber risk management automation and tools standards help reduce the cost and complexity of implementing cybersecurity solutions. Just as the International Electrotechnical Commission (IEC) and other standards bodies underscore, organizations can leverage economies of scale and reduce duplication of effort by adopting standardized approaches and technologies.[4] Using the right tools can lead to cost savings and improved efficiencies across industries and within your organization while ensuring that cyber risk management solutions meet industry best practices and quality standards.

You cannot overstate the importance of cyber risk management automation and tools. Such tools provide a basis for designing, implementing, and managing cyber risk management solutions and promote interoperability, consistency, and reliability. By automating, organizations can improve the effectiveness of their cybersecurity solutions, reduce costs, and enhance their ability to leverage ECRM as a value creator.

It is essential to include a section in your ECRM Program and Cybersecurity Strategy document that covers ECRM automation and technology tools standards, policies, and procedures and how you will manage your automation and tools. The chief output of the work discussed in this section is your organization's ECRM automation and technology tools standards, policies, and procedures.

ECRM Third-Party Risk Management

In recent years, third-party supply chain cyberattacks have become a significant concern for organizations of all sizes and industries. These attacks occur when hackers target a company's supply chain partners, such as vendors, contractors, and other third-party providers, to gain access to the primary target's network and data. These attacks can be devastating, leading to significant financial losses, reputational damage, and legal consequences. In addition to the SolarWinds attack in December 2020[5] and the Target attack in 2013,[6] two other significant attacks include Capital One and Maersk. Capital One suffered a data breach that exposed the personal information of over 100 million customers, where the vulnerability was traced back to a misconfigured firewall rule in Capital One's cloud infrastructure, which a third-party vendor provided.[7] In 2017, Maersk suffered a significant cyberattack that disrupted its operations for several weeks. The attack, attributed to the Russian military, began with a phishing email sent to a third-party vendor that provided IT services to Maersk.[8]

These examples demonstrate the severe consequences of third-party supply chain cyberattacks. These attacks can be challenging to detect and prevent, as they often exploit vulnerabilities in the networks and systems of third-party partners.

An increasing number of regulations explicitly call for supply chain cyber risk management. Supply chain risk management has existed in the healthcare ecosystem since the original promulgation of the HIPAA Privacy[9] and Security Rule[10] in the early 2000s. The SEC final disclosure rule includes a specific disclosure item of whether the organization *"... has processes to oversee and identify such risks from cybersecurity threats associated with its use of any third-party service provider."*[11]

Another clear focus on supply chain risk management emanates from the Defense Federal Acquisition Regulation Supplement (DFARS) and the Cybersecurity Maturity Model Certification (CMMC) requirements. These requirements are being finalized by the US Department of Defense (DoD) to ensure the cybersecurity of its supply chain. The certification process includes assessing the contractor's ability to manage cybersecurity risks in their supply chain. Compliance with these requirements is crucial for businesses that want to work with the DoD, and lack of compliance can result in the loss of contracts and potential legal repercussions.[12] Finally, in Section 500.11 Third Party Service Provider Security Policy, NYDFS requires a third-party service provider policy that specifies, *"Each Covered Entity shall implement written policies and procedures designed to ensure the security of Information Systems and Nonpublic Information that are accessible to, or held by, Third Party Service Providers. Such policies and procedures shall be based on the Risk Assessment of the Covered Entity."*[13]

Third-party supply chain cyberattacks are challenging to detect and prevent. Therefore, organizations must implement standard best practices, processes, and tools to mitigate such attacks' potential risks, promote transparency and accountability, and streamline operations for timely reporting. A common approach to third-party risk management across your organization is essential for ensuring effectiveness, efficiency, completeness, and consistency. Timely compliance with the legal and regulatory requirements cited in this chapter is critical to avoid penalties and reputational damage.

Given the increase in law, regulations, and enforcement, including a section in your ECRM Program and Cybersecurity Strategy document that covers ECRM third-party risk management standards, policies, and procedures is essential. By conducting thorough risk assessments and compliance gap assessments of third-party vendors, implementing stringent access controls, monitoring continuously, auditing third-party vendors, and developing an incident response plan, your organization can protect itself from the devastating impact of third-party supply chain cyberattacks. The chief output of the work discussed in this section is your organization's ECRM third-party risk management standards, policies, and procedures.

ECRM Recordkeeping and Reporting

Because of increasingly more stringent regulatory requirements, litigation, and enforcement actions, your organization must develop, implement, and enforce robust recordkeeping and reporting standards, policies, and procedures. You do not want your organization to fail to retain the necessary information. You must be able to rapidly report or disclose essential information about your ECRM Program and Cybersecurity Strategy.

All organizations have long wrestled with statutory recordkeeping and records retention requirements. Scale that up to an international company operating in countries worldwide, and we're into profound complexity. I recall these challenges from my global executive assignments at General Electric (NYSE: G.E.), Johnson & Johnson (NYSE: JNJ), and Healthways (NASDAQ: HWAY). You may find a sample Record Retention Schedule for Businesses on the Postlethwaite & Netterville website.[14] It illustrates the complexity of recordkeeping for any business.

Many types of ECRM data may require reporting or disclosure. Think about all the information generated across the six functions of the NIST Cybersecurity Framework, using that as a model—Govern, Identify, Protect, Detect, Respond, and Recover. This potentially reportable information may include, but not be limited to, strategies, policies, procedures, asset information, risk and opportunity assessments, risk response measures, safeguards implemented, incident detection and reporting, incident response, recovery plans, etc. Consider the disclosure requirements required by the SEC regarding your ECRM Program and Cybersecurity Strategy that I have discussed.

You would be wise to document and keep records of every action, activity, or assessment required by your policies and procedures and those required by applicable regulations. There are many stakeholders to whom specific ECRM information reporting is required. These include and are not limited to customers/patients, employees, credit reporting agencies, the media, insurers, attorneys, regulators, the courts, etc.

In Chapter 3, I discussed various cases, including an important 1996 ruling by the Delaware Court of Chancery. This decision dealt with a board's duties related to "reporting or information system or controls." The case established the so-called Caremark standard.[15]

Establishing ECRM recordkeeping and reporting standards, policies, and procedures helps implement meaningful "reporting or information system or controls." While there are many other existing (e.g., HIPAA Security Rule Implementation Specification: Response and Reporting)[16] and emerging reporting requirements (e.g., Cyber Incident Reporting for Critical Infrastructure Act of 2022 [CIRCIA])[17] seeking different content and timing, the SEC disclosure requirements further underscore the importance of ECRM recordkeeping and reporting. Remember, the SEC is addressing growing concerns about apparent underreporting and untimely reporting of cyber incidents by requiring registrants to "disclose material cybersecurity incidents in a current report on Form 8-K within four business days after the registrant determines that it has experienced a material cybersecurity incident."[18]

Additionally, without going into detail, global regulations like GDPR,[19] state regulations like the California Consumer Privacy Act,[20] and the proposed NYDFS rules,[21] federal laws like CIRCIA and, for organizations in the Defense Industrial Base, DFARS Safeguarding Covered Defense Information and Cyber Incident Reporting,[22] whistleblower cases, and other litigation are driving the requirement for comprehensive recordkeeping and reporting capabilities.

Again, the increase in laws, regulations, enforcement actions, and good business practices drives the need for a section in your ECRM Program and Cybersecurity Strategy document that covers ECRM recordkeeping and reporting policies and procedures.

Standards, Plans, Policies, and Procedures

Your education and training, automation and technology tools, third-party risk management, and recordkeeping and reporting standards, plans, policies, and procedures should spell out how you will conduct the work in each area, when it is delivered, by whom it will be provided, and what materials and methods will be used.

As I discussed in Chapter 11, your policy statements should indicate what you plan to do, why you plan to do so, the values of your organization, and what is expected of members of your workforce, that is, what your course of action will be and why you've chosen this course of action. Your policy statement establishes your good faith intent.

The following is an example of an ECRM education and training policy statement:

[YOUR COMPANY NAME HERE] is committed to establishing, implementing, and maturing an enterprise cyber risk management (ECRM) program, safeguarding all sensitive stakeholder data, systems, and devices against compromising confidentiality, integrity, and availability. International, federal, state, and local laws and regulations have established standards by which [YOUR COMPANY NAME HERE] achieves acceptable ECRM, privacy, security, and compliance. To support our commitment to ECRM, all workforce members, including executive management and the board of directors of [YOUR COMPANY NAME HERE], will receive appropriate ECRM education and training, as detailed in our ECRM education and training plans and procedures. All workforce members must attend ECRM education and training relevant to their role and pass knowledge and competency checks upon completion. In some instances, training will include active on-the-job training.

As discussed in Chapter 11, procedures bring your policy statements to life by providing the required actions to deliver on your policy. If policies are higher-level addressing "what" and "why," procedures provide the much-needed detail as to "how," "by whom," "when," "where," "using what," etc. the policy will be implemented. You should expand and elaborate on these elements and steps such that those responsible for receiving education and training and those responsible for delivering it will successfully provide education and training if they follow all your process steps in your documented procedures.

The following are several factors you should consider when developing your standards, plans, policies, and procedures:

- Formalize governance over the development work.

- Indicate the C-suite executive responsible for the policy and procedure.

- Leverage your cross-functional ECRM Working Group to serve as your development task force.

- Create an overall methodology to develop, review, test, and approve each procedure.

- Utilize your organization's standard policy and procedure template.

- Use your ECRM Guiding Principles, business strategic objectives, and ECRM strategic objectives to guide your work.

- Conduct an internal compliance gap assessment vis-à-vis your regulatory requirements.

- Incorporate and cite all applicable regulatory mandates and requirements into your plans, policies, and procedures.

- Incorporate change management considerations into your procedures.

- Integrate policy and procedure training into colleague onboarding and ongoing training.

- Call on cyber risk and opportunity management and regulatory compliance experts for assistance.

You should expand and elaborate on these elements and steps such that those responsible for managing ECRM third-party risk management will be successful if they follow all your process steps in your documented procedures.

Conclusion

Given the increase in laws, regulations, and enforcement and their specific requirements, it is essential to include sections in your ECRM Program and Cybersecurity Strategy document that cover education and training, automation and technology, third-party risk management, and recordkeeping and reporting standards, policies, and procedures.

I discussed the cybersecurity disclosure final rule from the SEC in Chapter 2 and several other chapters. It mandates registrants to give more comprehensive and informative disclosure about their cybersecurity risk management and strategy. Your ECRM education and training plan, automation and technology tools, third-party risk management, and recordkeeping and reporting standards, policies, and procedures will help meet this and other emerging disclosure requirements.

You can visit my YouTube channel, Stop the Cyber Bleeding | Putting ECRM Into Action, which includes brief video clips covering many of the topics in this book. It may help guide the development of your ECRM Program and Cybersecurity Strategy and can be accessed and subscribed to at https://www.youtube.com/@stopthecyberbleeding/videos.

I have covered a great deal of material and recommended numerous actions throughout the book. For those looking for an "immediate next steps plan," in Chapter 13, I provide ten recommended implementation steps to help you jump-start your new program or resuscitate a languishing one with fresh, new ideas.

Questions Management and the Board Should Ask and Discuss

1. Do your standards, policies, and procedures in the areas covered in this chapter meet the requirements of SEC's Cybersecurity Risk Management, Strategy, Governance, and Incident Disclosure final rule or your other regulatory requirements?

2. Do you have the internal resources with the appropriate skills, knowledge, and experience to facilitate the development of your education and training, automation and technology, third-party risk management, and recordkeeping and reporting standards, policies, and procedures?

3. Would engaging an experienced, reputable ECRM partner be valuable to establishing, implementing, and maturing these standards, policies, and procedures?

4. Has your organization developed ECRM third-party risk management standards, policies, and procedures, including continuous monitoring and auditing of third-party vendors? Are they of a high enough quality to disclose?

Endnotes

1.   Franklin, Benjamin. "The way to secure peace is to be prepared for war. They that are on their guard, and appear ready to receive their adversaries, are in much less danger of being attacked, than the supine, secure, and negligent." 1809. Accessed October 3, 2023. Available at https://www.azquotes.com/quote/914275

2.   Educate. Dictionary.com. (n.d.) Accessed February 27, 2023. Available at https://www.dictionary.com/browse/educate

3.   Train. Dictionary.com. (n.d.) Accessed February 27, 2023. Available at https://www.dictionary.com/browse/train

4.   International Electrotechnical Commission (IEC). "Benefits of using IEC standards." 2023. Available at https://www.iec.ch/standards-development/benefits-using-iec-standards

5.   Temple-Raston, Dina. All Things Considered. NPR. "A 'Worst Nightmare' Cyberattack: The Untold Story Of The SolarWinds Hack." April 16, 2021. Available at https://www.npr.org/2021/04/16/985439655/a-worst-nightmare-cyberattack-the-untold-story-of-the-solarwinds-hack

6. McCoy, Kevin. USA Today. "Target to pay
    $18.5M for 2013 data breach that affected 41
    million consumers." May 23, 2017. https://
    www.usatoday.com/story/money/2017/05/23/
    target-pay-185m-2013-data-breach-affected-
    consumers/102063932/.

7. Neto, Nelson Novaes et al. Cybersecurity at MIT
    Sloan. MIT Sloan School of Management. "A Case
    Study of the Capital One Data Breach." January 2020.
    Available at https://web.mit.edu/smadnick/www/
    wp/2020-07.pdf

8. Leovy, Jill. Los Angeles Times. "Cyberattack cost
    Maersk as much as $300 million and disrupted
    operations for 2 weeks." August 17, 2017. Available
    at https://www.latimes.com/business/la-fi-
    maersk-cyberattack-20170817-story.html

9. Privacy of Individually Identifiable Health
    Information. 45 CFR Part 164 Subpart E. Available
    at https://www.ecfr.gov/current/title-45/
    subtitle-A/subchapter-C/part-164/subpart-E

10. Security Standards for the Protection of Electronic
    Protected Health Information. 45 CFR Part 164
    Subpart E. Available at https://www.ecfr.gov/
    current/title-45/subtitle-A/subchapter-C/
    part-164/subpart-E

11. SEC. "Final Rule: Cybersecurity Risk Management,
    Strategy, Governance, and Incident Disclosure."
    July 26, 2023. Accessed July 30, 2023. Available
    at https://www.sec.gov/files/rules/
    final/2023/33-11216.pdf

12. Summit7.com. "What is DFARS 7021?" (n.d.)
    Available at https://www.summit7.us/dfars-7021

13. New York State Department of Financial Services.
    "New York State Department of Financial Services
    23 NYCRR 500, Cybersecurity Requirements
    for Financial Services Companies." March
    8, 2023. Accessed July 10, 2023. Available at
    https://www.dfs.ny.gov/system/files/
    documents/2023/03/23NYCRR500_0.pdf

14. Postlethwaite & Netterville. "Record Retention
    Schedule for Businesses." (n.d.) Available at
    https://www.pncpa.com/resources/record-
    retention-business/

15. Micheletti, Edward B. and Lindsay, Ryan
    M. Skadden, Arps, Slate, Meagher & Flom LLP. "The
    Risk of Overlooking Oversight: Recent Caremark
    Decisions From the Court of Chancery Indicate
    Closer Judicial Scrutiny and Potential Increased
    Traction for Oversight Claims." December 15,
    2021. https://www.skadden.com/insights/
    publications/2021/12/insights-the-delaware-
    edition/the-risk-of-overlooking-oversight.

16. Response and reporting Implementation
    Specification. 45 CFR §164.308(a)(6)(ii) (Security
    Standards for the Protection of Electronic Protected
    Health Information, Administrative Safeguards).
    Available at https://www.ecfr.gov/current/
    title-45/subtitle-A/subchapter-C/part-164/
    subpart-C/section-164.308

17. CISA. Cybersecurity & Infrastructure Security Agency. "Cyber Incident Reporting for Critical Infrastructure Act of 2022 (CIRCIA)." March 2022. Available at https://www.cisa.gov/circia

18. SEC. "Proposed Rule Cybersecurity Risk Management, Strategy, Governance, and Incident Disclosure." March 9, 2022. Available at https://www.sec.gov/rules/proposed/2022/33-11038.pdf

19. GDPR FAQs. EU GDPR.org. Accessed March 6. 2023. Available at https://gdpr.eu/faq/

20. California Consumer Privacy Act (CCPA). February 15, 2023. Available at https://oag.ca.gov/privacy/ccpa

21. New York State Department of Financial Services (NYDFS). "DFS Superintendent Adrienne A. Harris Announces Updated Cybersecurity Regulation." November 9, 2022. Available at https://dfs.ny.gov/reports_and_publications/press_releases/pr20221109221

22. 48 CFR 252.204-7012 Safeguarding Covered Defense Information and Cyber Incident Reporting. Available at https://www.ecfr.gov/current/title-48/chapter-2/subchapter-H/part-252/subpart-252.2/section-252.204-7012

CHAPTER 13

Ten Recommended Implementation Steps

Cheers to a new year and another chance for us to get it right.

—Oprah Winfrey[1]

Throughout this book, in each chapter, I have provided specific recommendations to establish, implement, and mature your ECRM Program and Cybersecurity Strategy. Additionally, I offered the section "Questions Management and the Board Should Ask and Discuss" at the end of each chapter. That material provided practical, tangible, actionable steps to develop and document your program and strategy.

In this chapter, I bring together those recommendations and action items into ten implementation steps you should consider launching your transformational ECRM Program and Cybersecurity Strategy initiative. You can take these steps to jump-start a new ECRM program or reinvigorate an existing one. The actions I recommend align with the NIST approach to cyber risk management. As I have emphasized throughout this book, I highly recommend the guidance and resources available from NIST. NIST offers an industry-recognized, technology-agnostic approach and compendium available resources at no cost. (See Appendix C for more details about the advantages of using NIST-based methods.)

© Bob Chaput 2024

B. Chaput, *Enterprise Cyber Risk Management as a Value Creator*,
https://doi.org/10.1007/979-8-8688-0094-8_13

You do not need to implement steps presented sequentially. Depending on the maturity of your program, internal strategic requirements, or external regulatory requirements, you may need to perform specific actions ahead of others. For example, suppose your financial services organization is being investigated or audited by the New York Department of Financial Services for alleged cybersecurity issues. In that case, you may need to accelerate Implementation Step #8: Conduct a comprehensive, NIST-based enterprise-wide risk and opportunity assessment as your top priority.

As you consider taking these actions within your organization, it is essential to remember that establishing, implementing, and maturing your ECRM program should be regarded as a long-term, ongoing, iterative initiative—not a short-term project with a start date and an end date. Think journey, not destination.

Implementation Step #1: Establish ECRM Governance

Throughout the book, I have emphasized the importance of formalizing how you will develop, lead, and oversee your ECRM work. Recall governance is about interrelated questions: Who makes what decisions? How and when do they make those decisions? And what data and facts do they use to make those decisions? Too many organizations fail because they have not clarified and documented decision-making. You need to make decisions about numerous aspects and capabilities of your program. These include but are not limited to foundational decisions about governance; your ECRM Guiding Principles; your ECRM strategic objectives; your ECRM Framework, Process, and Maturity Model; your ECRM education and training; your ECRM standards, policies, and procedures; etc.

I discussed the importance of governance and provided a three-tier governance model as an example of how you might establish governance in your organization in Chapter 9. You must decide your structure, but in any case, each tier (e.g., board, Executive Steering Committee, Working Group, etc.) should have a formal, written charter. Ensure that all teams are cross-functional. Consider external resources for your teams (e.g., advisors, consultants, insurance brokers, external audit firms, etc.)

If your organization has a Project Management Office (PMO), the PMO can help with chartering and facilitating the groups. Ensure that each governance group has the appropriate training and access to ECRM expertise sourced internally or externally.

After establishing the appropriate governance structure for your organization, the next step is to create your organization's ECRM Program and Cybersecurity Strategy document as outlined in Chapter 8. As an example of a get-started project, the ECRM Cross-Functional Working Group would be responsible for drafting elements of the ECRM Program and Cybersecurity Strategy. The Executive Steering Committee would review and request revisions to the documentation as needed and ultimately recommend it to the board committee for approval.

Implementation Step #2: Design and Deliver Ongoing ECRM and Cybersecurity Education

I wrote this book to create a call to arms by providing basic education on ECRM and cybersecurity. While your implementation effort is underway and throughout your journey, formalize and offer education and training appropriate to the roles of C-suite executives, board members, leaders, managers, and workforce members.

In Chapter 8, I discussed the importance of establishing an ECRM Glossary for your organization. Consider this task a critical part of your education program. As I discussed, when the executive team and board are discussing this quarter's financial results, everyone must understand terms like "revenue," "operating margin," and "net income." Any ambiguity in the understanding of those terms can lead to miscommunication. Likewise, to have a meaningful and productive conversation about cyber risk and cybersecurity, everyone at the table needs to speak with precision and understand the differences between a risk, a vulnerability, a threat, and a cyber opportunity (especially!) among other terms. As I discussed, to have meaningful and productive ECRM and cybersecurity conversations, avoiding the confusion and misinformation circulating over the most basic terms and concepts is vital. One of the best references on the terminology is the glossary compiled by the Computer Security Resource Center (CSRC) at NIST. You can access this comprehensive glossary online at https://csrc.nist.gov/glossary/. Feel free to use the content of Appendix D.

To the matter of board education as an example of one of your key audiences, opportunities exist in and out of board meetings. With typically precious little time offered to discuss cybersecurity in entire board or even committee meetings, consider options outside of board meetings, especially in the early stages of your implementation work. I would encourage you to consider two components of board education: (a) ECRM-relevant current events and (b) general ECRM education.

Regarding the former, the overall objective of addressing current events is to keep your board apprised of internal and external relevant events that may affect your risk posture. You must inform the board promptly (not waiting until the quarterly ECRM agenda item) about any internal incidents related to compromising the confidentiality, integrity, or availability of your assets. It's also essential to make the board aware of any high-profile external events, such as data breaches in peer organizations or regulatory enforcement actions that have been taken against other similar organizations in your industry. Cite lessons learned from these external incidents or enforcement actions.

For general board ECRM education, consider this expanded list of potential topics from Chapter 12:

- Hiring outside experts to brief the board on ECRM 101 or cybersecurity 101

- Having internal advisors, such as your chief audit executive or general counsel, provide in-depth briefings

- Engaging outside counsel to discuss the legal implications of a breach vis-à-vis your regulatory requirements

- Engaging your organization's executive risk insurance broker to discuss potential gaps, clashes, and redundancies in your liability policy portfolio

- Engaging outside and inside experts to forecast the cyber risk landscape one, three, and five years out

- Inviting external advisors, such as FBI representatives or SEC staff, to discuss your cyber risk environment

- Providing a briefing on the National Association of Corporate Directors (NACD) CERT Certificate in Cyber-Risk Oversight Program (`https://www.nacdonline.org/education-and-events/elearning-courses-on-demand-courses/CERT-cyber-riskoversight/`) or similar educational offerings to validate the importance of ECRM and encourage board members to pursue continuing education in cyber risk

- Providing a briefing on the NIST Cybersecurity Framework, including information on how adopting the framework encourages the integration of ECRM into the overall business strategy

Implementation Step #3: Establish and Document ECRM Guiding Principles

In Chapter 9, I discussed the value of having your board set forth principles by which your organization will undertake its ECRM work. Principles provide the guardrails, provide a foundation, and set the tone at the top. I provided examples from two NACD publications, "Cyber-Risk Oversight 2020: Key Principles and Practical Guidance for Corporate Boards"[2] and the 2021 "Principles for Board Governance of Cyber Risk."[3] You can review those principles in Chapter 9.

Here's an updated set to consider. NACD's *2023 Director's Handbook on Cyber-Risk Oversight*,[4] published in collaboration with the Internet Security Alliance, reiterates and refines previous guiding principles, and those principles are presented here as reminders:

1. Directors need to understand and approach cybersecurity as a strategic, enterprise risk, not just an IT risk.

2. Directors should understand the legal implications of cyber risks as they relate to their company's specific circumstances.

3. Boards should have adequate access to cybersecurity expertise, and discussions about cyber risk management should be given regular and adequate time on board meeting agendas.

4. Directors should set the expectation that management will establish an enterprise-wide, cyber risk management framework and reporting structure with adequate staffing and budget.

5. Board-management discussions about cyber risk should include identification and quantification of financial exposure to cyber risks and which risks to accept, mitigate, or transfer, such as through insurance, as well as specific plans associated with each approach.

6. Boards should encourage systemic resilience through collaboration with their industry and government peers and encourage the same from their management teams.

The wording of the preceding first NACD principle in the 2023 version regressed back to a seemingly pure risk focus without consideration of opportunities. I reiterate—insist on including a guiding principle that emphasizes your pivot from thinking about cybersecurity only in the context of risks and "managing the downside" to include opportunities and "managing the upside."

As suggested in Chapter 9, perhaps something like the following: "ECRM is viewed as a business value creator a means to create a competitive advantage. Business value is created from treating our cyber risks and leveraging our cyber opportunities." It is important to emphasize value creation.

Do not simply adopt these principles as presented. Take the time to discuss these and other principles and use them to create what makes the most sense for your organization, given where you are in your ECRM journey.

Implementation Step #4: Establish and Document Strategic Business and ECRM Objectives

In Chapter 4, I cited a definition of strategy as *"the means to create economic value by gaining competitive advantage through a unique value proposition."*[5] Specific objectives support a strategy. Strategic goals or objectives may be defined as specific financial and non-financial objectives and results a company aims to achieve over a particular period, usually the next three to five years.[6]

Strategic Business Objectives

Based on your industry; your stage as a company; your unique vision, mission, strategy, values, and services; and your regulatory requirements, among other considerations, you will typically articulate 10–12 strategic objectives. These will likely include financial (e.g., increase revenue by x%, lower the cost of capital, etc.), market (e.g., expand product offerings, co-develop new offerings with customers), innovation (e.g., protect IP with patents, introduce a new innovative service), customer service (e.g., increase account management, increase net promoter scores by x%), operational (e.g., increase factory utilization by x%, increase business resilience), or perhaps regulatory (e.g., complete an NYDFS-required security risk assessment, ensure compliance with new SEC cyber disclosure rules).

Consider whether you can find a cyber strength in your ECRM program that you can use to help your customers' strategic goals. Can you *"create economic value by gaining competitive advantage through a unique value proposition"* for your customers using that strength?

Whatever your strategic objectives are, they must be documented and used by your ECRM Working Group to ensure your ECRM Program and Cybersecurity Strategy aligns with these strategic business objectives. That is, your cybersecurity strategy fully supports the business strategy.

Strategic ECRM Objectives

You should consider strategic ECRM objectives in two categories: a) those that directly support the business strategic objectives and b) those that support the establishing, implementing, and maturing of your ECRM program.

To support business strategic objectives, leverage the new Govern function in the NIST Cybersecurity Framework 2.0 Core. It emphasizes the importance of articulating your ECRM and cybersecurity objectives only after you have set the organizational context by understanding the corporate mission, legal obligations, compliance requirements, and critical strategic goals.[7]

You should also use your enterprise-wide risk and opportunity assessment, discussed under Implementation Step #8 in the following, to identify cyber risks and opportunities related to these business objectives. For example, if one of your operational, strategic objectives is to improve resilience, set a strategic ECRM objective to conduct your risk and opportunity assessment on those information assets most critical to providing your most profitable services. As another example, if one of your strategic business objectives is to introduce a new innovative service, leverage your risk and opportunity assessment to ensure your ECRM and cybersecurity strengths are packaged and marketed as part of the service.

To establish, implement, and mature your program, your C-suite and board need to develop strategic ECRM objectives that address five critical core capabilities of your organization: governance, people, processes, technology, and engagement. Focusing on this specific and finite set of capabilities keeps it high level and sets the stage for the ECRM transformation your organization is about to undertake. Establishing and working toward strategic objectives in these five areas will help your organization grow and mature a cyber-risk- and cyber-opportunity-aware culture that supports your ECRM program. A sample strategic ECRM objective around governance would be requiring that ECRM be part of strategic decision-making and ongoing business planning. A strategic ECRM objective around people would be to establish a high degree of knowledge of your chosen ECRM Framework, Process, and Maturity Model among the people throughout your organization responsible for execution. A strategic ECRM objective around engagement would be to ensure line-of-business, process, and functional leaders are engaged in the ECRM program.

Implementation Step #5: Set the Scope of Your ECRM Program

As of this writing, the NIST Cybersecurity Framework 2.0 is not finalized, so I will refer to version 1.1 of the NIST "Framework for Improving Critical Infrastructure Cybersecurity."[8] It includes section 3.2 on implementation, "Establishing or Improving a Cybersecurity Program," and the first step is Prioritize and Scope. That implementation step calls for organizations to identify business objectives and priorities to inform decision-making around cybersecurity implementation and the scope of systems and assets to be included.

In Chapter 9, I discussed several dimensions by which scope can be set, including business units within your organization, geography, business functions (e.g., finance, manufacturing, human resources, etc.), the criticality of business processes, an entity's contribution to profitability, external requirements, etc. To set the scope of your ECRM program, you must also consider your strategic business objectives and external requirements from your legal, regulatory, and contractual obligations.

Implementation Step #6: Establish and Document Your ECRM Budget Philosophy

Joe Biden is attributed with saying, "Don't tell me what you value, show me your budget, and I'll tell you what you value."[9] Politics aside, the statement makes an important point and implies you show how much you value your ECRM Program and Cybersecurity Strategy work by way of your budget.

In Chapter 5, I discussed ECRM funding at length, called for a change in thinking and philosophy, and guided the building of an ECRM Budget Philosophy. I presented a set of six maxims to discuss and debate to help formulate a budget philosophy that works for your organization. As a quick reminder, I labeled these maxims that I presented: "part of the ordinary course of doing business," "risk-based expenditure," "an ounce of prevention," "business ownership," "security-by-design," and "business enabler."

I also discussed what I believe to be the "Single Most Important Cybersecurity Question for the Board to Ask." Whether OpEx, CapEx, or a resource allocation, the question is, "Will this expenditure reduce our risks or create business value?"

Use the maxims and this fundamental question to help in setting your ECRM Budget Philosophy. In any case, where you land must suit your organization's needs. Most importantly, you must take up the ECRM Budget Philosophy subject entirely and transparently.

Implementation Step #7: Formally Adopt Your ECRM Framework, Process, and Maturity Model

In Chapter 10, I characterized your ECRM Framework, Process, and Maturity Model as three critical building blocks in establishing your ECRM Program and Cybersecurity Strategy. With proper adoption and implementation, they enable your organization to conduct its ECRM work and incorporate ECRM into ongoing strategic decision-making and business planning.

As a reminder, a framework provides a high-level model that assists you in defining your desired cyber risk and opportunity management outcomes in alignment with your overall organization vision, mission, strategy, values, and services. The framework that I recommend is the Cybersecurity Framework created by NIST.[10] The ECRM Framework defines the "what" of your ECRM program: What outcomes are you setting out to achieve?

The ECRM Process, on the other hand, describes the "how" of your ECRM program. What specific, repeatable actions will your organization take to achieve the cybersecurity outcomes you described in your framework? The cyber risk and opportunity management process I recommend is provided in "Managing Information Security Risk" (NIST Special Publication 800-39).[11]

A maturity model is a "tool that helps people assess the current effectiveness of a person or group and supports figuring out what capabilities they need to acquire next to improve their performance."[12] Another way of describing how a maturity model is used is that it helps the organization identify its current maturity level in relation to specific capabilities (e.g., governance, people, process, technology, and engagement), facilitates the establishment of goals for performance improvement, and helps organizations set priorities for improvements aimed at achieving the desired maturity level. I discussed commonly used maturity models and cases where some organizations use tools that don't quite meet the definition of a maturity model. You must sort this out and adopt a model that best meets your needs. Measuring program maturity (not controls list maturity) is the third critical ECRM program building block. NIST lets me down a bit in this area because I cannot recommend a specific NIST maturity model. At the same time, in the absence of a particular NIST maturity model, you might consider an adaptation of the NIST Cybersecurity Framework using COBIT levels that some have offered.[13]

Implementation Step #8: Conduct a Comprehensive, NIST-Based Enterprise-Wide Risk and Opportunity Assessment

Underscoring the importance of "managing the downside," "managing the expected," and "managing the upside," when you conduct your risk assessment, you must remember that it is an opportunity assessment as well. What are the opportunities to leverage your ECRM and cybersecurity strengths to increase customer trust and brand loyalty, improve social responsibility, drive revenue growth, lower the cost of capital, attract higher-quality investments, create competitive advantage, attract and retain talent, or facilitate M&A activity?

The reason to conduct an enterprise-wide, comprehensive risk and opportunity assessment is simple. Before making decisions regarding cyber risk and opportunity management investments and taking meaningful action to manage your organization's cyber risks or leverage your cyber opportunities, you must first identify and prioritize your unique risks. Risk identification begins with conducting a comprehensive inventory of your data, systems, and devices and then assessing the risks and opportunities associated with each asset.

To conduct your risk and opportunity assessment, I recommended and discussed using NIST SP 800-30 "Guide for Conducting Risk Assessments"[14] as your guide and starting point in Chapter 12. There is no doubt that the NIST risk assessment process is focused on "managing the downside." When conducting your risk assessment for your ECRM scope of assets, remember that you must focus on the opportunities in "managing the upside" also and adapt the process accordingly.

One final thought is that you might not want to do an enterprise-wide risk and opportunity assessment on your own, at least not the first time. The data on the failure to complete comprehensive, enterprise-wide risk assessments is very compelling. Comprehensive NIST-based risk assessments are not being performed very well at all. I encourage C-suite executives and board members to seek outside assistance completing their first NIST-based risk and opportunity assessments for their teams. Risk and opportunity assessment skills are not typically part of even the best security organizations. Organizations often engage outside partners to assist with functions outside the organization's core activities. Risk and opportunity assessment and management is one such area. Partnering with an experienced, reputable organization can help you complete your first risk and opportunity assessment and management steps efficiently and effectively and help you achieve your cyber risk and opportunity management goals.

Implementation Step #9: Establish Your Cyber Risk Appetite, Opportunity Threshold, and Complete Risk and Opportunity Treatment

Conducting a comprehensive, enterprise-wide risk and opportunity assessment described in Implementation Step #8 is not the end of the story. As discussed in Chapter 8, setting your risk appetite and opportunity threshold and requiring cyber scenarios to be rated when new business initiatives or programs are planned is essential. Risk appetite is generally defined in the context of "managing the downside" as the level of risk an organization is willing to assume to achieve a desired result. Opportunity threshold is defined in the context of "managing the upside" and involves creating business value.

You can also adapt the risk appetite concept to establish your opportunity threshold. That is, when your risk and opportunity assessment produces stellar results in the form of low rating scores, you can think of these low risks as potential high opportunities. If you set your risk appetite at 15 on a 1–25 rating scale, you would avoid, mitigate, or transfer risks with a rating of 15 or above 15. Suppose you set your opportunity rating at 8. In that case, you should carefully review all items in your risk and opportunity register with a value of 8 or below for leverage to increase customer trust and brand loyalty, improve social responsibility, drive revenue growth, lower the cost of capital, attract higher-quality investments, create competitive advantage, attract and retain talent, or facilitate M&A activity. That is, create value or a competitive advantage in some way.

Setting, communicating, and adjusting your organization's risk appetites and opportunity threshold is one of the most important C-suite and board responsibilities concerning your organization's ECRM program. It provides overarching guidance to the teams in identifying and prioritizing risks and opportunities.

Risk and opportunity treatment is at the heart of your ECRM program. Decisions made here drive investments. An example of risk avoidance would be to stop allowing access to non-company, public Wi-Fi networks. An example of risk mitigation would be to implement multifactor authentication. An example of risk transfer would be increasing an organization's cyber liability insurance limits to help cover potential damages.

An example of opportunity leverage would be demonstrating the robustness of your privileged access management (PAM) solution to your credit agencies to help lower the cost of capital. Another opportunity leverage opportunity would be packaging and selling a SaaS solution your organization has developed for SEC materiality assessments.

Implementation Step #10: Formally Document Your ECRM Program and Cybersecurity Strategy

You should document your ECRM Program and Cybersecurity Strategy during your implementation process. Throughout the book, I emphasized the importance of documentation in standards, plans, policies, procedures, business continuity plans, incident response plans, and training programs, among other artifacts. Your documentation shows the effort you put forth as an organization and may serve you well as part of an affirmative defense. On an operational level, it is your first line of defense as it provides clarity to everyone in the organization as to what the organization is trying to achieve, how it will achieve its goals, and what is expected of everyone.

Appendix E includes a sample table of contents for your ECRM Program and Cybersecurity Strategy documentation. Whatever outline or document management solution you use, maintain current up-to-date documentation, past versions, and version control.

Conclusion

There are many possible actions to launch your transformational ECRM Program and Cybersecurity Strategy initiative. The ones provided here are based on my experience working with C-suites and boards. The approach to establishing, implementing, and maturing such a program is not one-size-fits-all. For some, the implementation steps provided in this chapter provide a perfect fit and plan. For others, perhaps the best initial first step is to complete a baseline inventory and assessment of your current ECRM projects. Consider the maturity of your organization at a high level vis-à-vis the core capabilities of governance, people, process, technology, and engagement.

In all cases, as they say, don't just stand there—do something. Your cyber risks are not lessening, and your cyber opportunities are only likely increasing.

Questions Management and the Board Should Ask and Discuss

1. Of the implementation steps presented in this chapter, which are the most important for your organization at this time?

2. Do you have a formal enough ECRM governance structure to assure a successful transformational ECRM effort?

3. What is your internal ability to undertake the implementation steps presented in this chapter?

4. How will you conduct the work to decide on the scope of your ECRM program? What internal and external factors will you consider?

5. What team will lead your effort to establish and document your ECRM Budget Philosophy?

6. What criteria will you use to formally select and adopt your ECRM Framework, Process, and Maturity Model?

7. How urgent and important is it for your organization to conduct a comprehensive, NIST-based enterprise-wide risk and opportunity assessment?

8. Have you set, documented, and communicated your cyber risk appetite and opportunity threshold?

9. What is the state of your ECRM Program and Cybersecurity Strategy documentation? Will it meet the regulatory requirements with which you must comply?

Endnotes

1. BrainyQuote. "*Cheers to a new year and another chance for us to get it right.*" (n.d.) Accessed August 31, 2023. Available at https://www.brainyquote. com/quotes/oprah_winfrey_676234

2. Clinton, Larry, Higgins, Josh, and van der Oord, Friso. National Association of Corporate Directors (NACD). "Cyber-Risk Oversight 2020: Key Principles and Practical Guidance for Corporate Boards." February 2022. https://nacdonline.org/ insights/publications.cfm?ItemNumber=67298

3. NACD. "Principles for Board Governance of Cyber Risk". March 2021. Available at https:// www.nacdonline.org/applications/ secure/?FileID=319863

4. National Association of Corporate Directors (NACD) and Internet Security Alliance (ISA). *2023 Director's Handbook on Cyber-Risk Oversight.* March 20, 2023. Available at https://www.nacdonline.org/ insights/publications.cfm?ItemNumber=74777

5. Blue Ribbon Commission Series. National
    Association of Corporate Directors
    (NACD). "Report of the NACD Blue Ribbon
    Commission on Strategy Development."
    October 13, 2014. Available at `https://www.`
    `nacdonline.org/insights/publications.`
    `cfm?ItemNumber=12161&aitrk=nacd-1`

6. "Strategic goals." BDC. (n.d.) Accessed July 18, 2023.
    Available at `https://www.bdc.ca/en/articles-`
    `tools/entrepreneur-toolkit/templates-`
    `business-guides/glossary/strategic-goals`

7. National Institute of Standards and Technology
    (NIST). "Discussion Draft of the NIST Cybersecurity
    Framework 2.0 Core." April 24, 2023. Accessed July
    16, 2023. Available at `https://www.nist.gov/`
    `system/files/documents/2023/04/24/NIST%20`
    `Cybersecurity%20Framework%202.0%20Core%20`
    `Discussion%20Draft%204-2023%20final.pdf`

8. National Institute of Standards and Technology
    (NIST). "Framework for Improving Critical
    Infrastructure Cybersecurity, Version 1.1." April
    16, 2018. Accessed December 16, 2019. `https://`
    `nvlpubs.nist.gov/nistpubs/CSWP/NIST.`
    `CSWP.04162018.pdf`

9. Biden, Joe. Goodreads. "Don't tell me what you
    value, show me your budget, and I'll tell you what
    you value." (n.d.) Accessed July 18, 2023. Available at
    `https://www.goodreads.com/quotes/10478-don-`
    `t-tell-me-what-you-value-show-me-your-budget`

10. National Institute of Standards and Technology (NIST). " Framework for Improving Critical Infrastructure Cybersecurity, Version 1.1." April 16, 2018. Accessed April 12, 2020. `https://nvlpubs.nist.gov/nistpubs/CSWP/NIST.CSWP.04162018.pdf`

11. National Institute of Standards and Technology (NIST). NIST Special Publication 800-39. "Managing Information Security Risk." March 2011. Accessed November 11, 2019. `https://nvlpubs.nist.gov/nistpubs/Legacy/SP/nistspecialpublication800-39.pdf`

12. Fowler, Martin. MaturityModel. August 26, 2014. Accessed October 24, 2019. `https://martinfowler.com/bliki/MaturityModel.html#targetText=A%20maturity%20model%20is%20a,order%20to%20improve%20their%20performance.`

13. Charles, Foster. "Why NIST CSF Maturity is Important for All Organizations." July 26, 2022. Accessed July 18, 2023. Available at `https://blog.charlesit.com/why-nist-csf-maturity-is-important-for-all-organizations`

14. National Institute of Standards and Technology (NIST). NIST Special Publication 800-30, Revision 1. "Guide for Conducting Risk Assessments." September 2012. Accessed July 18, 2023. `https://nvlpubs.nist.gov/nistpubs/Legacy/SP/nistspecialpublication800-30r1.pdf`

APPENDIX A

What to Look for in an ECRM Company and Solution

Some of the content found in this appendix first appeared in *Stop the Cyber Bleeding*.[1] It is now updated to reflect the cybersecurity challenges, opportunities, and changes we've experienced over the last three years.

In this book and *Stop the Cyber Bleeding*, I outlined the key concepts C-suite executives and board members need to understand to provide leadership and oversight for their organization's ECRM efforts. I have offered specific, tangible, and actionable recommendations to get started. As C-suite executives and board members have become more engaged in their organization's ECRM program, they often need to augment their organization's internal resources with outside support to establish, implement, and mature a comprehensive and effective ECRM program. Outside assistance is usually required for organizations pivoting from "managing the downside" to also "managing the upside."

---

[1] Chaput, Bob. *Stop the Cyber Bleeding: What Healthcare Executives and Board Members Must Know About Enterprise Cyber Risk Management (ECRM)*. 2021. Clearwater. Available at https://amzn.to/33qr17n

ECRM is a specialty area that requires expertise beyond what is typically found in most organizational IT, security, or risk management departments. Your IT and risk management departments may be excellent at meeting your organization's tactical and operational needs. Still, they may not have the time, experience, or strategic expertise to establish an ECRM program focused on business value creation.

If this is the case for your organization, you may consider hiring a third-party service provider to help you build your organization's ECRM program. But beware since ECRM consultants and service providers are not regulated or evaluated by a reliable, objective third party. This absence of rating systems means that anyone can call themselves a "cyber risk and opportunity management expert." Therefore, it is incumbent on your organization to exercise due diligence before contracting with a cyber risk and opportunity management consultant or service provider.

The following considerations and questions will help you evaluate the depth of expertise, experience, and service you may expect from the prospective service providers you are considering.

Alignment with Your Organization's Strategic ECRM Objectives

Building an effective ECRM program begins with analyzing your organization's unique vision, mission, strategy, values, and services (i.e., organizational context). Next, you identify all the information assets that enable you to achieve your mission. It is critically important to use the context of your organization to identify your organization's "crown jewel" assets. Identifying your organization's most valuable information assets is critical to establishing an ECRM program that prioritizes the protection of those assets and creating business value.

Evaluate prospective service providers who understand executive leadership and board oversight. Ensure, for example, that they know the three core board responsibilities: (1) talent management, (2) strategy, and (3) risk management. Discuss their views on how your ECRM Program and Cybersecurity Strategy can create a competitive advantage for you. Test their abilities to treat ECRM as a value creator and business enabler.

If a prospective service provider comes to you with a one-size-fits-all security checklist, I recommend you look elsewhere for help. Likewise, keep looking if a prospective service provider does not offer a risk and opportunity-based ECRM program approach that can be tailored to your unique organization. A one-size-fits-all checklist or a controls-based process will not protect your organization's unique assets, create a competitive advantage, or align with your organization's specific, strategic business objectives.

The following questions can help you determine whether a prospective provider is offering a cookie-cutter approach or an authentic, risk- and opportunity-based system:

1. Will the prospective service provider's proposed ECRM solution be adaptable to and aligned with your organization's unique vision, mission, strategy, values, and services?

2. How will the prospective service provider facilitate identifying opportunities to create value, enable your business to grow, and develop a competitive advantage?

3. Is the prospective service provider proposing a risk-based ECRM approach or a controls checklist? If they offer a controls checklist, I suggest you walk away and keep looking!

4. Will the prospective service provider's proposed
    ECRM Process result in identifying your
    organization's data, systems, and devices?

5. Will the prospective service provider's proposed
    ECRM Process result in identifying all risks to your
    organization's data, systems, and devices?

6. Will the prospective service provider's proposed
    ECRM Process result in identifying all opportunities
    to leverage your cybersecurity strengths?

7. Is the prospective service provider offering a
    comprehensive, asset-based, enterprise-wide,
    NIST- or ISO-based risk assessment an essential,
    foundational component of your organization's
    cyber risk and opportunity management work?
    (This question is a canary-in-the-coal-mine
    question that you must answer affirmatively.)

8. Will the prospective service provider's proposed
    ECRM solution result in practical, tangible
    deliverables that your organization can use as
    evidence that you are exercising your fiduciary
    responsibility?

9. How will the prospective service provider present
    cybersecurity opportunities to leverage along with
    cybersecurity risks to treat?

Competency and Expertise

Competency and expertise are essential table-stakes qualities in any prospective service provider. But how do you determine whether a potential service provider has the skills, knowledge, and experience to establish, implement, and mature an effective ECRM Program and Cybersecurity Strategy successfully and efficiently? Asking the following questions can help you determine the nature and depth of their competence and expertise:

1. Is the prospective service provider's ECRM methodology based on an industry-standard process and framework, such as NIST's Managing Information Security Risk[2] and the NIST Cybersecurity Framework[3]?

2. Does the prospective service provider's specific risk and opportunity assessment solution and methodology produce as output both cybersecurity risks and cybersecurity opportunities?

3. Does the prospective service provider demonstrate industry experience in regulatory compliance relevant to your organization's needs?

---

[2] National Institute of Standards and Technology. NIST Special Publication 800-39. "Managing Information Security Risk." March 2011. Accessed April 12, 2020. https://nvlpubs.nist.gov/nistpubs/Legacy/SP/ nistspecialpublication800-39.pdf

[3] National Institute of Standards and Technology (NIST). "Framework for Improving Critical Infrastructure Cybersecurity, Version 1.1." April 16, 2018. Accessed April 12, 2020. https://nvlpubs.nist.gov/nistpubs/CSWP/NIST. CSWP.04162018.pdf

4. What are the qualifications of the prospective service provider's cyber risk and opportunity management professionals?

   a. What are their qualifications in terms of expertise (e.g., what industry-recognized certifications and credentials have they earned?)

   b. What are their qualifications in terms of experience (e.g., how many previous ECRM program implementation projects have they led?)

   c. Have they established ECRM programs in similarly sized organizations as yours, in your industry sector or subsector?

   d. Have they created business value by leveraging cybersecurity strengths?

5. Does the prospective service provider have evidence that relevant regulators have accepted work products for previous ECRM clients during enforcement actions?

6. Does the prospective service provider have evidence that work products created value, enabled business, or developed a competitive advantage?

Capability and Capacity to Scale to Enterprise

Capability and capacity speak to the depth and power of the resources the prospective service provider has to offer to scale and extend to serve an organization of your size. Cyber risk and opportunity management must be scalable and extensible to your organization to be effective. Therefore, a prospective service provider must be able to facilitate enterprise-wide deployment of your ECRM program.

1. Does the prospective service provider have the ability and leadership sophistication to engage in appropriate talent management, strategy, and risk and opportunity management discussions with the C-suite and board?

2. Does the prospective service provider offer all the tools and services needed to establish, implement, and mature a comprehensive ECRM system (i.e., a proven methodology based on industry standards, comprehensive consulting services, and a software solution)?

3. Does the prospective service provider offer a scalable software solution to facilitate and automate an ECRM program? (See Appendix B for more information about choosing an ECRM software solution.)

4. Does the prospective service provider's solution provide multiple reporting levels and delegation of responsibility (e.g., by facility, line-of-business, process, etc.) to enable engagement and accountability across your entire enterprise?

5. Does the prospective service provider's solution facilitate the continuous improvement (i.e., maturity) of your ECRM program?

6. Does the prospective service provider's solution facilitate ongoing monitoring and change management to adapt your ECRM program as your organization's vision, mission, strategy, values, and services evolve?

7. Should your organization decide to proceed independently after an initial engagement, does the prospective service provider's solution equip your organization to become self-sufficient in conducting ECRM?

Industry Commitment

Cyber risk and opportunity management is critical across all industries—manufacturing, financial services, utilities, education, transportation, and healthcare. As such, common approaches and best practices (often as articulated by NIST) apply across all industries. Cyber risk and opportunity management within each sector can be nuanced due to each industry's unique regulatory environment (e.g., NYDFS, CMMC, FERPA, HIPAA, etc.), distinctive ecosystem or supply chain, and what's at stake (e.g., in healthcare, possibly patients' lives). Therefore, prospective service providers must demonstrate expertise and commitment to your industry.

1. How has the prospective service provider given back to your industry (e.g., through industry association participation, NIST collaboration, and advocacy group support)?

2. What is the depth and breadth of the prospective service provider's ECRM experience in your industry?

    a. How many years have they worked in your industry?

    b. How many different clients have they served in your industry?

    c. Have they published customer success stories about business value creation?

3. How has the prospective service provider been a thought leader, contributing to increased awareness and education about cyber risk and opportunity management within your industry? For example, does the provider educate, inform, and give back to your industry, above and beyond the commercial services they provide?

Reputation

Henry Ford once said, "You can't build a reputation on what you are going to do." The reputation of your prospective service provider matters because it represents what the company has already accomplished. That is, reputation speaks to promises kept, not promises made.

1. Do peers in your industry have any experience with the service provider you are considering? If so, was their experience a good one?

2. Has the prospective service provider earned significant industry recognition, endorsements, or awards for cyber risk mitigation and leveraging cyber opportunities?

3. How long has your prospective service provider
    worked in cyber risk and opportunity management?
    Do they have years of experience, or are they a
    brand-new company with a bit of history?

4. If the prospective service provider has a history
    of working with organizations like yours, what
    has been their ECRM track record with those
    organizations? That is, have the client companies
    of the prospective service provider suffered any
    severe data breaches since the engagement of the
    prospective provider's cyber risk and opportunity
    management services?

5. Does the prospective service provider have a
    track record for implementing robust defensive
    cybersecurity strategies and value-creating leverage
    opportunities?

Customer Service

An effective service provider will have an established process for
implementation and measuring customer satisfaction. ECRM is a journey,
not a destination, so you will want to engage the services of a provider
whose methodology indicates a collaborative, long-term, business-
building partnership rather than a once-and-done approach.

1. Has the prospective service provider offered a clear
    and measurable description of the tangible ECRM
    work products (i.e., risk mitigation and opportunity
    leverage) your organization will receive because of
    the engagement?

2. Do the tangible ECRM work products described include those that create shareholder value, drive growth, enable business, or produce competitive advantage?

3. Has the prospective service provider offered a timeline, including benchmarks and a transparent process for communication, so that they will fully inform your organization about every step in the ECRM implementation process and every milestone achieved?

4. Has the prospective service provider identified the individuals who will lead the partnership with your organization and identified the means of communication with those individuals? Do these individuals have the business savvy to generate a competitive advantage for your organization?

5. Is the prospective service provider well-known in the industry for customer satisfaction? What is the evidence? Have they been recognized and rewarded by independent evaluators? If they have been so recognized, what kinds of customer comments have they garnered?

6. Does the prospective service provider establish a formal customer feedback process to track customer satisfaction? For example, do they conduct annual or periodic surveys or reviews to collect customer feedback? How do they incorporate that feedback into their solutions and services?

7. Can the prospective service provider provide you with independently verifiable customer references that can discuss their creation of business value beyond cybersecurity defense? Are they willing to provide you with contact information for previous and existing customers?

I advise finding the answers to all these questions before your organization contracts with a cyber risk and opportunity management service provider. Executing due diligence at the front end will help ensure that the resulting engagement with a cyber risk and opportunity management solution provider will result in an ECRM program that reduces risk and increases opportunity leverage for your organization.

APPENDIX B

Enterprise Cyber Risk Management Software (ECRMS)

Some of the content found in this appendix first appeared in *Stop the Cyber Bleeding.*[1] It is now updated to reflect the cybersecurity challenges, opportunities, and changes we've experienced over the last three years.

The right software can simplify and facilitate conducting enterprise-wide risk and opportunity assessment and cyber risk management. The wrong software—or worse, no cyber risk management software solution—makes it nearly impossible to establish, implement, and mature an effective ECRM Program and Cybersecurity Strategy.

I've seen organizations try to use office software suites—word processors, presentation software, or spreadsheets—to try to establish, implement, and mature their ECRM program. The work products from these ostensible solutions are typically dead on arrival, as they are no longer relevant when these generic tools have been customized enough to accept the data and all the data is entered. The information is outdated

---

[1] Chaput, Bob. *Stop the Cyber Bleeding: What Healthcare Executives and Board Members Must Know About Enterprise Cyber Risk Management (ECRM).* 2021. Clearwater. Available at https://amzn.to/33qr17n

© Bob Chaput 2024
B. Chaput, *Enterprise Cyber Risk Management as a Value Creator,*
https://doi.org/10.1007/979-8-8688-0094-8

by the time the document is complete. Likewise, governance, risk, and compliance (GRC) platforms are equally unsuited to ECRM. GRC platforms aren't architected to provide the conceptual infrastructure, address assets, threats, and vulnerabilities or drive risk management workflows to support an ECRM Program and Cybersecurity Strategy.

ECRM in all industries is complex and multi-layered. Risk and opportunity assessment and risk management must not only aim to protect your organization. They must also identify opportunities that can be leveraged to create value and grow your business. It isn't possible to conduct and document a NIST-based risk assessment and implement an ECRM Program and Cybersecurity Strategy without an appropriate software solution. Establishing and managing an ECRM program without the right software tool would be like using an Excel spreadsheet to track a fleet of over-the-road trucks, manage inpatient care at a hospital, or facilitate customer accounting in a brokerage firm. It just doesn't work.

Many competing vendors offer software to simplify and document risk and opportunity assessment and management tasks. These vendors include GRC vendors, who typically deliver an open platform on which you must build your solution. To be clear, a platform—GRC or otherwise—means that your organization will be doing a lot of additional work, designing and "programming" the solution before the actual work of ECRM can begin.

Therefore, before purchasing a specific software package, you must exercise due diligence to ensure that your chosen solution will support all risk and opportunity management requirements out of the box—that is, identifying what parts of your ECRM program create value, enable business, or create a competitive advantage. For example, if you have a strong identity access management program that protects your banking clients, identify that strength and use it in marketing.

A comprehensive ECRMS solution must include all the components of an ECRM program to serve your organization. That means functionality that supports complete risk and opportunity assessments, compliance assessments, and adoption of the NIST methodologies. In addition, like any helpful solution designed for enterprise-wide use, the solution should be user-friendly, include accessible dashboards, offer actionable reporting capabilities, facilitate enterprise-wide ECRM collaboration, and provide for C-suite and board governance.

The following questions will help you evaluate whether the ECRMS solution you are considering is comprehensive enough to support your organization's ECRM Program and Cybersecurity Strategy.

Risk and Opportunity Assessment Features and Functionality

As I emphasized throughout this book, the only effective means of establishing an ECRM program is to take a risk- and opportunity-based approach. That means inventorying all your organization's information assets, considering all reasonably anticipated threats and vulnerabilities, and identifying all your cybersecurity strengths.

Essential questions to ask about risk and opportunity assessment features and functionality include the following:

1. Does the ECRMS solution support enterprise-wide risk and opportunity assessment by offering

    a. The scalable capacity to inventory all ePHI assets and components across your enterprise?

    b. The ability to associate specific, reasonably anticipated threats and vulnerabilities with each asset-component category? (Note this functionality should include pre-populated threats and vulnerabilities related to assets and the ability to catalog unique-to-your-organization threats and vulnerabilities.)

    c.   A method to identify your cybersecurity strengths?

    d.   The ability to differentiate and highlight risks and opportunities?

2.   Does the ECRMS solution facilitate the establishment of your organization's risk appetite and opportunity threshold?

3.   Does the ECRMS solution provide an enterprise-wide view of your top exposures?

4.   Does the ECRMS solution provide an enterprise-wide view of your top opportunities that leverage your cybersecurity strengths?

5.   Does the ECRMS solution offer the functionality to manage risk remediation at the individual asset or asset-component level?

6.   Does the ECRMS solution provide the functionality to manage and leverage opportunities identified in risk and opportunity assessments?

7.   Does the ECRMS solution facilitate ongoing, continuous ECRM work with version control?

8.   Does the ECRMS solution automate the completion of regulatory compliance gap assessments?

Compliance and Technical Testing Assessment Features and Functionality

A good ECRM Program and Cybersecurity Strategy includes compliance, cyber risk, and opportunity management. In addition to comprehensive risk and opportunity assessment, many regulations require that organizations conduct periodic technical and nontechnical evaluations of their compliance with those regulations. For example, the HIPAA Security Rule requires both.[2] Your ECRMS solution should be able to support these nontechnical evaluations (sometimes called compliance gap assessments) that align with the various regulations you must comply with.

1. Does the ECRMS solution enable you to assess your organization's compliance posture against all regulations with which your organization must comply?

2. Does the ECRMS solution enable you to identify the gaps in compliance with these regulations?

3. Does the ECRMS solution enable you to manage remediation actions with these regulations?

Cybersecurity Framework Support

For reasons detailed in Appendix C, I highly recommend adopting the National Institute of Standards and Technology (NIST) Cybersecurity Framework. A comprehensive ECRMS solution should support your organization's adoption of the NIST Cybersecurity Framework.

---

[2] Evaluation Standard. 45 CFR §164.308(a)(8) (Security Standards for the Protection of Electronic Protected Health Information, Administrative Safeguards). Available at https://www.ecfr.gov/cgi-bin/text-idx?SID=b3f494 6246df559b9785dc48625e59a4&mc=true&node=se45.2.164_1308&rgn=div8

1. Does the ECRMS solution support a business-focused operationalization and adoption of the NIST Cybersecurity Framework?

2. Does the ECRMS solution incorporate all aspects of the structure and language of the NIST Cybersecurity Framework?

3. Does the ECRMS solution enable you to assess and document the current state of your organization's adoption of the NIST Cybersecurity Framework?

4. Does the ECRMS solution enable you to set the desired future state of your organization's adoption of the NIST Cybersecurity Framework and assess the gaps and opportunities?

5. Does the ECRMS solution enable you to define your goals for NIST Cybersecurity Framework adoption (e.g., to set your desired tier, as articulated in the Framework)?

6. Does the ECRMS solution enable you to manage and document your progress toward your NIST Cybersecurity Framework adoption goals?

General Additional Features and Functionality

In addition to offering support for compliance and cyber risk and opportunity management and supporting the adoption of a cybersecurity framework, your ECRMS solution should also enable efficient ECRM by providing the following features and functionality:

1. Does the ECRMS solution provider offer unlimited, complimentary training in using their solution?

2. Does the ECRMS solution offer accessible, user-friendly dashboards that provide actionable insight into

   a. Your organization's progress on risk identification and assessment?

   b. Your organization's progress on opportunity identification and assessment?

   c. Your organization's most profound and likely threats?

   d. Your organization's most critical vulnerabilities?

   e. Your organization's control deficiencies?

   f. Your organization's real-time remediation/risk mitigation efforts?

   g. Your organization's progress leveraging opportunities where there are strengths in your ECRM Program and Cybersecurity Strategy?

3. Does the ECRMS solution offer dashboards and reporting functionality that support leadership-level ECRM governance and oversight (i.e., dashboards and reports that provide valuable cyber risk and opportunity information to C-suite executives and board members)?

4. Does the ECRMS solution offer dashboards and reporting functionality that support tactical-level ECRM program activities (i.e., dashboards and reports that provide valuable information to other

managers and professionals engaged in risk and opportunity management at the facility, division, or department level)?

5. Does the ECRMS solution include dashboards that feature

    a. Configurable views?

    b. Configurable reporting capabilities?

    c. Real-time analytics capabilities?

6. Does the ECRMS solution facilitate enterprise-wide collaboration via the following functionalities and workflow tools?

    a. The ability to assign tasks (e.g., control evaluations, risk mitigation action items, opportunity action items, etc.)

    b. The ability of users to view and update work performed toward the completion of assigned tasks

    c. The ability of risk managers to monitor users' progress toward task completion via real-time reports

7. Does the ECRMS solution provide for cascading/inheritance of data capabilities so that parent entities can share information with child entities, thus reducing duplicative data entry and analysis?

A Word About Cloud-Based Software Solutions, Software-as-a-Service (SaaS)

Cloud-based software solutions (Software-as-a-Service, or SaaS) offer many advantages over on-premise software systems. They typically entail a lower total cost of ownership (TOC) because organizations do not have to purchase and maintain the hardware to host them. ECRMS is particularly well suited to be a cloud-based solution. Using a cloud-based solution shortens implementation time—your organization can put the solution to work soon after signing a contract. This quick start-up is a plus, considering the urgency with which ECRM needs to be implemented. In addition, the cyber threat landscape is changing constantly. A cloud-based solution can be updated (with overall feature and functionality upgrades, as well as risk-related data and algorithms) regularly and automatically. For these reasons, a cloud-based SaaS solution makes more sense for ECRMS.

1. Is the ECRMS solution offered as Software-as-a-Service (SaaS) to enable you to realize lower TOC, faster implementation and updates, anytime-anywhere access, and other SaaS benefits?

2. Is the ECRMS solution accessible through multiple browsers and devices, anytime, anywhere on the globe?

Reputation

The software industry is replete with stories of so-called vaporware: software products that are billed as offering every feature and functionality your organization might desire. However, after implementation, it became clear that some of those claims were aspirational and those features and functions aren't in place yet. That's why verifying a vendor's reputation is crucial in the due diligence.

1. Do your peers in the industry have any experience with the ECRMS solution you are considering? If so, was their experience a good one?

2. Has the specific ECRMS solution you are considering earned any significant industry recognition, endorsements, or awards?

3. How long has the ECRMS solution you are considering been on the market? Has it been used in the industry long enough to prove its value? Or is it a beta version, which may be riddled with unresolved problems?

4. Can the vendor provide you with independently verifiable customer references? Are they willing to provide you with contact information for previous and existing customers?

Customer Service

It is a truism that even the most carefully designed, so-called turnkey software solutions require more than the flip of a switch to implement effectively. This truism especially comes to life if you acquire a GRC platform. With a valid out-of-the-box ECRMS solution, you will need excellent support but not a development team to create a solution. By now, it should be clear that establishing an ECRM Program and Cybersecurity Strategy requires much more than simply populating a database or ticking off boxes on a controls checklist. Therefore, your ECRMS solution vendor must provide strong customer service support.

1. Is the vendor of the ECRMS solution well-known in the industry for customer satisfaction? What is the evidence? For example, have independent, third-party evaluators recognized and rewarded the vendor? If they have been so recognized, what kinds of customer comments have they garnered?

2. Does the ECRMS solution vendor have a formal customer feedback process and metrics established to track customer satisfaction with the product? For example, do they conduct annual or periodic surveys or reviews to collect customer feedback? How do they incorporate that feedback into their ECRM solution?

3. Sometimes, an organization will require more than just customer service support for an ECRMS solution. If this is the case, it is essential to know whether the vendor provides services above and beyond the provision of an ECRMS solution. For example, in addition to the software, does the vendor provide

    a. A documented methodology for implementing the ECRMS solution?

    b. Consulting services to support the implementation of the solution?

    c. Consulting services to assist your organization in conducting the risk and opportunity assessment on your organization's behalf, conducting a security assessment, managing the adoption of the NIST Cybersecurity Framework, etc.?

The Benefits of Using an ECRMS Solution

With software solutions, the wrong or inadequate tool is just as useless as no tool. Make sure you acquire a proper solution and not just a vacant platform. Asking these questions before you contract with an ECRMS solution provider will help ensure that you invest in a solution that provides the breadth of functionality you need to establish, implement, and mature an effective ECRM program across your organization. The right ECRMS solution offers many benefits to your organization, like the ones listed here:

- Enables consistent ECRM across the enterprise, eliminating redundant, non-interoperable, and siloed tools

- Enables leadership to make informed decisions about where to deploy controls or leverage strengths to achieve the best outcomes

- Enables leadership to make informed risk and opportunity treatment decisions based on real-time information about your organization's unique requirements

- Promotes cross-functional risk management collaboration across all stakeholders by providing a "single source of truth" for enterprise-wide risk and opportunity management efforts

- Provides ECRM documentation for auditors, such as your outside audit firm or regulators

- Provides ECRM documentation for insurers, which may result in lower insurance premiums (see Chapter 1)

- Provides ECRM documentation for credit-rating agencies, which may improve your credit ratings and lower your cost of capital (see Chapter 1)

The right ECRMS solution can facilitate establishing, implementing, and maturing your organization's ECRM Program and Cybersecurity Strategy. But beyond that, the right ECRMS solution can also enhance the results of your organization's ECRM efforts by making it easier to make more informed, strategic decisions about ECRM investments, increasing efficiency, and enabling ECRM efforts across your organization to work toward the achievement of the same, strategic ECRM goals.

APPENDIX C

The Benefits of a NIST-Based ECRM Approach

Cyber risks are real; cyber opportunities are equally real. They are here now, and no matter your industry, your organization must mitigate these risks and leverage these opportunities. The best way to address weaknesses (cybersecurity risks) or leverage strengths (cybersecurity opportunities) of your current posture is to establish, implement, and mature an ECRM Program and Cybersecurity Strategy.

Your organization's ECRM program begins with you. As C-suite and board members, in addition to regulatory requirements, you have a fiduciary responsibility and duty of care to take actions (such as establishing your ECRM program!) that protect your organization, customers/clients/patients, employees, and other stakeholders. More importantly, as C-suite and board members, you have the big-picture perspective and oversight powers that enable you to provide the leadership and guidance necessary to establish, implement, and mature an effective ECRM program.

Notwithstanding my comments that the NIST approach does not expressly consider cyber opportunities, that can be addressed. Its flexibility and adaptability make it a robust set of methodologies to follow.

© Bob Chaput 2024
B. Chaput, *Enterprise Cyber Risk Management as a Value Creator*,
https://doi.org/10.1007/979-8-8688-0094-8

A Strong ECRM Program and Cybersecurity Strategy Creates Competitive Advantage

To provide effective leadership for your organization, you must first understand the value and benefits of ECRM. In addition, C-suite and board members must communicate this value throughout your organization. This communication also includes external stakeholders.

I have emphasized the importance and benefits of ECRM throughout this book. In the first part of this appendix, I want to refresh on some of the key advantages your organization will realize by implementing an effective ECRM program.

As I have emphasized throughout this book, the benefits of implementing a robust ECRM Program and Cybersecurity Strategy extend beyond the traditionally important responsibility of "managing the downside" and protecting your organization against compromising confidentiality, integrity, and availability of your critical information assets. You must also leverage your cybersecurity strengths by "managing the upside" to create shareholder value, enable your business, and create a competitive advantage whenever possible.

In Chapter 1, I discussed several ways in which you may accentuate the positives of your program and create business value. These value creators included increasing customer trust and brand loyalty, improving social responsibility, driving revenue growth, lowering the cost of capital, attracting higher-quality investments, creating competitive advantage, attracting and retaining talent, and facilitating M&A work.

I now turn to several important reasons to use the NIST approach to establishing, implementing, and maturing your ECRM Program and Cybersecurity Strategy using the resources available from NIST.

The Benefits of Implementing a NIST-Based ECRM Program and Cybersecurity Strategy

Throughout this book, I have emphasized that, for your ECRM program to be effective, it must be risk-based. It cannot be controls-checklist-based. The National Institute of Standards and Technology (NIST) developed the best, most comprehensive risk-based approach. This appendix offers a more in-depth look at why a NIST-based ECRM program is the best choice for your organization.

The NIST Approach Was Developed Using an Open, Inclusive Process

One of NIST's core principles is *"Inclusivity: We work collaboratively to harness the diversity of people and ideas inside and outside of NIST to attain the best solutions to multidisciplinary challenges."*[1] NIST designed its development process of standards, guidelines, and methodologies to be as open and inclusive as possible. Think about the NIST Cybersecurity Framework as an example. The genesis of the Framework was Presidential Executive Order 13636, issued on February 12, 2013.[2] The executive order focused on sharing cybersecurity threat information across industries. Another goal was to develop a framework for reducing risks to critical sectors of US infrastructure.

---

[1] About NIST. National Institute of Standards and Technology (NIST). (n.d.) Updated March 16, 2023. Accessed October 6, 2023. Available at https://www.nist.gov/about-nist

[2] History and Creation of the (NIST Cybersecurity) Framework. National Institute of Standards and Technology (NIST). Created February 8, 2018, Updated March 16, 2023. Accessed July 11, 2023. https://www.nist.gov/cyberframework/online-learning/history-and-creation-framework

The initial framework development and subsequent updates included the participation of more than 2,000 people across a wide range of impacted industries. The strength, relevance, and effectiveness of the NIST Cybersecurity Framework are directly related to the open, inclusive process used to develop and update it. In August 2023, NIST released the "Public Draft: The NIST Cybersecurity Framework 2.0," produced using an open, inclusive approach and hundreds of organizations.[3]

All NIST development efforts are open and collaborative, including many guides discussed in this book, such as NIST SP 800-39, NIST SP 800-30, etc. Public and private organizations participate extensively.

The NIST Approach Uses Accessible Language That All Stakeholders in Your Organization Can Understand

The NIST Cybersecurity Framework is built around six core functions: Govern, Identify, Protect, Detect, Respond, and Recover. These six words encompass the entire scope of cybersecurity. They are also intentionally accessible words so that all stakeholders in any organization—from board members to clinicians to hospital volunteers—can understand and contribute to your organization's cybersecurity efforts.

The NIST cyber risk management process, which I referred to as the ECRM Process, similarly uses precise, understandable eight-grade verbs to describe the critical process steps: Frame, Assess, Respond, and Monitor.

---

[3] National Institute of Standards and Technology. "Public Draft: The NIST Cybersecurity Framework 2.0." August 8, 2023. Accessed August 28, 2023. Available at https://nvlpubs.nist.gov/nistpubs/CSWP/NIST.CSWP.29.ipd.pdf

The NIST Approach Facilitates Information Governance

The NIST Cybersecurity Framework has governance built into it because it outlines both a "top-down" and a "bottom-up" response. Per the Framework, your organization's technical people may collect data and identify what is working and what is not. At the same time, it is up to the leadership—including C-suite executives and board members—to look at that data and decide how it will change your organization's approach to security. The NIST model includes people at every level of governance: from the front-line technical people operating your organization's Security Operations Center (SOC) to mid-management (including your ECRM Cross-Functional Working Group), the ECRM Executive Steering Committee, and the board. It encompasses all levels of ECRM activity, from tactical to policy and procedures to oversight.

Similarly, as we saw in "Managing Information Security Risk" (NIST Special Publication 800-39),[4] the purpose of the first step, Frame, includes *"making explicit and transparent the risk perceptions that organizations routinely use in making both investment and operational decisions."* Recall that governance is all about who makes what decisions using what data and facts.

---

[4] National Institute of Standards and Technology. NIST Special Publication 800-39. "Managing Information Security Risk." March 2011. Accessed August 6, 2023. https://nvlpubs.nist.gov/nistpubs/Legacy/SP/ nistspecialpublication800-39.pdf

The NIST Approach Leverages Current Standards, Guidelines, and Best Practices from Multiple Internationally Recognized Sources

Although security controls don't constitute a cybersecurity framework, they provide necessary guidance in the tactical implementation of safeguards once your unique risks are identified. For example, the NIST Cybersecurity Framework includes cross-references to other industry requirements and, in some cases, global standards related to cybersecurity (e.g., COBIT 5, ISA 62443, ISO/IEC 27001, NIST SP 800-53), which provide the safeguards to be considered for a more robust security program.[5]

Numerous Industries Align with and Have Adopted the NIST Approach

Numerous industries, including financial services, technology, manufacturing, healthcare, business services, etc., have adopted the NIST approach to ECRM. For example, because of standard requirements within industries, several critical infrastructure sectors have created profiles that align with the NIST framework. You will find a diversity of industry sectors collaborating to create profiles such as Cybersecurity Framework Manufacturing Profile, Election Infrastructure Profile, Smart Grid Profile, Liquefied Natural Gas, Communications Sector, Maritime Cybersecurity Framework Profiles, Connected Vehicle Environments, and

---

[5] National Institute of Standards and Technology (NIST). "Framework for Improving Critical Infrastructure Cybersecurity: Where We Are & Where We Are Going." October 29, 2015. Accessed July 11, 2023. https://www.nist.gov/system/files/documents/cyberframework/Dell-Webinar-Oct2015.pdf

Hybrid Satellite Networks (HSN) that you may be able to leverage. NIST defines a profile, one of the three components of the framework, as *the alignment of the Functions, Categories, and Subcategories with the business requirements, risk tolerance, and resources of the organization.*[6]

In other cases, regulatory agencies have mapped their requirements into the NIST Functions, Categories, and Subcategories. For example, in February 2016, OCR released a document entitled "HIPAA Security Rule Crosswalk to NIST Cybersecurity Framework."[7] The 35-page document maps the administrative, physical, and technical standards and implementation specifications in the HIPAA Security Rule to the relevant categories in the NIST Cybersecurity Framework. OCR's publication of this document provides further validation that adopting the NIST approach to ECRM can assist your organization with HIPAA compliance and reduce regulatory compliance risk.

According to a 2019 survey by Gartner, Inc., a research and advisory firm, 73% of organizations worldwide have implemented and currently use the NIST Cybersecurity Framework.[8] This widespread adoption is vital for all organizations because of interdependencies on other sectors, including the energy, financial services, information technology, and emergency services sectors. Communication about cybersecurity needs to be precise and efficient both within and across sectors. As different sectors adopt the NIST Cybersecurity Framework, it will continue enhancing cross-sector cybersecurity communications.

---

[6] Examples of Framework Profiles. National Institute of Standards and Technology (NIST). Created May 14, 2021, Updated June 8, 2023. Accessed July 11, 2023. Available at https://www.nist.gov/cyberframework/examples-framework-profiles

[7] US Department of Health and Human Services, Office for Civil Rights (OCR). "HIPAA Security Rule Crosswalk to NIST Cybersecurity Framework." February 22, 2016. Accessed March 9, 2023. https://www.hhs.gov/sites/default/files/nist-csf-to-hipaa-security-rule-crosswalk-02-22-2016-final.pdf

[8] Pratap, Khushbu, Thielemann, Katell, and Predovich, Brent. Implement 4 Essentials—NIST Cybersecurity Framework. (ID:G00464751). Retrieved from Gartner database. December 30, 2019.

The NIST Cybersecurity Framework Has Become the Standard for the US Government

The NIST Cybersecurity Framework, as initially released in 2014, was voluntary. An executive order issued in May 2017 by the president changed that.[9] All agencies of the US government are now required to use the NIST Cybersecurity Framework to manage cybersecurity risk. Using the same cybersecurity framework as peers and partners can facilitate cyber intelligence sharing across information systems and expedite collaborative approaches to threat analysis and response. With this requirement established at the federal level, I expect ongoing trickle-down requirements for organizations doing business with federal agencies.

The NIST Approach Is Customizable

The NIST Cybersecurity Framework provides a template for your organization's framework. It is neither one-size-fits-all nor rigidly prescriptive. It simply provides a foundation for developing an ECRM program specifically suited to any organization's assets and risks. As discussed in "Managing Information Security Risk" (NIST Special Publication 800-39),[10] *"The application of the risk management process across the three risk management tiers described in this publication is*

---

[9] CISA. "Executive Order (EO 13800) on Strengthening the Cybersecurity of Federal Networks and Critical Infrastructure." May 11, 2017. Accessed August 31, 2023. Available at https://www.cisa.gov/topics/cybersecurity-best-practices/ executive-order-strengthening-cybersecurity-federal-networks-and- critical-infrastructure#:~:text=President%20Trump%20issued%20 Executive%20Order,face%20of%20intensifying%20cybersecurity%20threats

[10] National Institute of Standards and Technology. NIST Special Publication 800-39. "Managing Information Security Risk." March 2011. Accessed August 6, 2023. https://nvlpubs.nist.gov/nistpubs/Legacy/SP/ nistspecialpublication800-39.pdf

flexible, allowing organizations to effectively accomplish the intent of the specific tasks within their respective organizational structures to best manage risk."

The NIST Cybersecurity Framework Is Scalable

There are enormous variations in organization size within all industries, from small businesses to large, multinational corporations. For example, the NIST Cybersecurity Framework is flexible enough to accommodate organizations at both ends of the spectrum and every organization in between—for example, one subcategory of the framework that requires your organization to establish and communicate its business objectives and priorities. A well-resourced organization might fulfill that subcategory with a 100-page business plan, while a smaller organization might capture that in a page or a paragraph. The extent to which each organization meets a given subcategory is not prescribed, which makes the NIST Cybersecurity Framework scalable.

The NIST Approach Is Affordable

Unlike commercial frameworks, all the resources your organization needs to adopt and implement the NIST Cybersecurity Framework are available for free. The Framework and supporting documentation, video presentations, FAQs, industry-specific resources, and implementation guides are available at https://www.nist.gov/cyberframework. Some organizations may hire an outside vendor to assist in implementing the Framework across a large, complex enterprise, but this is not required.

The NIST Cybersecurity Framework Does Not Require Certification

Some cybersecurity framework vendors offer "certification" services for a fee. The implication is that "certification" will protect an organization in the event of a cybersecurity breach or incident. Certification does not ensure that your organization is secure or compliant with regulations.

The NIST Approach Is Designed to Accommodate Changes in Technology

A preliminary version of the first Framework was released on July 1, 2013.[11] After a comprehensive, inclusive development process, Version 1.0 of the NIST Cybersecurity Framework was released on February 12, 2014. However, the development of the Framework did not end with its initial release. After NIST incorporated additional stakeholder input, Version 1.1 was released on April 16, 2018. Per the original directive, NIST continues to develop the Framework through active dialogue and community outreach.[12] NIST plans to publish a significant update to the Framework, CSF 2.0, in 2024.[13]

---

[11] Evolution of the (NIST Cybersecurity) Framework. National Institute of Standards and Technology (NIST). Updated April 2, 2019. Accessed March 11, 2023. https://www.nist.gov/cyberframework/evolution

[12] History and Creation of the (NIST Cybersecurity) Framework. National Institute of Standards and Technology (NIST). Updated November 21, 2019. Accessed March 12, 2023. https://www.nist.gov/cyberframework/online-learning/history-and-creation-framework

[13] Updating the NIST Cybersecurity Framework—Journey to CSF 2.0. National Institute of Standards and Technology (NIST). Created May 26, 2022, Updated April 25, 2023. https://www.nist.gov/cyberframework/updating-nist-cybersecurity-framework-journey-csf-20

In addition, irrespective of version number, the NIST Cybersecurity Framework is intentionally designed to accommodate technological and threat landscape changes. It is intended to be agile and adaptable over time to keep pace with the ever-changing risk landscape.

For additional perspectives/testimonials on the value of the NIST Cybersecurity Framework from experts across a variety of industries, visit `https://www.nist.gov/cyberframework/general-perspectives`.

APPENDIX D

Twenty-Five Essential Terms for Your ECRM Glossary

This appendix defines vital terms, phrases, and concepts you need to understand to provide appropriate leadership and oversight for your organization's ECRM program. Feel free to use this content to develop your ECRM Glossary.

Clarifying the definition of enterprise cyber risk management and cybersecurity terms is crucial to avoid misunderstandings. To have a constructive discussion about ECRM and cybersecurity, everyone must communicate accurately and comprehend the distinctions between risk, vulnerability, threat, opportunity, and other relevant risk components and terms.

The fact is that cyber risk and opportunity management and cybersecurity encompass so many different terms and concepts that one could write an entire book on terminology alone. (It's been done. One of the best references on the subject—and my primary resource in writing this appendix—is the glossary compiled by the Computer Security Resource Center (CSRC) at NIST. You can access this comprehensive glossary online at https://csrc.nist.gov/glossary/.)

© Bob Chaput 2024
B. Chaput, *Enterprise Cyber Risk Management as a Value Creator*,
https://doi.org/10.1007/979-8-8688-0094-8

In your free time, you might find it interesting to browse that NIST Glossary. I've summarized the most critical terms, phrases, and concepts in the following pages to save time. Understanding these terms and concepts will enable you to provide your organization with meaningful and appropriate cybersecurity guidance and oversight.

Key ECRM and Cybersecurity Terminology

1. *Risk (cyber risk)*

   In Chapter 4, I cited COSO, NIST, and NACD definitions of risk. When focusing on "managing the downside," risk is considered the possibility of loss or harm. Risk is a function of the *likelihood* of a given *threat* triggering or exploiting a particular *vulnerability* and the resulting *impact* on the organization. (The terms in *italics* are further defined in the following.) Risk is not, therefore, one single factor or event but the combination of variables (assets, threats, vulnerabilities, controls, likelihood, impact) that, when considered together, can harm your organization or its stakeholders. Cyber risk arises by compromising your data, systems, or devices' confidentiality, integrity, or availability (CIA).

   Usage Example: "Have we assessed our enterprise-wide cyber risk?"

2. *Resilience*

   Resilience is the ability to (i) operate under adverse conditions or stress, even if in a degraded or debilitated state, while maintaining essential operational capabilities and (ii) recover to an effective operational posture in a time frame consistent with mission needs.[1] The ultimate goal of your ECRM program is to make your organization more resilient to ensure the continuity of services to your customers.

Usage Example: "Do we have an ECRM program to support our organization's resilience requirements in case of a cyberattack?"

3. ***Opportunity (cyber opportunity)***

NIST defines an opportunity as "A condition that may result in a beneficial outcome."[2] That definition facilitates you to think about opportunity management as "managing the upside." While the tragic Russian attack on Ukraine represents a significant loss, harm, or risk to thousands of individuals and businesses, it meant great upside opportunities to the oil industry as prices and profits soared.[3]

You need to think about your organization's cyber opportunities that arise through the strengths in your assuring the confidentiality, integrity, and

---

[1] National Institute of Standards and Technology (NIST). NIST Special Publication 800-53, Revision 5. "Security and Privacy Controls for Information Systems and Organizations." December 2020. Accessed August 6, 2023. https://nvlpubs. nist.gov/nistpubs/SpecialPublications/NIST.SP.800-53r5.pdf

[2] "Opportunity." Glossary. Computer Security Resource Center (CSRC). National Institute of Standards and Technology (NIST). Accessed August 3, 2023. https:// csrc.nist.gov/glossary/

[3] Global Witness. "Crisis year 2022 brought $134 billion in excess profit to the West's five largest oil and gas companies." February 9, 2023. Accessed August 8, 2023. Available at https://www.globalwitness.org/en/campaigns/fossil-gas/ crisis-year-2022-brought-134-billion-in-excess-profit-to-the-wests- five-largest-oil-and-gas-companies/

availability of your data, systems, or devices (see the preceding *risk* definition). Similar to the assessment of risks, you must (1) identify and then prioritize all of your organization's unique cyber opportunities; (2) discuss, debate, and settle on your threshold for cyber opportunities, that is, determine what level of opportunity your organization is prepared to leverage; and (3) make informed decisions about which opportunities you will leverage and then execute on that plan.

4. *Cybersecurity*

Cybersecurity describes the ability to safeguard, protect, and defend the confidentiality, integrity, and availability (CIA) of all your data, systems, and devices against all reasonably anticipated threats and vulnerabilities. When your unique risks are rated based on all your reasonably expected threats and vulnerabilities, your goal is to keep risks below your risk appetite (see the following definition #16).

Usage Example: "Have we integrated cybersecurity into our enterprise risk and opportunity management program?"

5. *Assets and information assets*

Assets may include major applications, general support systems, high-impact programs, the physical plant, mission-critical systems, personnel, equipment, or another logically related group of systems.[4] System or information assets include any software, hardware, data, or administrative, physical, communications, or personnel resources within an information system. In its cybersecurity disclosure final rule, the SEC defined information systems as

... electronic information resources, owned or used by the registrant, including physical or virtual infrastructure controlled by such information resources, or components thereof, organized for the collection, processing, maintenance, use, sharing, dissemination, or disposition of the registrant's information to maintain or support the registrant's operations.[5]

As you can see, the SEC's definition of an information system is broad. The typical organization has hundreds of information systems or assets when you include all the different categories of assets that exist:

- Traditional information assets: Traditional information assets include IT systems and applications. As an example, in a healthcare organization, they have EHRs, clinical information applications, lab and medical specialty applications, medical-billing and claims-processing applications, email applications, company

---

[4] "Asset." Glossary. Computer Security Resource Center (CSRC). National Institute of Standards and Technology (NIST). Accessed August 3, 2023. https://csrc.nist.gov/glossary/

[5] SEC. "Final Rule: Cybersecurity Risk Management, Strategy, Governance, and Incident Disclosure." July 26, 2023. Accessed July 30, 2023. Available at https://www.sec.gov/files/rules/final/2023/33-11216.pdf

intranet websites, human resources management applications, network file-sharing applications, electronic data interchange (EDI) applications, fax applications, payment-processing applications, financial management and reporting applications, and other applications and systems.

- Internet of Things (IoT) information assets: For example, in a healthcare organization, IoT assets consist of biomedical equipment and Internet-connected assets like facilities security and building management. Additionally, there are real-time location services (RTLS) for assets, employees, patients, and visitors, as well as networking hardware, software, security, and services.

Usage Example: "When we complete our acquisition of XYZ Company, we will need to inventory all their information assets to incorporate them into our ECRM program."

6. ***Risk and opportunity owner***

Risk ownership is one of the most essential terms and concepts for organizations to define and agree to use. It is crucial to expand the definition to include opportunity ownership. I suggest starting with the NIST definition of a risk executive (function) because it encourages risk ownership at the executive level. The definition is "an individual or group within an organization that helps to ensure that (i) security risk-related considerations for individual information systems, to include the authorization decisions for those systems, are viewed from an organization-wide perspective with regard to the overall strategic goals and objectives of the organization in carrying out its missions and business functions; and (ii) managing risk from individual information systems is consistent across the organization, reflects organizational risk tolerance, and is considered along with other organizational risks affecting mission/business success."[6]

7. ***Threats, threat sources, and threat events***

A threat is any circumstance or event with the potential to adversely impact organizational operations (including mission, functions, image, or reputation), organizational assets, or individuals through an information system via unauthorized access, destruction, disclosure, modification of information, or denial of service.[7] Threats come from a variety of sources. A common way to categorize threat sources is as follows:

- Accidental: Accidental threats occur without malice or intent on the part of the user. Examples of accidental threat sources include an employee who sends out a group email containing sensitive personal information to the wrong recipients or an equipment operator at a nearby construction site

---

[6] "Risk Executive (function)." Glossary. Computer Security Resource Center (CSRC). National Institute of Standards and Technology (NIST). Accessed August 31, 2023. Available at https://csrc.nist.gov/glossary/.

[7] "Threat." Glossary. Computer Security Resource Center (CSRC). National Institute of Standards and Technology (NIST). Accessed August 3, 2023. https://csrc.nist.gov/glossary/

cutting fiber-optic cable connecting you to your cloud-based information assets.

- Adversarial: The malicious intent of the perpetrator characterizes adversarial threats. The perpetrator may be an individual, a group, a competing organization, or a hostile nation-state. A common type of adversarial threat is an "insider threat," which originates inside the organization (e.g., a disgruntled or untrained employee).

- Environmental: Environmental threat sources include natural or man-made disasters (fire, flood, earthquake, tornado, etc.) and unusual natural events (e.g., sunspots/solar flares, pandemic).

- Structural: Structural threats include IT equipment or utility service failure, such as a failed hard drive, poorly written code in a software application, or loss of telecommunications infrastructure or electrical power.

An effective ECRM program will consider all reasonably anticipated threat sources and possible threat events. It's essential to base your ECRM program on a comprehensive assessment of your organization's unique threats rather than simply responding to the latest "threat *du jour*." The specific threats that are making headlines today (malicious URLs, web attacks, form-jacking attacks, crypto-jacking, and ransomware) will be replaced by new threats tomorrow.[8] Your organization's best defense is proactively assessing risk rather than reacting to today's headlines.

A threat event is an event or situation that can potentially cause undesirable consequences or impact.[9] When conducting a risk and opportunity assessment (refer to the following definition #13), it's crucial to brainstorm and consider all potential threat events, regardless of how unlikely they may seem or if they've never been encountered. For example, although California has experienced accidental power outages before, 2019 marked the first year preemptive power outages were used so frequently and on such an expansive scale. All businesses, especially healthcare providers, have had to rethink their disaster protocols to deal with this new environmental threat.[10]

Usage Examples: "Does our ECRM program address relevant environmental threats?"

---

[8] 2019 Internet Security Threat Report (ISTR). Symantec. February 2019. Accessed August 3, 2023. https://www.symantec.com/security-center/threat-report

[9] "Threat Event." Glossary. Computer Security Resource Center (CSRC). National Institute of Standards and Technology (NIST). Accessed August 8, 2023. https://csrc.nist.gov/glossary/

[10] Ostrov, Barbara Feder. Kaiser Health News. "California hospitals and nursing homes brace for wildfire blackouts." September 11, 2019. Accessed August 8, 2023. https://khn.org/news/california-hospitals-and-nursing-homes-brace-for-wildfire-blackouts/?utm_source=STAT+Newsletters&utm_campaign=e1b5d35314-MR_COPY_01&utm_medium=email&utm_term=0_8cab1d7961-e1b5d35314-150885145

"As we develop our ECRM program, we must consider all possible threat events that our organization might encounter."

8. *Vulnerability*

A vulnerability is a flaw or weakness in system security procedures, design, implementation, or internal controls that could be exercised (accidentally triggered or intentionally exploited) and result in a security breach or a violation of the system's security policy.[11]

Security engineers and operations staff often confuse conducting *vulnerability scans* with completing a *risk assessment* (see the following definition #13). Vulnerability scans are essential but do not comprise accurate risk assessment. Vulnerability scans provide a long list of weaknesses but fail to consider the other crucial factors in the risk equation. Consider a home example for a moment: If you do not have a deadbolt lock on one of your exterior doors, that could be a vulnerability. But you don't just run out and install deadbolt locks. Live in a gated community (a control) and have external motion detectors in your home security system (another control). The likelihood of a burglar exploiting the lack of a deadbolt on a single door may be very low.

---

[11] "Vulnerability." Glossary. Computer Security Resource Center (CSRC). National Institute of Standards and Technology (NIST). Accessed August 8, 2023. https://csrc.nist.gov/glossary/

Various vulnerabilities could affect your information assets, such as inactive user accounts, accounts with excessive permissions, insufficient encryption for devices or data, flawed code in custom applications, weak passwords, inadequate governance for ECRM programs, and the absence of a cybersecurity strategy.

You can determine your organization's specific vulnerabilities by conducting a comprehensive, enterprise-wide risk and opportunity assessment.

Usage Example: "I am concerned about the lack of encryption on the laptops and mobile devices that store PHI. Do you think this vulnerability creates a risk we ought to treat?"

9. ***Controls***

As a reminder, risk exists only when an asset, a threat, and a vulnerability are present simultaneously (see the preceding definition #1). One of your ECRM program's goals is to implement reasonable and appropriate controls to ensure your risks are rated below your risk appetite. Controls (also called *safeguards* or *countermeasures*) are the tools your organization uses to mitigate risks to an acceptable level.

Security controls are the management, operational, and technical controls (i.e., safeguards or countermeasures) prescribed for an information system to protect the CIA of the system and its information.[12] NIST defines security and privacy controls, respectively, as follows in NIST SP 800-53, Revision 5, "Security and Privacy Controls for Information Systems and Organizations":

Security controls are the safeguards or countermeasures employed within a system or an organization to protect the confidentiality, integrity, and availability of the system and its information and to manage information security risk.

Privacy controls are the administrative, technical, and physical safeguards employed within a system or an organization to manage privacy risks and to ensure compliance with applicable privacy requirements.[13]

Note that technical safeguards are only one of three types of safeguards or controls. Establishing and maturing your organization's ECRM program is, arguably, your most critical administrative control. You can't achieve cybersecurity by engaging in a technical controls arms race. For controls to be adequate, your organization needs to take a considered approach based on examining your unique business and your organization's unique assets, threats, and vulnerabilities.

---

[12] "Security Controls." Glossary. Computer Security Resource Center (CSRC). National Institute of Standards and Technology (NIST). Accessed August 8, 2023. https://csrc.nist.gov/glossary/

[13] National Institute of Standards and Technology (NIST). NIST Special Publication 800-53, Revision 5. "Security and Privacy Controls for Information Systems and Organizations." December 2020. Accessed August 6, 2023. https://nvlpubs.nist.gov/nistpubs/SpecialPublications/NIST.SP.800-53r5.pdf

Usage Example: "I know we've discussed purchasing a new intrusion detection system, but before we discuss that, are we sure we have the appropriate administrative controls in place?"

10. ***Likelihood***

Likelihood is the chance of something happening.[14] The first step in conducting a comprehensive, enterprise-wide risk and opportunity assessment is identifying possible risk scenarios {asset-threat-vulnerability}; the next step is to rate them. Likelihood is one of two factors (the other being "impact," defined in the following) used to rate risks. In the context of insurance, the analogous terms you will likely hear are "frequency" and "severity." Your Chief Risk Officer and professional liability insurance broker usually use these terms.

NIST explains that the likelihood of occurrence is a weighted risk factor based on analyzing the probability that a given threat can exploit a given vulnerability (or set of vulnerabilities).[15] I show an example of a scale on which to assess likelihood in Table D-1.

---

[14] "Likelihood." Glossary. Computer Security Resource Center (CSRC). National Institute of Standards and Technology (NIST). Accessed October 24, 2019. https://csrc.nist.gov/glossary/

[15] "Likelihood of Occurrence." Glossary. Computer Security Resource Center (CSRC). National Institute of Standards and Technology (NIST). Accessed October 24, 2019. https://csrc.nist.gov/glossary/

Table D-1. *Risk Likelihood Scale*

RATING	DESCRIPTION	PERCENT LIKELIHOOD IN NEXT 12 MONTHS	FREQUENCY MAY OCCUR
1	Rare	5%	Once every 20 years
2	Unlikely	25%	Once every 4 years
3	Moderate	50%	Once every 2 years
4	Likely	75%	Once every 16 months
5	Almost Certain	100%	Multiple times per year

For example, suppose you are assessing the likelihood of one of your organization's unencrypted laptops being lost by a careless employee in the {laptop-careless employee-no encryption} risk scenario. It's been estimated that a laptop is lost every 53 seconds![16] Given this statistic, it is likely that all organizations will lose at least one laptop each year. In that case, the likelihood rating would be "Almost Certain," a "5." In assessing likelihood, you should consider what controls you have in place. In this risk scenario, while the laptops may not be encrypted, the organization may have a robust password policy to lower the likelihood of accessing the laptop's data.

Usage Example: "What is the likelihood that one of our employees will lose a laptop containing ePHI this year?"

---

[16] Mah, Paul. CIO. "10 things to do before you lose your laptop." September 10, 2015. Accessed October 24, 2019. https://www.cio.com/article/2981970/10-things-to-do-before-you-lose-your-laptop.html

11. *Impact*

Impact from a threat event is the magnitude of
loss or harm that can be expected to result from
the consequences of unauthorized disclosure of
information, unauthorized modification of data,
unauthorized destruction of information, or loss
of information or information system availability.[17]
In other words, the impact assessment is based
on the extent of compromise of the CIA of your
organization's data, systems, or devices.

Like with likelihood, you can use a scale to assess
the impact, as shown in Table D-2.

Table D-2. *Risk Impact Scale*

RATING	DESCRIPTION	EXAMPLE CONSIDERATIONS		
--------	-------------	# RECORDS BREACHED	DOWNTIME	ORGANIZATION COST IN $
1	Insignificant	<100	Minutes	$10,000
2	Minor	100-499	2 hours	$20,000
3	Moderate	500	4 hours	$200,000
4	Major	5,000	8 hours	$2,000,000
5	Severe	50,000	24 hours	$20,000,000

Continuing with the {laptop-careless employee-
no encryption} risk scenario from the preceding
likelihood definition, if that lost laptop were
known to contain 5,000+ records with personal
information, a rating of "Major" or "4" would be
assigned. Similarly, when considering impact, you

---

[17] "Impact." Glossary. Computer Security Resource Center (CSRC). National
Institute of Standards and Technology (NIST). Accessed October 24, 2019.
https://csrc.nist.gov/glossary/

should consider what controls you have in place. In this risk scenario, while the laptops may not be encrypted, the organization may have a mobile device management solution that remotely wipes the laptop's data. Such a control may reduce the impact of this risk scenario.

Usage Example: "What is the impact on our organization from one lost, unencrypted laptop?"

12. ***Risk or opportunity rating***

The risk or opportunity rating for each risk scenario {asset-threat-vulnerability} is determined by considering both the likelihood (definition #10 previously) and the impact (definition #11 previously) of the threat event occurring. In the {laptop-careless employee-no encryption} risk scenario I described in the last two definitions, the rating would be "5" (likelihood scale) multiplied by "4" (impact scale), resulting in a total rating of 20 for this particular risk scenario. (Note that since both the likelihood and impact scales have five rating levels, the highest possible rating would be 5 × 5, or 25.) Calculating the rating for all scenarios results in an initial, natural ranking of risks from most serious to least severe, as shown in Table D-3.

Table D-3. *Sample Excerpt from a Risk and Opportunity Register*

ASSET	THREAT SOURCE/ EVENT	VULNERABILITY	LIKELIHOOD	IMPACT	SCENARIO RATING
Laptop	Burglar steals laptop	No encryption	High (5)	High (5)	25
Laptop	Burglar steals laptop	Weak password	High (5)	High (5)	25
Laptop	Burglar steals laptop	No asset tracking	High (5)	High (5)	25
Laptop	Careless user drops laptop	No data backup	Medium (3)	High (5)	15
Laptop	Lightning strikes home	No surge protection	Low (1)	High (5)	5
Laptop	Shoulder-surfer views screen	No privacy screen	Low (1)	Medium (3)	3
Etc.	*There are dozens more risk scenarios to consider with each category of laptops.*				

This information may inform the C-suite and board members' deliberations when determining the organization's risk appetite or opportunity threshold. Or the C-suite and board members may set a risk appetite or opportunity threshold before their organization conducts its first risk assessment. The ratings also provide an inherent starting point for the prioritization of risks.

Usage Example: "What risk or opportunity rating did we calculate for the risk scenario in which a laptop is lost or stolen?"

13. *Risk and opportunity assessment*

Risk and opportunity assessment is the process of identifying, estimating, and prioritizing risks and opportunities to organizational data, systems, and devices.[18] The biggest issue facing most organizations today is the failure or inability to identify all their unique risks or opportunities, that is, the failure to complete a comprehensive risk and opportunity assessment. While many organizations are to be commended for making progress in conducting NIST-quality risk analyses, there is still too little emphasis and discussion on cyber opportunities. How will you possibly treat your cyber risks or leverage your cyber opportunities if you do not know what they are?

Usage Example: "Has our organization completed a comprehensive enterprise-wide risk and opportunity assessment?"

14. ***Risk and opportunity management***

Risk and opportunity management refers to the broader ongoing program and supporting processes deployed to manage risks and opportunities to organizational operations (including mission, functions, image, and reputation), organizational assets, individuals, and other organizations.[19] Most organizations are focused on maturing their processes for managing cyber risks. Few organizations have brought the same level of attention to leveraging cyber opportunities.

---

[18] "Risk Analysis" and "Risk Assessment." Glossary. Computer Security Resource Center (CSRC). National Institute of Standards and Technology (NIST). Accessed October 24, 2019. https://csrc.nist.gov/glossary/

[19] "Risk Management." Glossary. Computer Security Resource Center (CSRC). National Institute of Standards and Technology (NIST). Accessed August 8, 2023. https://csrc.nist.gov/glossary/

Usage Example: "Our risk and opportunity management program focuses too much on our cyber risks and needs to spend more time identifying and leveraging our cyber opportunities."

15. *Enterprise cyber risk management (ECRM)*

ECRM is (or should be) incorporated into your enterprise risk management program. ECRM deals specifically with the *cyber* risks and opportunities that can affect your organization. ECRM has multiple components, including developing a risk and opportunity register from your risk and opportunity assessment that serves as the basis for informed decision-making related to cyber risks and opportunities. The countermeasures or controls implemented to treat risks at or above your organization's risk appetite (see the following definition) and the investments to leverage your cybersecurity strengths form the basis of your organization's cybersecurity strategy.

Usage Example: "Our ECRM program enables us to deploy our resources effectively to manage all high cyber risk and cyber opportunities."

16. *Risk appetite and opportunity threshold*

Once you identify and rate your risks and opportunities, you must decide how to treat your risks (see the following definition #17) and leverage your cyber opportunities. Risk appetite is the level of risk an organization is willing to assume to achieve a desired result.

Setting, communicating, and adjusting your organization's risk appetite is one of the most important C-suite and board responsibilities concerning your organization's ECRM program. For example, in the risk scenario where a careless employee loses an unencrypted laptop, if that risk is assigned a likelihood of 5/5 and an impact of 4/5, then the rating for that scenario is 20. If the organization's risk appetite is set at 15, it will not accept this risk but treat it somehow (i.e., avoid, mitigate, or transfer it). But if you set your organization's risk appetite at 22, the organization would simply accept this risk.

Opportunity threshold is not well-defined, so I suggest the following: the rating value at which an opportunity represents strength to the organization that can be exploited to increase customer trust and brand loyalty, improve social responsibility, drive revenue growth, lower the cost of capital, attract higher-quality investments, create competitive advantage, attract and retain talent, or facilitate M&A activity. In the context of the rating scale discussed previously, your organization might set its opportunity threshold at 6 or 8 on a 25-point scale.

Usage Example: "What percent of the risks we identified and rated in our most recent risk and opportunity analysis are above our risk appetite? What percent are at or below our opportunity threshold?"

17. ***Risk and opportunity treatment choices (a.k.a. risk and opportunity response choices)***

Once your organization has rated all your possible risks and opportunities (see the preceding definition #12), you must decide how to treat risks and leverage opportunities by considering the likelihood and impact of each scenario.

For risk treatment, the risks rated below your risk appetite are risks you will typically simply *accept*. For risks at or above your risk appetite, you must determine whether you will *avoid, mitigate,* or *transfer* that risk. These four choices—accept, avoid, mitigate, or transfer—are standard in treating any type of risk. An example of risk mitigation would be to implement encryption on all laptops so that, even if a careless employee lost a laptop, whoever found it could not access the data on it. An example of risk transfer is increasing an organization's cyber liability insurance limits to help cover any potential damages.

For opportunity treatment, discuss and prioritize opportunities with the most significant potential to create business value up to and including a competitive advantage. As an example, if your risk and opportunity assessment shows you have implemented robust controls such as multifactor authentication, endpoint detection and response, and secure backups, among other essential safeguards cyber liability underwriters are demanding,[20] then plan to meet with your broker as soon as possible to negotiate a more favorable premium.

Usage Example: "Given that this particular risk is rated right at the risk appetite we defined, what risk or opportunity treatment choice would you recommend?"

18. ***Risk acceptance***

Acceptable risk is "A level of residual risk to the organization's operations, assets, or individuals that falls within the defined risk appetite and risk tolerance by the organization."[21] Therefore, risk acceptance is the appropriate risk response when the identified risk is within the organizational risk appetite. For example, an organization may accept the risk of bring-your-own-devices (BYOD) if they require owners of these devices to install and use the organization's mobile device management solution.

Usage Example: "Given our access controls for all mobile devices, we accept the risk of field service engineers carrying company-issued laptops and tablets."

---

[20] Global Data Systems. "Cyber Insurance Checklist: 12 Essential Security Controls." (n.d.) Accessed August 8, 2023. Available at https://www.getgds.com/resources/blog/cybersecurity/cyber-insurance-checklist-12-essential-security-controls

[21] "Acceptable Risk." Glossary. Computer Security Resource Center (CSRC). National Institute of Standards and Technology (NIST). Accessed October 6, 2023. https://csrc.nist.gov/glossary/

19. *Risk avoidance*

Risk avoidance involves taking specific actions
to eliminate the activities or technologies that
are the basis for the risk to avoid the potential for
unacceptable risk. Continuing to use BYOD as an
example, some organizations do not allow access
to their organization's information assets by any
company-issued devices, thereby avoiding any risks
associated with BYOD.

Usage Example: "Given the difficulty in securing
non-company-issued laptops and tablets, we
will avoid this risk by not allowing access to any
company information assets."

20. *Risk mitigation*

Risk mitigation is "prioritizing, evaluating, and
implementing the appropriate risk-reducing
controls/countermeasures recommended from the
risk management process."[22] It is the appropriate
risk response for that portion of risk that cannot
be accepted, avoided, shared, or transferred.
Implementing technical controls such as encryption
or a mobile device management (MDM) solution
on all mobile devices would be considered risk
mitigation in the BYOD scenario.

---

[22] "Risk Mitigation." Glossary. Computer Security Resource Center (CSRC).
National Institute of Standards and Technology (NIST). Accessed October 6, 2023.
https://csrc.nist.gov/glossary/

Usage Example: "We will mitigate the risk of allowing the use of non-company-issued laptops and tablets by requiring the use of our MDM and VPN solutions to supplement our acceptable use policy."

21. **Risk transfer**

Risk transfer shifts the risk liability from one organization to another organization. Using cyber liability insurance transfers risk from organizations to insurance companies. This treatment choice is often selected in combination with risk mitigation actions.

Usage Example: "In addition to the encryption, MDM, and VPN controls, we will transfer some risk by increasing the limits on our cyber coverage related to BYOD."

22. **Opportunity leverage**

When your risk and opportunity assessment highlights strengths, it is essential to consider investing to leverage those opportunities. If you have implemented an incredibly secure BYOD program, can you package it, sell it, and generate revenue?

Usage Example: "We have implemented a medical device security solution that continuously scans your network and gathers device utilization data. We can leverage this strength to improve capacity planning and reduce equipment purchases, creating business value."

23. **ECRM Framework**

A framework provides a high-level model that assists organizations in defining their desired cyber risk and opportunity management outcomes in alignment with their overall organization vision, mission, strategy, values, and services. The framework that I recommend is the Cybersecurity Framework created by NIST.[23]

At the highest level, the NIST Cybersecurity Framework identifies six essential functions your ECRM program must perform: Govern, Identify, Protect, Detect, Respond, and Recover. Appendix C covers the advantages of using the NIST Cybersecurity Framework.

Usage Example: "I recommend we consider adopting the NIST Cybersecurity Framework to help align and articulate our desired ECRM program outcomes with our organization's vision, mission, strategy, values, and services."

24. **ECRM Process**

Your ECRM Framework defines the "what" of your ECRM program: what outcomes are you setting out to achieve? The ECRM process, on the other hand, describes the "how" of your ECRM program. What specific, repeatable actions will your organization take to achieve the cybersecurity outcomes you described in your framework?

---

[23] National Institute of Standards and Technology. "Public Draft: The NIST Cybersecurity Framework 2.0." August 8, 2023. Accessed August 28, 2023. Available at https://nvlpubs.nist.gov/nistpubs/CSWP/NIST.CSWP.29.ipd.pdf

The cyber risk and opportunity management process I recommend is based on guidance provided in "Managing Information Security Risk" (NIST Special Publication 800-39)[24] and is composed of four basic steps, each of which informs the other steps in the process:

1. *Frame risk.* That is, establish the context for risk-based decisions and your overall approach to and your desired outcomes of your ECRM program discussed previously. Adopting and implementing your ECRM Framework is completing this framing step. I also recommended you expand your scope to establish the context for opportunity-based decisions.

2. *Assess risk.* In other words, identify your exposures via an enterprise-wide, comprehensive risk assessment. NIST has published a separate guide for risk assessments, NIST SP 800-30 "Guide for Conducting Risk Assessments."[25] Keeping with our theme of value creation, you must identify and assess your cyber opportunities.

---

[24] National Institute of Standards and Technology. NIST Special Publication 800-39. "Managing Information Security Risk." March 2011. Accessed August 6, 2023. https://nvlpubs.nist.gov/nistpubs/Legacy/SP/nistspecialpublication800-39.pdf

[25] National Institute of Standards and Technology (NIST). NIST Special Publication 800-30, Revision 1. "Guide for Conducting Risk Assessments." September 2012. Available at https://nvlpubs.nist.gov/nistpubs/Legacy/SP/nistspecialpublication800-30r1.pdf

3. *Respond to risk.* In this step, your organization focuses on making risk treatment decisions and executing risk treatment actions. As I will discuss further, this step involves deciding whether to accept, avoid, mitigate, or transfer risk. As a reminder, you must treat or manage the cyber opportunities you identify.

4. *Monitor risk on an ongoing basis.* Risk management is more than just a once-and-done proposition. It is a continuous process, which includes a feedback loop for process improvement and consideration of internal and external changes. The feedback loop must monitor opportunities. Although "Managing Information Security Risk" (NIST Special Publication 800-39) focuses more on risks than opportunities, it is adaptable to manage both.

Usage Example: "We need to ensure that we have established and documented an effective, enterprise-wide ECRM Process to ensure we execute ECRM consistently."

25. ***ECRM Maturity Model***

A maturity model is a "tool that helps people assess the current effectiveness of a person or group and supports figuring out what capabilities they need to acquire next to improve their performance."[26] Another way of describing how a maturity model is used is that it helps the organization identify its

---

[26] Fowler, Martin. Maturity Model. August 26, 2014. Accessed October 24, 2019. https://martinfowler.com/bliki/MaturityModel.html#targetText=A%20 maturity%20model%20is%20a,order%20to%20improve%20their%20performance.

current maturity level concerning specific capabilities (e.g., ECRM), facilitates the establishment of goals for performance improvement, and allows organizations to set priorities for improvements aimed at achieving the desired maturity level.

A typical approach to the maturity process is the four-step management model, sometimes called the Deming Cycle. The four steps in this model are Plan, Do, Check, and Act.[27] The maturity model provides a mechanism for determining whether your ECRM program is improving over time. Based on my work with organizations across multiple industry sectors, I recommend focusing your ECRM maturity model on improving five key capabilities:

1. *Governance* (and Awareness of the Benefits and Value of ECRM)

2. *People* (Skills, Knowledge, and Experience)

3. *Process* (Discipline and Repeatability)

4. *Technology* (Standards, Technology Tools, and Scalability)

5. *Engagement* (including Delivery and Operations)

Usage Example: "As we mature our ECRM program, I would like to see more focus on the governance and engagement capabilities in our maturity model. In our current program, those are two areas where I am seeing the greatest weakness."

---

[27] US Department of Health and Human Services, Agency for Healthcare Research and Quality, Health Information Technology. "Plan-Do-Check-Act Cycle." (n.d.) Accessed October 24, 2019. https://healthit.ahrq.gov/health-it-tools-and-resources/evaluation-resources/workflow-assessment-health-it-toolkit/all-workflow-tools/plan-do-check-act-cycle

Bringing It All Together

How do these terms and concepts work together? Figure D-1 illustrates many key terms and concepts related to risk and their relationship to each other.

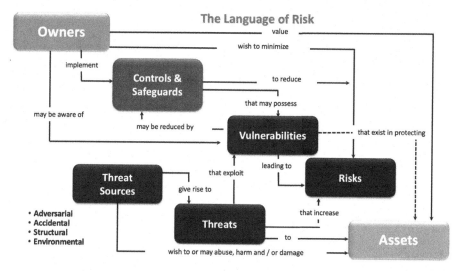

Figure D-1. *How It All Works Together*

As C-suite executives and board members, you are the de facto "owners" of your organization's assets. As discussed in Chapter 3, with that responsibility comes a requirement that you exercise a *duty of care*. That responsibility includes understanding your organization's unique cyber risks and opportunities and providing the leadership and oversight to manage those risks rated above your risk appetite and leverage your cyber opportunities rated below your opportunity threshold.

APPENDIX E

Sample ECRM Program and Cybersecurity Strategy Table of Contents

This appendix contains a sample table of contents to provide a sense of what you should consider, decide upon, and create in your ECRM Program and Cybersecurity Strategy documentation. Certain items in the table of contents may look like technobabble for some. Worry not because in Part 2 of the book, I discuss what should be covered in each section to enable you to establish, implement, and mature your ECRM Program and Cybersecurity Strategy. A well-documented set of standards, plans, policies, procedures, and practices is crucial to the success of your ECRM program.

© Bob Chaput 2024
B. Chaput, *Enterprise Cyber Risk Management as a Value Creator*,
https://doi.org/10.1007/979-8-8688-0094-8

It is critically important that this work be completed by a Cross-Functional Working Group under the supervision of the C-suite, with oversight by the board. Do not delegate this foundational work to a single person or role in your organization—not the Chief Risk Officer, Chief Information Officer, or Chief Information Security Officer.

The following is the sample table of contents for your ECRM Program and Cybersecurity Strategy documentation:

1. Document Management

2. Table of Contents

3. Executive Summary

4. Introduction

5. ECRM Guiding Principles

6. ECRM Budget Philosophy

7. Scope of the ECRM Strategy

8. Business Strategic Objectives

9. ECRM Strategic Objectives

10. Responsibility for and Governance of the ECRM Program

11. ECRM Framework

12. ECRM Process

13. ECRM Maturity Model

14. Risk Appetite and Opportunity Threshold

15. Risk and Opportunity Framing Standards, Policies, and Procedures

16. Risk and Opportunity Assessment Standards, Policies, and Procedures

Index

A

B

© Bob Chaput 2024
B. Chaput, *Enterprise Cyber Risk Management as a Value Creator*,
https://doi.org/10.1007/979-8-8688-0094-8

Printed in the United States
by Baker & Taylor Publisher Services